Between Apocalypse and Eschaton

Between Apocalypse and Eschaton

History and Eternity in Henri de Lubac

Joseph S. Flipper

Fortress Press
Minneapolis

BETWEEN APOCALYPSE AND ESCHATON
History and Eternity in Henri de Lubac

Cover image © Thinkstock; *Ruins of Dresden* by rglinsky

Cover design: Alisha Lofgren

Library of Congress Cataloging-in-Publication Data

Print ISBN: 978-1-4514-8456-4

eBook ISBN: 978-1-4514-9663-5

The paper used in this publication meets the minimum requirements of American National Standard for Information Sciences — Permanence of Paper for Printed Library Materials, ANSI Z329.48-1984.

Manufactured in the U.S.A.

This book was produced using PressBooks.com, and PDF rendering was done by PrinceXML.

Contents

Acknowledgements   vii

Introduction   1

Part I. Eschatology as the "Storm Center"

1. An Eschatological Modernity   *21*

2. Time and Eternity in the *Nouvelle Théologie*   *47*

Part II. Temporal Ruptures

3. Scripture and the Structure of History   *91*

4. Christ is the Center of History   *129*

5. Between Apocalypse and Eschaton   *151*

Part III. The Eschatological Structure of De Lubac's Thought

6. Sacraments of the Eschaton   *209*

7. Eschatology in the Theology of the Supernatural   *257*

Conclusion: Eternity in Time   *301*

Bibliography   311
Index   327

Acknowledgements

Although the road that led from idea to book has been long and challenging, I have not walked it alone. I am grateful to Susan K. Wood, SCL, of Marquette University, my dissertation adviser, who has been a source of encouragement for this project and whose work is an inspiration. I am particularly indebted to Rev. Joseph G. Mueller, SJ, of Marquette for his invaluable engagement with and criticism of my research. D. Stephen Long and Rev. David G. Schultenover, SJ, of Marquette, Katy Leamy of Mount Angel Seminary, and Matthew Gerlach of University of Mary also each helped me immensely through conversation and by pointing me to new ideas and new sources. I am thankful to my wife Karen, whose close reading of several chapters contributed immensely to key sections of the book. I am grateful for the help of Shelby Eriksson of Bellarmine University, who assisted me in proofreading and indexing of the book.

I would not have been able to complete my dissertation, on which this book is based, without the support of the 2011–2012 dissertation fellowship from the Ford Foundation and a summer 2012 postdoctoral fellowship at the University of Wisconsin-Milwaukee (UWM), French, Italian, and Comparative Literature Department. I am grateful to my mentor at UWM, Peter Y. Paik, for his advice and encouragement of my project. Bellarmine University and its Department of Theology have been fantastic supporters of my work. Bellarmine University's 2014 Faculty Development Fellowship enabled me to complete the book.

Introduction

Henri Sonier de Lubac, SJ (1896–1991) remains a puzzling figure for interpreters of twentieth-century Catholicism. In the twenty years since his death, interest in de Lubac has not faded. In part, this is because his scholarship had a considerable influence on the shape of Catholic theology prior to the Second Vatican Council (1962–1965). As the meaning of the Council has become contested, so has the interpretation of de Lubac's theology and the *nouvelle théologie*, the loosely affiliated group of scholars with whom de Lubac associated.[1] The *nouvelle théologie* remains critical for understanding the theological and pastoral shifts leading to the Second Vatican Council. Increasingly, scholarship on de Lubac and the *nouvelle théologie* has come from authors of Protestant and Anglo-Catholic traditions, who appeal to the *nouvelle théologie* as a resource for ecumenical engagement and for the renewal of their own theological traditions.

---

1. For recent studies on the *nouvelle théologie* and *ressourcement* see Gabriel Flynn and Paul D. Murray, eds., *Ressourcement: A Movement for Renewal in Twentieth-Century Catholic Theology* (New York: Oxford University Press, 2012); Jürgen Mettepenningen, *Nouvelle Théologie—New Theology: Inheritor of Modernism, Precursor to Vatican II* (New York: T & T Clark, 2010); Hans Boersma, *Nouvelle Théologie and Sacramental Ontology: A Return to Mystery* (New York: Oxford University Press, 2009); Hans Boersma, "Sacramental Ontology: Nature and the Supernatural in the Ecclesiology of Henri de Lubac," *New Blackfriars* 88, no. 1015 (2007): 242–73; Brian Daley, "The Nouvelle Théologie and the Patristic Revival: Sources, Symbols and the Science of Theology," *International Journal of Systematic Theology* 7, no. 4 (October 2005): 362–82.

Henri de Lubac was one of the most visible theologians of the *nouvelle théologie* movement, and, beginning in the 1940s, drew controversy for his theology and his work as an editor of early Christian writings. His proposals concerning nature and grace in *Surnaturel* (1946) made him suspect to the theological establishment in Rome, and he became the subject of intense debate.[2] Contemporary interpreters have suggested that de Lubac's primary theological contribution was to dismantle a secular ontology hidden within much of modern Catholic theology and to recover a "Christianized ontology" inspired by the early church. John Milbank has painted de Lubac as a protopostmodern theologian whose metaphysics of nature and grace underlies his radical integration of faith and reason. Milbank's highly influential interpretation confirms the deepest suspicions of contemporary neothomists, who fear that de Lubac's theology demolishes the ontological difference between nature and the supernatural. While the neothomists are generally appreciative of Lubac's other intellectual contributions (e.g., his ecclesiology and his recovery of patristic and medieval biblical interpretation), they echo the criticism of de Lubac's controversial work *Surnaturel* from over sixty years ago: de Lubac's ontology fails to respect the relative autonomy of nature and undermines the gratuity of grace.[3] A Christianized ontology remains at the center of the debate over de Lubac's theological contribution.

However, the theme that occupies the majority of de Lubac's writings is not ontology, but rather history and its fulfillment. His

2. See Matthew Bernard Mulcahy, OP, *Aquinas's Notion of Pure Nature and the Christian Integralism of Henri de Lubac: Not Everything Is Grace*, American University Studies (New York: Peter Lang, 2011); Lawrence Feingold, *The Natural Desire to See God according to St. Thomas and His Interpreters* (Washington, DC: Sapientia Press, 2010); Serge-Thomas Bonino, *Surnaturel: A Controversy at the Heart of Twentieth-Century Thomistic Thought* (Ave Maria, FL: Sapientia Press of Ave Maria University, 2009).

3. Feingold, *The Natural Desire to See God*, 2010; Mulcahy, *Aquinas's Notion of Pure Nature*.

first book, *Catholicisme* (1938), outlined a Christian understanding of salvation as an historical process, contrasting this understanding of history with Platonism, on the one hand, and historical immanentism, on the other. *Histoire et esprit: l'intelligence de l'Écriture d'après Origène* (1950) recovered a Christian understanding of history embedded within the practice of "spiritual interpretation" of Scripture. The four volumes of *Exégèse médiévale* (1959–64) traced the history of spiritual interpretation of Scripture from the patristic to medieval periods. In de Lubac's interpretation, the spiritual interpretation of Scripture functioned as both a theological method and an implicit understanding of the history of salvation. His two-volume *La Posterité spirituelle de Joachim de Flore* (1979–81) outlined the transmutation of a patristic and medieval understanding of history through the influence of Joachim of Fiore. He traced the evolution of Joachim's thought to political and secular forms in modernity. De Lubac's interest in a Christian understanding of history was more than an isolated undertaking. His various theological projects are all shaped by his preoccupation with history and its fulfillment, arguably the same preoccupation that shaped his generation's spiritual outlook and theological interests.

An Enigmatic Theologian

While it is generally agreed that Henri de Lubac was one of the most influential Catholic theologians of the twentieth century, it remains difficult to assess the nature of his theological contribution and the inner coherence of his work. It is how de Lubac wrote rather than what he wrote that makes him difficult to interpret. David Williams declared that "a less systematic systematician is difficult to imagine."[4] His body of writings remains difficult to interpret due to his idiosyncratic methods, his "third person style," and the occasionality and sheer diversity of his writings.

First, de Lubac did not fit naturally into any rigid theological discipline, as he specialized in neither "dogmatic" nor "historical" theology. His initial academic appointment was as a professor of fundamental theology at the *Institut catholique de Lyon* in 1929. The opening lecture for his course on fundamental theology, published as "Apologétique et théologie" in 1930, was programmatic for de Lubac's future scholarship.[5] "Apologétique et théologie" argued that doctrine sheds its light on the whole of human reality. Doctrine's intelligibility derives from the orientation of the soul to God. The discipline of apologetics must not be seen as a purely rationalistic exercise, but must involve the presentation of the faith in its wholeness and beauty. De Lubac's subsequent scholarship sought to present the faith of the early church to a new generation. His first book, *Catholicisme*, suggested new directions for Catholic ecclesiology through the recovery of patristic thought.[6] His book *Corpus mysticum* (1944) sought a recovery of an ancient notion of church and sacrament for the present day.[7] De Lubac's proposals concerning the supernatural took the form of historical research on the history of patristic and scholastic thought. In general, his writings reflect an assumption of the unity among the disciplines of dogmatic theology and historical theology. These writings were historical

4. David M. Williams, *Receiving the Bible in Faith: Historical and Theological Exegesis* (Washington, DC: Catholic University of America Press, 2004), 132.

5. Henri de Lubac, "Apologétique et théologie," *Nouvelle Revue théologique* 57 (1930): 361–78.

6. Henri de Lubac, *Catholicism: Christ and the Common Destiny of Man*, trans. Lancelot C. Sheppard and Sister Elizabeth Englund, OCD (San Francisco: Ignatius Press, 1988). Originally published as Henri de Lubac, *Catholicisme: les aspects sociaux du dogme*, Unam Sanctam 3 (Paris: Éditions du Cerf, 1938).

7. Henri de Lubac, *Corpus Mysticum: The Eucharist and the Church in the Middle Ages*, trans. Gemma Simmonds, CJ, Faith in Reason (Notre Dame, IN: University of Notre Dame Press, 2007). Originally published as Henri de Lubac, *Corpus mysticum: l'eucharistie et l'Église au Moyen âge. Étude historique*, Théologie 3 (Paris: Aubier, 1944).

studies with systematic theological intent; they were never a disengaged narration of the past.

Furthermore, de Lubac's historical research implied suggested new frameworks for doing theology. De Lubac and the *nouveaux théologiens* generally resisted the neoscholastic domination of theological discourse in favor of theological pluralism.[8] Although they were trained as neoscholastics, Marie-Dominique Chenu, Jean Daniélou, Yves Congar, and de Lubac were attentive to historical development and resisted the ahistorical methods of neoscholasticism in favor of methods attentive to historicity. The departure from neoscholasticism left a vacuum difficult for the *nouvelle théologie* to fill. As a result, it lacks the clarity of methods, sources, and foundations within neoscholasticism that gave theology the appearance of a science. These theologians were forced to improvise, drawing resources from the patristic and medieval periods and from the wider Christian tradition. The patristic and medieval periods offered "new" ways of thinking about the nature of theology, though prior to the Second Vatican Council (1962–1965), the implications of these shifts in theological methodology were uncertain. Because de Lubac's body of work developed during a time of radical upheaval in theological methodology, his methodology often appears to be unclear or idiosyncratic.

---

8. A growing body of literature examines the impact of the *nouvelle théologie*. See Mettepenningen, *Nouvelle Théologie—New Theology*; Boersma, *Nouvelle Théologie and Sacramental Ontology*; A. N. Williams, "The Future of the Past: The Contemporary Significance of the Nouvelle Théologie," *International Journal of Systematic Theology* 7, no. 4 (2005): 347–61; Daley, "Nouvelle Théologie and the Patristic Revival"; Étienne Fouilloux, "'Nouvelle Théologie' et Théologie Nouvelle (1930–1960)," in *L'histoire religieuse en France et en Espagne: Colloque international, Casa de Velázquez, 2–5 avril 2001: Actes*, ed. Benoît Pellistrandi, vol. 87, Collection de la Casa de Velázquez (Madrid: Casa de Velázquez, 2004), 411–25; Agnès Desmazières, "La nouvelle théologie, prémisse d'une théologie herméneutique? La controverse sur l'analogie de la vérité (1946–1949)," *Revue Thomiste* 104, no. 1/2 (2004): 241–72; Aidan Nichols, OP, "Thomism and the Nouvelle Théologie," *The Thomist* 64 (2000): 1–19.

Second, even in comparison with other *nouveaux théologiens,* de Lubac exhibited a particular allergy to theological systematization and methodological foundations. De Lubac often avoided speaking in his own voice, but rather expressed his opinions through the writings of other authors. Hans Urs von Balthasar explained that de Lubac wanted the voice of the ancient church to have a clear expression within his writings.[9] John Milbank, on the other hand, suggests that de Lubac's writings took on an increasingly historical and third-person form after 1950, when he was removed from teaching and his writings were under suspicion by the Catholic authorities. Milbank theorizes that de Lubac hid his authentic but heterodox theological opinions under the cover of historical studies.[10] Whatever the underlying cause may be for avoiding the first-person voice, his style of writing resists the easy discovery of the systematic considerations guiding his work.

Third, de Lubac's writings were responses to the problems of his day. Establishing theological coherence among his various writings remains a problem because these works are notoriously difficult to reduce to clear systematic positions. De Lubac described his writings as occasional, the choice of topics determined by situations imposed upon him rather than by some preconceived plan.[11] He likened the development of some of his writings to a disorderly evolution or autogenesis. In an interview with Angelo Scola, he admitted that *Exégèse médiévale* grew "in a rather vague order, without any

---

9. Hans Urs von Balthasar, *The Theology of Henri de Lubac: An Overview* (San Francisco: Ignatius Press, 1991), 26–27.

10. John Milbank, *The Suspended Middle: Henri de Lubac and the Debate Concerning the Supernatural* (Grand Rapids, MI: Eerdmans, 2005), 8. I fail to find any evidence for esotericism in de Lubac's work.

11. Henri de Lubac, *At the Service of the Church: Henri de Lubac Reflects on the Circumstances that Occasioned His Writings* (San Francisco: Communio Books, 1993), 369. Originally published as Henri de Lubac, *Mémoire sur l'occasion de mes écrits,* Chretiens aujourd'hui 1 (Namur, Belgium: Culture et Verité, 1989).

preconceived plan, and with enormous *lacunae*."[12] Furthermore, de Lubac's studies ranged across topics in early church history, medieval history, ecclesiology, medieval to modern scholasticism, modern atheistic thought, mysticism, fundamental theology, Renaissance studies, and literary criticism. Unifying features and foundational insights are not easy to pin down.[13]

A final obstacle to discerning the coherence of de Lubac's theological reflection is its incompleteness. In his autobiographical reflection, *At the Service of the Church*, he admitted that the idea at the center of his thought, which would be communicated in a projected book on Christ and mysticism, would never be completed: "I truly believe that for a rather long time the idea for my book on Mysticism has been my inspiration in everything. I form my judgments on the basis of it, it provides me with the means to classify my ideas in proportion to it. But I will not write this book. It is in all ways beyond my physical, intellectual, and spiritual strength."[14] This admission reflects de Lubac's notion that conceptual formulation always falls short of theological truth. It is consistent with his tendencies away from theological system.[15] The heart of his theology remains unexpressed; the center remains unarticulated. The incompleteness of de Lubac's work stands as a caveat against

---

12. Henri de Lubac, *De Lubac: A Theologian Speaks* (Los Angeles: Twin Circle, 1985), 32.

13. Rudolf Voderholzer writes, "Henri de Lubac left no masterpiece of systematic theology, no comprehensive summa of his thought. His work is both many-faceted and versatile. His writings do not carry out a long, preconceived plan." Rudolf Voderholzer, *Meet Henri de Lubac*, trans. Michael J. Miller (San Francisco: Ignatius Press, 2008), 107.

14. De Lubac, *At the Service of the Church*, 113.

15. It is more than coincidence that de Lubac's inability to express the center of his own thought reflects his theological anthropology, in which the human being, as the image of God, can only acquire self-knowledge in light of the transcendent mystery. He writes, "We shall understand more and more as we experience it, and as we see better and better that we do not yet understand it, and never shall understand it, what this astounding thing, the discovery of God, means—for it will never cease to astonish us." Henri de Lubac, *The Discovery of God*, trans. Alexander Dru (Grand Rapids, MI: Eerdmans, 1996), 166. Originally published as *Sur les chemins de Dieu* (Paris: Aubier, 1956).

excessively systematic interpretations of his thought. At the same time, it proposes something positive about his theological vision: authentic transcendence requires that complete synthesis occur only beyond the present horizon. The incompleteness of his work testifies to its eschatological character and its apophatic tone.

Ontology and History

Despite these obstacles, many have recognized signs of a consistent theological vision that permeates de Lubac's diverse writings. Instead of speaking of his "systematic theology," Voderholzer refers to his "synthetic thinking" and "synoptic presentation."[16] Hans Urs von Balthasar, in *The Theology of Henri de Lubac* (1991), spoke of an "organic unity" amidst a "multiplicity of themes."[17] Yet determining precisely what that organic unity consists in remains a difficulty. Two major interpretations have arisen in describing the coherence of de Lubac's corpus: an ontological interpretation and an historical interpretation.

One proposal relates de Lubac's theological method, ecclesiology, sacramental theology, and other theological themes to his ontology, particularly his account of the supernatural and the natural, that informs his entire theological project. This proposal was popularized by John Milbank's *The Suspended Middle: Henri de Lubac and the Debate Concerning the Supernatural* (2005), in which he argued that the core of de Lubac's work is the debate on the supernatural, most authentically articulated in de Lubac's 1946 book *Surnaturel: Études*

---

16. Voderholzer, *Meet Henri de Lubac*, 108–9. Susan K. Wood speaks of an "organic unity." Susan K. Wood, *Spiritual Exegesis and the Church in the Theology of Henri de Lubac* (Grand Rapids, MI: Eerdmans, 1998), 129.

17. Balthasar, *Theology of Henri de Lubac*, 10. The title of the German original is more suggestive of unity within diverse themes: *Henri de Lubac: Sein organisches Lebenswerk* (1976; Henri de Lubac: his organic life's work). The conclusion of *Theology of Henri de Lubac* was taken from Hans Urs von Balthasar, *Le cardinal Henri de Lubac, l'homme et son oeuvre*, (Paris: Éditions Lethielleux, 1983).

historiques. Milbank explains, "Most of de Lubac's other writing . . . in a sense works out the thesis of *Surnaturel* in relation to ecclesiology, exegesis, inter-religious dialogue, and secular social and scientific thought."[18] For Milbank, *Surnaturel* communicates a core theological insight: the rejection of a hierarchical duality between nature and grace, and nature and the supernatural. In sum, de Lubac saw nature and the supernatural as different intensities of being rather than as formally distinct. While Milbank admits that de Lubac never developed a formal ontology, he nevertheless proposes that de Lubac's fundamental vision was guided by an Augustinian-Neoplatonic account of being.

Milbank's account of the unity of de Lubac's theology has influenced an ontological interpretation of the unity of his work. Bryan C. Hollon's book on de Lubac, *Everything Is Sacred: Spiritual Exegesis in the Political Theology of Henri de Lubac* (2009), is a significant engagement with and corrective to Milbank. The title suggests an ontology of creation in which the partition between supernatural and natural has been dissolved.[19] Matthew Bernard Mulcahy, in *Aquinas's Notion of Pure Nature and the Christian Integralism of Henri de Lubac* (2011), appropriates Milbank's ontological interpretation of de Lubac's work and identifies the core inspiration of de Lubac with that of Milbank and Radical Orthodoxy.[20] The subtitle, *Not Everything Is Grace*, more provocatively captures the heart of the question as to whether de Lubac's ontology preserves the distinction between nature and grace.

18. Milbank, *The Suspended Middle*, 4.
19. Bryan C. Hollon, *Everything Is Sacred: Spiritual Exegesis in the Political Theology of Henri de Lubac* (Eugene, OR: Cascade Books, 2009). To be precise, however, Hollon's interpretation, "Everything is sacred," diverges considerably from Milbank. Hollon does not attribute to de Lubac an implicit Neoplatonic ontology of participation, as does Milbank. Instead, he frames the sacrality of creation in terms of the historical participation in the Christ event, a participation illuminated by the practice of "spiritual interpretation" of Scripture.
20. Mulcahy, *Aquinas's Notion of Pure Nature*.

Similarly, Hans Boersma interprets de Lubac, and *nouvelle théologie* as a whole, through the lens of ontology. He theorizes that de Lubac recovered a metaphysics—which he calls "sacramental ontology"—that functioned as a common systematic method.[21] Sacramental ontology concerns the "sacramental character of all created existence" and functions as the link between the theology of nature and the supernatural and the theology of the church in de Lubac's thought.[22] His recent book, *Nouvelle Théologie and Sacramental Ontology: A Return to Mystery,* expands these ideas in an effort to identify the internal coherence within the *nouvelle théologie* as a movement.[23]

There are merits to speaking of de Lubac's ontology or sacramental ontology. Yet there are also limitations. Ontology—whether in regard to a Christian-Neoplatonic ontology or a postmodern Christian ontology—suggests that the principal categories of de Lubac's theology are philosophical rather than historical. The predominant themes and discourses within his work revolve around *chronos* (time) or *kairos* (the opportune moment) rather than *ontos* (being). However, it is more accurate to say that the ontology found within de Lubac's account of the supernatural and natural is derivative of his understanding of the history of salvation and its fulfillment.

21. Boersma borrows the term *sacramental ontology* from Dennis Doyle, who writes that de Lubac's doctrine of the supernatural "provides an ontology that allows for speaking of knowledge of God in an historical and critical framework," which assumes that the historical nature of God's revelation does not occlude knowledge of God, but is a means to knowledge of God's self. Dennis M. Doyle, "Henri de Lubac and the Roots of Communion Ecclesiology," *Theological Studies* 60, no. 2 (1999): 209–27.

22. Boersma, "Sacramental Ontology," 243–4.

23. While Boersma admits that the theologians associated with the *nouvelle théologie* did not constitute a homogeneous theological school, he contends that their approach to diverse theological problems—including the interpretation of Scripture, the theology of history, the development of doctrine, nature and grace, and ecclesiology—evinced an underlying sacramental view of reality. He closely relates this sacramental view of reality with Neoplatonic ontology.

The second line of interpretation of de Lubac's work emphasizes *chronos* and *kairos* over *ontos* as the basic unifying features of de Lubac's thought. Balthasar suggests that the multiple themes in de Lubac's writings are systematically connected with the organic center: the natural desire of the creature for God. According to Balthasar, the "principal problem" that de Lubac addressed is that the finite creature tends through a "positive dynamism . . . toward a goal that cannot be reached 'from below' but is nevertheless necessary."[24] The dynamism of the creature for God permeates de Lubac's fundamental theology, his theology of salvation history, and cosmology-eschatology.[25] Adding that these theological themes cannot be reduced to each other, Balthasar contends that each theme shares a common "structural principle of the divine plan."[26] He notes that the structure of God's plan in history is the underlying subject of de Lubac's *Exégèse médiévale*, despite its focus on the development of biblical interpretation.[27]

Like Balthasar, Susan K. Wood contends that de Lubac's investigations into early Christian scriptural interpretation concern a theology of history.[28] Wood demonstrates the parallels articulated in de Lubac's writings between the senses of Scripture (literal, allegorical, anagogical), the multiple meanings of the "body of Christ" (historical, sacramental, ecclesial), and multiple significations of liturgical practice (memorial, presence, anticipation). According to Wood, the pattern of salvation history is the basic structure that informs de Lubac's theology of Scripture, sacraments, and the church.

24. Balthasar, *Theology of Henri de Lubac*, 12.
25. Ibid., 62.
26. Ibid., 63.
27. Ibid., 76.
28. Wood, *Spiritual Exegesis and the Church*; Susan K. Wood, "The Nature-Grace Problematic within Henri de Lubac's Christological Paradox," *Communio* 19, no. 3 (1992): 389–403; Susan K. Wood, "The Church as the Social Embodiment of Grace in the Ecclesiology of Henri de Lubac" (PhD diss., Marquette University, 1986).

Similarly, Brian Daley has suggested that the *nouvelle théologie*'s recovery of patristic and medieval exegetical practices—namely, the figural or spiritual interpretation of Scripture—was central to its shift away from both neoscholastic ecclesiology and theological methodology. Daley concludes that the patristic revival in the *nouvelle théologie* allowed for a broadening of theological methodology and a revival of a sacramental mentality. From the Greek and Latin fathers, the *nouvelle théologie*'s rediscovery of "sacramental modes of thought" through "figural exegesis . . . [as a] way of reading all history as really speaking of Christ, was the heart of the *nouvelle théologie*, the greatest lesson it had learned from reading the Fathers."[29] The recovery of spiritual exegesis in the *nouvelle théologie*—most evident in the work of Henri de Lubac and Jean Daniélou—explains its growing appeal to Protestant theologians as a resource for theology and ecumenism.[30]

Towards an Eschatological Unity

Building on the work of Balthasar, Wood, and Daley, I argue that the pattern of redemptive history and its eschatological fulfillment constitute the theological axes of de Lubac's work. De Lubac's eschatology remains an often-overlooked feature of his theological writings. Against the backdrop of a renewed awareness of the end in Roman Catholicism during the twentieth century, de Lubac's theology appears essentially eschatological.

Beginning in the late nineteenth century, Roman Catholicism communicated an apocalyptic interpretation of modern history and the church's place in the modern world through official church pronouncements and messages from the appearances of Mary. In

---

29. Daley, "Nouvelle Théologie and the Patristic Revival," 382.
30. For example, see Hollon, *Everything Is Sacred*; Hollon, "Ontology, Exegesis, and Culture in the Thought of Henri de Lubac" (PhD diss., Baylor University, 2006).

the twentieth century, apocalypticism in Roman Catholicism became more acute. The apocalyptic, the experience of evil, and God's judgment were also the subjects of literary reflection, for example, in Georges Bernanos's *Sous le soleil de Satan* (1926) and Paul Claudel's *Paul Claudel interroge l'apocalypse* (1952). In the mid-1940s, the question of the apocalyptic was addressed directly in the debate over the "theology of history" within the *nouvelle théologie*. During the German occupation of France, it became clear that an apocalyptic understanding of history was at the root of fascist ideology. Writers associated with the *nouvelle théologie*—Henri-Marie Féret, Gaston Fessard, Joseph Huby, and Jean Daniélou—began to rethink a Christian view of history, one that takes seriously God's ongoing presence in the world, in light of the philosophies of history promulgated both by fascists and Marxists. The central question that emerged concerned the relationship between the sacred history communicated in Scripture and historical experience punctuated by the war, the Shoah, and the liberation of Paris.

The debate over the theology of history within the *nouvelle théologie* in the 1940s is not unlike the current reflections on the recovery of the apocalyptic within Christian theology.[31] As Cyril O'Regan suggests, on the one hand, apocalyptic theology is a powerful "visionary option," transmitting an image of Christianity as a way of life, the anticipation of restoration, and the establishment of divine justice.[32] On the other hand, apocalyptic theology could be a dangerous tool of sectarianism, triumphalism, or worse. The debate over the theological meaning of history in the 1940s attempted to

---

31. See Cyril O'Regan, *Theology and the Spaces of Apocalyptic* (Milwaukee: Marquette University Press, 2009); Nathan R. Kerr, *Christ, History, and Apocalyptic: The Politics of Christian Mission* (Eugene, OR: Cascade Books, 2009).
32. O'Regan, *Theology and the Spaces of Apocalyptic*, 127.

address both the promises and dangers of the apocalyptic as a mode of interpreting Scripture and the world.

For the *nouvelle théologie*, representing the telos of history and the eternal in the present became an overarching concern. Especially for de Lubac, the theological meaning of history became the axis of his work. While de Lubac presented an outline of patristic historical and eschatological thought in *Catholicisme*, it was in *Exégèse médiévale* that he outlined the development of Christian thinking about history and its fulfillment. De Lubac's *La Posterité spirituelle de Joachim de Flore* traced a stream of apocalyptic theology from the medieval theologian Joachim of Fiore through the modern era. De Lubac also recognized an impulse opposed to Joachim within a stream of Christian mysticism that lacked the virtue of hope or the element of expectation. In a mysticism divorced from history and an apocalyptic understanding divorced from mysticism, Western modernity had inherited the pathological remains of a Christian understanding of "the end," reconstituting them in secular variants. De Lubac's work sought to recover an early Christian understanding of eschatology from the patristic period, a unity of historical expectation and mysticism.

De Lubac should not be interpreted in an overly systematic or foundational manner. He never elaborated a systematic eschatology that would coordinate the various aspects of his thinking. Yet de Lubac's various theological interventions evince a common structure organized around the relationship between redemptive history and its fulfillment. De Lubac's eschatology, which arose against the backdrop of diverse apocalyptic and eschatological streams in modernity, constitutes the organizing principle and guiding intuition of his diverse theological projects.

***

Between Apocalypse and Eschaton: History and Eternity in Henri de Lubac examines de Lubac's understanding of history and its fulfillment in light of the eschatological consciousness within twentieth-century Catholicism and the shifting methodology in Catholic theology during that period. The study is divided into three parts. Part 1, "Eschatology as the 'Storm Center,'" shows that the eschatological resurgence in early twentieth-century theology was part of a broader eschatological turn in modernity. The instability of the meaning of time and history characterized *fin-de-siècle* European culture. This instability manifested itself eschatologically. Antimodernist Catholics tended to interpret this instability in apocalyptic terms, reflecting the loss of a clear framework for discovering eternity in time. The *nouvelle théologie* movement, and particularly the post–World War II debate over the "theology of history," sought to reconcile a vibrant Catholic apocalyptic sensibility with a modern historical consciousness.

Part 2, "Temporal Ruptures," outlines de Lubac's formulation of a theology of history that responded to diverse eschatological strands within modernity. De Lubac recovered a Christian understanding of history from the patristic tradition, especially from the writings of the Egyptian theologian Origen (185–254 CE). For de Lubac, a Christian understanding of history was transmitted through ancient methods of interpreting the Bible, methods of spiritual interpretation that can be traced back to Origen. This Christian consciousness of history eroded with the erosion of spiritual interpretation in the Middle Ages. According to de Lubac, a modern apocalyptic consciousness can be traced to a rupture in the tradition of scriptural interpretation.

Part 3, "The Eschatological Structure of De Lubac's Thought," shows that de Lubac's historical-eschatological thinking constitutes the fundamental inspiration for his various theological projects and interventions. His theology of revelation, Christology, sacramental theology, ecclesiology, and understanding of the supernatural share a common structure inspired by his eschatology.

PART I

Eschatology as the "Storm Center"

Part 1 narrates the rise of an eschatological consciousness within twentieth-century Catholic theology. While Catholic theology of an earlier period produced systematic eschatologies in the form of treatises on the last things—death, judgment, heaven, and hell—twentieth-century ˙Catholic theology more explicitly articulated a consciousness of this present time as preceding and anticipating the end. By the early twentieth century, an eschatological renewal within Christian theology was already afoot, in part due to the rediscovery of the eschatological message of the Gospels by biblical scholars.[1] Soon, as Hans Urs von Balthasar claimed, these eschatological themes spread everywhere:

> Eschatology is the storm center of our times. It is the source of several squalls that threaten all the theological fields, and makes them fruitful, beating down or reinvigorating their various growths. Troeltsch's dictum, "The bureau of eschatology is usually closed," was true enough of the liberalism of the nineteenth century, but since the turn of the century the office has been working overtime.[2]

---

1. The work of Johannes Weiss and Albert Schweitzer was particularly a catalyst for rethinking the eschatological content of the Gospels.

There are reasons to believe that this eschatological storm was not solely a response to the traumatizing experience of World Wars I and II, as significant as these events were. This eschatological renewal in the twentieth century was the outgrowth of an intensifying historical consciousness within Christian theology in the nineteenth century. Furthermore, the eschatological renewal was in concert with a growing eschatological awareness outside of strictly theological or strictly Christian circles. It was being worked out and anticipated in cultural, ecclesial, literary, and political arenas before it reached European Christian theology. In many respects, the themes treated by Christian theologians intersected with a broader European eschatological imaginary and a broader feeling of living at the end of history.

In advance of the eschatological renewal in theology, a significant apocalyptic consciousness is manifest within Catholic magisterial documents of the nineteenth century and within the antimodernist movement. Roman Catholic culture and theology in the nineteenth to twentieth centuries reflected a broader struggle within European modernity over the meaning of time and eternity. Neoscholasticism and Catholic antimodernism not only suffered from an allergy to history but also contributed to an intense consciousness of the present as the last days. From the late nineteenth century, the popes condemned the contemporary age as the culmination of decadence. Catholics responded to modernity by combining a nostalgia for the unchanging and an apocalyptic sensibility.

This is the soil in which the *nouvelle théologie* grew and also to which it responded. The challenge to relate the changing and unchanging, time and eternity, and the historical and the eschaton figured prominently within the *nouvelle théologie*. If eschatology was

---

2. Hans Urs von Balthasar, *Explorations in Theology: The Word Made Flesh*, trans. A. V. Littledale and Alexander Dru, vol. 1 (San Francisco: Ignatius Press, 1989), 255.

the storm center, as Balthasar puts it, the *nouvelle théologie* became the eye of the storm in Roman Catholicism from the 1930s to the 1950s. The papal promulgation of documents like *Pascendi dominici gregis* (1907) and *Lamentabili sane exitu* (1907) had the intention of quashing Catholic Modernism and of supporting a homogeneous program of Catholic education grounded in the neothomist revival. The Modernist Crisis (1902–1907), a period of persecution of Modernist Catholics by ecclesial authorities, effectively suppressed the questions raised by the Modernists, namely the historically embedded nature of dogmatic statements, the critical interpretation of Scripture, the epistemological status of concepts, the role of apologetics, and the nature of divine revelation. However, as a result of the Modernist Crisis, similar conflicts reemerged at the center of Thomism itself and in the *nouvelle théologie*. At the heart of these conflicts was the interpretation of time and eternity, and the changing and unchanging.

Chapter 1, "An Eschatological Modernity," describes the emergence of eschatological and apocalyptic thinking in nonecclesial settings in the *fin de siècle* and the return of eschatology to the center of twentieth-century Catholicism. Chapter 2, "Time and Eternity in the *Nouvelle Théologie*," examines the World War II debate over the theology of history in the *nouvelle théologie*—specifically the work of Henri-Marie Féret, Joseph Huby, Gaston Fessard, and Jean Daniélou—as a struggle over the interpretation of time and eternity.

1

_____

An Eschatological Modernity

Eschatology—that is, a religious interpretation of the fulfillment of God's plan (the eschaton)—reemerged as an important theme in twentieth-century European Christianity. Biblical studies led the way in the work of Johannes Weiss (1863–1914) and Albert Schweitzer (1875–1965). For Weiss, the predominant theme within the preaching of Jesus was the imminence of the "kingdom of God." Schweitzer states that the earliest Christians believed in the impending end of the world and, as a result, in the urgency of responding to the gospel message. According to Joseph Ratzinger, the rediscovery of the eschatological character of Jesus's preaching in the work of Johannes Weiss and Albert Schweitzer impacted biblical studies but had little immediate impact on systematic theology: "As far as systematic theology was concerned, they had not the faintest idea of what to do with their discovery."[1] However, as Ratzinger explains, Karl Barth's 1919 *Commentary on the Letter to the Romans*

1. Joseph Ratzinger, *Eschatology, Death and Eternal Life*, 2nd ed. (Washington, DC: Catholic University of America Press, 1988), 47.

initiated a revolution. Barth stated, "A Christianity that is not wholly eschatology and nothing but eschatology has absolutely nothing to do with Christ."[2] Barth's radical break with liberal Protestantism and his eschatological turn is often associated with a disillusionment with modern ideologies of progress triggered by the experience of the World War I. The war indeed acted as a ferment for a theological reawakening to eschatology among many Christian theologians.

Yet this reawakening also occurred in the midst of a period of reevaluation of the meaning of time and eternity, beginning in the nineteenth century. From around the mid-nineteenth century to the mid-twentieth century, a broad crisis of adequately representing temporality and the eternal was unfolding within scientific, literary, economic, philosophical, and artistic spheres. Stephen Kern explains,

> The structure of history, the uninterrupted forward movement of clocks, the procession of days, seasons, years, and simple common sense tells us that time is irreversible and moves forward at a steady rate. Yet these features of traditional time were also challenged as artists and intellectuals envisioned times that reversed themselves, moved at irregular rhythms, and even came to a dead stop. In the *fin de siècle*, time's arrow did not always fly straight and true.[3]

No single theoretical model accounts for all the different shifts in temporal representation and eschatological consciousness during the period. It suffices, for my purposes, to indicate that the modern West experienced a confusion over the meaning of time and its end, a confusion that effected an eschatological consciousness during the *fin de siècle* and following. Additionally, this confusion affected the experience and representation of time and eternity in Roman Catholicism.

2. Karl Barth, *Epistle to the Romans*, trans. Edwyn C. Hoskyns, 6th ed. (Oxford: Oxford University Press, 1933), 314.
3. Stephen Kern, *The Culture of Time and Space, 1880–1918* (Cambridge, MA: Harvard University Press, 1983), 28.

Representing Time in a Changing World

According to David Harvey, prior to the mid-nineteenth century, an Enlightenment sense of space and time was dominant among the bourgeoisie. Enlightenment thinkers emphasized the rational, objective, quantifiable, and universal characteristics of time and space.[4] For example, the production of maps increasingly represented the earth in those aspects necessary for navigation and commerce, evacuating space of the "sensuous" qualities developed in medieval cartography: "Maps, stripped of all elements of fantasy and religious belief, as well as any sign of the experiences involved in their production, had become abstract and strictly functional systems for the factual ordering of phenomena in space." The Enlightenment gave a "totalizing" sense of space insofar as the whole world could be conceived as existing in a "single spatial frame."[5] The Enlightenment conception and production of time was similarly totalizing in its prioritization of the neutral, objective, quantifiable, and infinite qualities of time. The chronometer provided a fixed division for time's flow, allowing its exact measurement and, significantly, the conception of time as a linear progress. Newton's *Principia* envisioned space as a kind of envelope or container for materially extended things, and time was a receptacle for change. Absolute time was mathematical in its qualities and extended into the past and future infinitely. Although Newtonian space and time had its challengers in Leibniz and Kant, they left undisturbed the emphasis on the universal, neutral, and quantifiable temporal qualities.

From the sixteenth to eighteenth centuries, economic and colonial expansion required mastery over space. As Dana Sobel narrated in *Longitude* (1995), mastery over space, and specifically mastery of

4. David Harvey, *The Condition of Postmodernity: An Enquiry into the Origins of Cultural Change* (Cambridge, MA: Blackwell, 1989), 245.
5. Ibid., 249–50.

the oceans, necessitated a system for accurately determining longitude. She notes that means to determining latitude had been available for centuries through the position of the stars. But determining longitude with any accuracy remained a problem until the eighteenth century. While great strides were made to solve this problem through astronomy, the simplest solution come through a mechanical clock that could withstand travel, changes in temperature, and weather, while remaining accurate. By comparing the time of a known location to the solar time of a new location, one could determine the degree hour difference between the two, and thus one's longitude. The mastery of space required a mastery over time. This mastery over time did not happen quickly or uniformly. It took until 1884 for the International Meridian Conference to make Greenwich the prime meridian and standardize the measurement of longitude and world time on the basis of it. Sobel notes that it took the French another twenty-seven years to recognize Greenwich as the prime meridian instead of Paris.[6]

The end of the nineteenth century experienced the victory of the Enlightenment conception of temporality through technological advancements in mechanical clocks and systems of measurement. Ironically, this same period experienced a serious challenge to the Enlightenment sense of time with the genesis of literary, artistic, and cultural phenomena known as *modernism*. Technological development is significant to the story of modernism because new technologies reordered how Westerners experienced their world and how they experienced time. In brief, the increasing speed of communication and transportation during the nineteenth to twentieth centuries led to a shrinking world. As a result, heterogeneous local practices of measuring time—often governed

---

6. Dana Sobel, *Longitude: The True Story of a Lone Genius Who Solved the Greatest Scientific Problem of His Time* (New York: Walker and Company, 1995), 168.

by agricultural, local commercial, liturgical-religious, and seasonal cycles—were put in conflict. The development of the telegraph and the expansion of railways joined different local times together, exposing their differences. Kern notes that travelers on a cross-continental journey by railroad in 1870 would pass through over two hundred different local times. In 1870, there were over eighty time zones used by the railroads in the United States.[7] The confusion between different systems had a detrimental effect on the efficiency of railroads and, in 1883, a uniform system of measuring time for the railroads was created. In the following year, the Prime Meridian Conference organized the twenty-four time zones. The increased speed of communication and transportation led to various systematic orderings of time across space, joining previously separated peoples and economies. This was a vast but chaotic reorganization and creation of public time, the uniform and measurable progression of moments to which local times would have to conform.

According to Harvey, modernism as a "cultural force" formed under the "crisis of representation . . . derived from a radical readjustment in the sense of time and space in economic, political, and cultural life."[8] The interconnectedness of the international economy, the increased speed of commerce, the unification of monetary systems, and the development of new communication technologies were elements of "time-space compression."

> Enlightenment thought operated within the confines of a rather mechanical "Newtonian" vision of the universe, in which the presumed absolutes of homogeneous time and space formed limiting containers to thought and action. The breakdown in these absolute conceptions under the stress of time-space compression was the central story in the birth of nineteenth- and twentieth-century forms of modernism.[9]

7. Kern, *Culture of Time and Space*, 12.
8. Harvey, *Condition of Postmodernity*, 260.
9. Ibid., 252.

Thus, "time-space compression" brought the tensions between public time and private time, the universal and the particular, the international and the local into the foreground.

The awareness of new configurations of space and time played out in art and literature, notably in the writings of James Joyce, Gustave Flaubert, and Charles Baudelaire. Joyce and Flaubert expressed the "simultaneity" of modern life, in which actions and events in different places paralleled and affected one another. Just as different places were being absorbed under a single economy, these authors tried to represent the relationship between heterogeneous "times." Closely related to simultaneity was the feeling that modern life was riddled by constant change, insecurity, and ephemerality. Baudelaire's attempt to reconcile "the transient, the fleeting, the contingent" with "the eternal and the immutable" was characteristic of the "aesthetic thrust of modernism" as a whole "to strive for this sense of eternity in the midst of flux."[10]

The attempt to reconcile time and eternity in literary modernism is consonant with the work of French philosopher Henri Bergson. For Bergson, the discrete units of mathematical or clock time fail to capture the dynamic flow of reality, life as a dynamic energy, and of the experience of *durée* (duration). According to Bergson, consciousness is a stream rather than a "conglomeration of separate faculties or ideas."[11] He distinguished between a relative knowledge of reality through the symbols or language that ultimately distort it, by breaking it up into various pieces, and the absolute knowledge of reality through a form of intuition. In his conception of *durée*, he appealed to a mystical experience of time and of reality beyond our power to represent. In a sense, Bergson's temporal mysticism was an

10. Ibid., 10, 206.
11. Kern, *Culture of Time and Space*, 24.

attempt to reconcile the sense of eternity with an evolutionary view of a constantly changing world.[12]

The technological advancements that were the cause of economic and cultural unification brought about a struggle to reconcile the eternal with the contingent, changing world. Similarly, modern life brought about a rethinking of the historical plane, particularly the relationship between the present and the future.

Representing the Future

Enlightenment representations of the future depended upon a conception of time as straight and uniform in direction. Progress was a straight line from myth to reason, ignorance to knowledge, and bondage to freedom.[13] The future of humanity was already emerging in the present day through the emergence of new forms of governance, science, and knowledge. In *fin-de-siècle* Europe, the Enlightenment version of the future became increasingly contested. Not only did challenges to Enlightenment notions of uniformity and progress emerge, but apocalyptic understandings of time took center stage in cultural, literary, and political arenas. Like the Enlightenment era, these new conceptions of time and history depicted qualitatively different times and caesuras between eras. Yet they announced different ruptures between the past and present, and between the present and future. The apocalyptic sentiment of living just before

---

12. Bergson is known to have had a keen antipathy toward clocks. As Kern notes, Bergson's appeal to the experience of temporality and his emphasis on intuition is consonant with Charles Péguy, who "explained the spiritual death of Christianity by its mindless repetition of fixed ideas: layers of habit stifle the dynamic energies of true faith." Ibid., 26. Bergson's lectures inspired Christian thinkers like Pierre Rousselot, Jacques Maritain, and Gabriel Marcel.
13. Immanuel Kant's essay "An Answer to the Question 'What is Enlightenment?'" exemplifies the Enlightenment faith in a slow growth of humanity toward the independent use of reason, liberty, and knowledge. Kant states that enlightenment is the emergence of humanity from its immaturity. Enlightenment, he says, needs liberty to reason publicly.

the end was a wide-ranging cultural expression of this contested "future."

A version of this sentiment is manifested in the Italian Futurist Movement's admiration of technology, speed, and violence that ushered in a new world. The introduction to Filippo Tommaso Marinetti's "Fondazione e Manifesto del futurismo" (Futurist foundation and manifesto, 1909) reads almost like an apocalyptic text in which the seer glimpses through the veil of this world to the drama that lies beyond it.[14] Marinetti narrates a drunken escapade that results in overturning his automobile in a muddy ditch. Emerging injured from the muck, he announces the principles of Futurism: live dangerously without fear; awaken to the "beauty of speed," exemplified in the racing car; aggressiveness and violence are the media of creativity; reject antiquarianism, museums, and the past; glorify youthfulness. Marinetti declares that we are living at the last point of history. Human beings, as the creators of speed, have broken down the barriers to the impossible. He claimed to be ushering in the age of the "impossible" and the "absolute." Although Marinetti's glimpse of a glorious future is in continuity with Enlightenment thought, he does not propose a slow evolution toward maturity. The future breaks violently with the past and, indeed, violence and technology bring about this future. The Futurist infatuation with a new humanity or posthumanity united to technology spilled over into politics; many Futurists became fascists.[15]

---

14. Filippo Tommaso Marinetti, "Fondazione e manifesto del Futurismo," *Gazetta dell'Emilia*, February 5, 1909.

15. See Günter Berghaus, *Futurism and Politics: Between Anarchist Rebellion and Fascist Reaction, 1909–1944* (Oxford: Berghahn Books, 1996). Mark Antliff argues that the arts mediated fascism in France prior to the Second World War, particularly insofar as they expressed the expectation of a new humanity, the "New Man," and the desire to overthrow all institutions. Mark Antliff, *Avant-Garde Fascism: The Mobilization of Myth, Art, and Culture in France, 1909–1939* (Durham, NC: Duke University Press, 2007).

The awareness of the near future was not always the expectation of a glorious future era. In some cases, it was an expectation of a decline. The theory of the heat death of the universe, embodied in the second law of thermodynamics, exercised an influence over popular imagination, particularly in the French Decadent Movement of the late nineteenth century. The entropy of all available energy in the universe—no matter how far in the future it would occur—symbolized a feeling of being on the verge of the end. David Weir states, "Whether the late nineteenth century was actually a period of decadence is open to debate; but it clearly was perceived as such, as a time when all was over, or almost over: not the end, but the ending."[16] H. G. Wells's *Time Machine* foretold a catastrophic future in which humanity would degenerate, "overpowered by the forces of nature and society, leading to . . . an ultimate extinction of the species."[17] The protagonist first arrives in a posthuman future and then travels in his time machine farther into the future to witness a barren planet tumbling through space. Oswald Spengler's *The Decline of the West* (1918) echoed the theme of the degeneration of society. Like all civilizations, Western civilization follows an evolutionary course of life and death. Having reached its apex, it is now experiencing its final season. "The theory of Entropy signifies today [the] world's end as completion of an inwardly necessary evolution."[18] According to Spengler, the modern world is uniquely obsessed with time and the future; moderns measure the meaning of the present by its projected end.

In fields of art, politics, and history, a dominant trope was emerging. *Fin-de-siècle* interpretations of the present moment ranged

16. David Weir, *Decadence and the Making of Modernism* (Amherst, MA: University of Massachusetts Press, 1996), 17.
17. Kern, *Culture of Time and Space*, 91.
18. Ibid., 105.

from intoxicated enthusiasm to despair. Furthermore, the imaginary future of society represented the telos of the present, the age right before the end. Whether the coming era was perceived as the dawn of a new era of history, or the initial winding down of a tired universe, the present age was seen to be one of transition to a new era.

Eternalism in Catholic Neoscholasticism and Anti-Modernism

A new historical consciousness arising within various fields posed the vital challenge to Christian theology in the nineteenth to twentieth centuries. Roman Catholic theology and culture manifested a particular allergy to historical consciousness, particularly in the neoscholastic theological movement and among antimodernist Catholics. *Neoscholasticism* refers to a Catholic theological movement that arose in the middle of the nineteenth century as a recovery of medieval theology. Pope Leo XIII's encyclical *Aeterni Patris* (1879) endorsed medieval theology, preeminently the theology of Thomas Aquinas, as the primary intellectual vehicle for a Catholic response to the challenges to Christian belief in the modern world. Based on *Aeterni Patris*, theological schools employed neoscholastic theology for the theological formation of priests, which held a quasi–official status within Catholic teaching for over seventy years. Neoscholasticism is historically related to what Joseph Komonchak calls the "construction" of Roman Catholicism, a distinct subculture or sociological form that Catholicism took as a response to modernity.[19] Resistance to the modern world was characteristic of this subculture. *Antimodernist* refers to those authors and their writings who suppressed Catholic Modernists, that is, those considered overly sympathetic toward modern philosophy, critical

---

19. Joseph A. Komonchak, "Modernity and the Construction of Roman Catholicism," *Cristianesimo nella Storia* 18, no. 2 (1997): 353–85.

methods, political philosophy, and culture during the early twentieth century, particularly during the Modernist Crisis (1903–1907).

Historical consciousness is a multifaceted and ambiguous term that refers to the awareness that human beings are historically situated, that historical circumstances affect our experience of the world, and that our historical experience affects the categories of our thinking. Lawrence F. Barmann describes historical consciousness by distinguishing between "thinking about history" from "thinking with history." *Thinking about history* denotes the endeavor to recover the past by analyzing evidence available to the historian. *Thinking with history*—properly speaking, historical consciousness—denotes the perception of ourselves within the stream of history:

> In this mode one perceives the past as a process, of which process we are the most recent expressions. It is this sense of history as a process in which we ourselves are located consciously and culturally that is what I would mean by "historical consciousness." And it is this sense that forces one to acknowledge the relativity of all finite reality, i.e., of all that ordinarily impinges on our human consciousness, because it is always and necessarily in flux, moving, unstable, incomplete, partial.[20]

Historical consciousness, for Barmann, implies that human knowledge is not a "view from nowhere," but rather is somehow tied to its particular and localized conditions.[21]

At the turn of the century, Catholic theology in its neoscholastic and antimodernist forms resisted historical consciousness.[22] First, it

---

20. Lawrence F. Barmann, "Defining Historical Consciousness" (paper presented at the Annual Meeting of the American Academy of Religion, Denver, November 2001), 2.

21. In a 1966 lecture, Bernard F. Lonergan made a similar observation when he distinguished between a "classicist world-view" and "historical-mindedness" as "differences in horizon, in total mentality." Bernard J. F. Lonergan, "The Transition from a Classicist World-View to Historical-Mindedness," in *A Second Collection* (Toronto: University of Toronto Press, 1996), 2. The classicist worldview takes the unchanging as the starting point for rational inquiry, whereas historical mindedness takes the changing world of experience as its starting point: "One may work methodically from the abstract and universal towards the more concrete and particular" or "begin from people as they are" concretely. Ibid., 3.

was reluctant to accept the results of historical research and the relative independence of historical investigation from theological truth claims. This was a resistance to questions about the historical accuracy of the Scriptures and to recognizing the difference between the content of the Bible and that of later Christian doctrine. Second, this theology opposed the idea of historical development or evolution, especially when it appeared to challenge the "unchanging" nature of truth. Scholasticism's model of scientific knowledge prioritized unchanging essences over changing events. History and particularity did not fit well within this model.

The scholastic systems were more prepared to respond to the attacks on revealed religion by the rationalists than they were to face the challenge of historical research into the continuity of Christian dogma with the Bible. The idea of development, change, or evolution within doctrine and theological systems in the theology of John Henry Cardinal Newman in the 1840s was met with anathema by the papal encyclicals *Pascendi* and *Lamentabili* half a century later. Indeed, Newman was considered suspect by many antimodernists. It is not that the neoscholastics rejected all development of doctrine. Rather, Newman's organic model of doctrinal or theological development was rejected in favor of a theory of logical development: theological development results from the application of metaphysics to biblical propositions, resulting in a syllogistic growth from premise to conclusion. Historical research into Scripture threatened not only the truthfulness of certain revealed propositions found in the Bible, but also this model of conceiving doctrine. Thus, the work of Bible scholars like Marie-Joseph Lagrange was alarming because it assumed a relative independence of historical research from theology.

---

22. See Gerald McCool, *Nineteenth-Century Scholasticism: The Search for a Unitary Method*, 2nd ed. (New York: Fordham University Press, 1989), 9–11; T. M. Schoof, *A Survey of Catholic Theology, 1800–1970* (Glen Rock, NJ: Paulist Newman Press, 1970), 35–36.

Although neoscholasticism in the nineteenth century appears to be "classicist" due to its rejection of historical development, it also had much in common with the empirical turn within the sciences and history in the nineteenth century. T. M. Schoof states that during the mid-nineteenth century, there was a philosophical and cultural shift away from German Idealism and toward trust in empirical data, from synthetic methods toward analytic.[23] The shift toward analytic methods within neoscholasticism, however, did not include the reevaluation of historicity.

Antimodernist arguments against the Modernists and the later neoscholastic grievances against the *nouvelle théologie* almost always returned to the same theme: the loss of *unchanging* truth. Pope Pius X's *Lamentabili sane exitu* (1907) condemned a host of errors attributed to Modernist Catholics, which were perceived as undermining the authority of the "teaching church" and orthodox doctrine. Among the theses proscribed are the following:

> 53. The organic constitution of the Church is not immutable.

> 58. Truth is no more immutable than man himself, since it evolved with him, in him, and through him.

> 64. Scientific progress demands that the concepts of Christian doctrine concerning God, creation, revelation, the person of the Incarnate Word, and redemption be recast.[24]

The follow-up encyclical, *Pascendi Dominici gregis* (1907), targeted the Kantian philosophical assumptions of the Modernists, in which human minds cannot rise beyond "phenomena," and the "representations of the object of faith are merely symbolical," since

---

23. Schoof, *A Survey of Catholic Theology*, 33.
24. Pius X, "The Errors of Modernists, on the Church, Revelation, Christ, the Sacraments" (*Lamentabili sane exitu*), in Henry Denzinger, *The Sources of Catholic Dogma*, trans. Roy J. Deferrari (Fitzwilliam, NH: Loreto Publications, 2004), 512–513.

the mind must construct these representations from the phenomenal and changing world. In sum, the preoccupation in these antimodernist encyclicals was to preserve the *constancy* of Christian doctrine and the *unchanging* nature of truth.

The condemnations against the Modernists and the end of the Modernist Crisis, generally traced to 1907, ended discussion on a range of philosophical, exegetical, and ecclesiological debates. It did not, however, resolve those debates by any means, but instead shifted the loci of these conversations to the safety of the papally endorsed Thomistic thought. Jean Daniélou suggested that the solutions of the Modernists were insufficient, but the questions that they asked were valid. Their condemnation only prolonged the crisis.[25] By stifling "modern" thought and expelling it to the periphery of the Catholic Church, and by dismantling pluralism through the enforcement of scholastic or Thomistic theology, the same debates and pluralism reemerged within Thomism itself, not even a generation later, in the work of the interpreters of St. Thomas.[26]

Nearly forty years later, the neoscholastic attacks on the *nouvelle théologie* returned to the same questions that drove the Modernists concerning historicity and the unchanging nature of truth. Marie-Michelle Labourdette's 1946 article, "Théologie et ses sources," raised questions over the recovery of the thought of the patristic period in the series Théologie and Sources Chrétiennes. While he did not object to the recovery of patristic theology, he suspected that the authors and editors of these series lacked a respect for theological truth in its "scientific state" as embodied in the neoscholastic system.

25. Jean Daniélou, "Les orientations présentes de la pensée religieuse," *Études*, no. 249 (1946): 5–21.
26. See Gerald McCool, *From Unity to Pluralism: The Internal Evolution of Thomism* (New York: Fordham University Press, 1992). Walter Cardinal Kasper's assessment that "the outstanding event in the Catholic theology of our century is the surmounting of neo-Scholasticism" is valid. Walter Kasper in Fergus Kerr, *Twentieth-Century Catholic Theologians: From Neoscholasticism to Nuptial Mysticism* (Malden, MA: Blackwell Publishing, 2007), vii. However, those theologians who most successfully surmounted it considered themselves as part of its tradition.

The implication of the recovery of an earlier theology in these series implied a historical relativism—that truth did not remain the same for each time period—and an "experiential relativism" in which the object of faith is an expression of an inner experience that might differ from person to person or from age to age.[27]

Reginald Garrigou-Lagrange, called the *monstre sacré* (the sacred monster) of Thomism, led the neoscholastic denouncement of what was called the "new theology."[28] In his article "La nouvelle théologie où va-t-elle?" (The new theology: where is it going?), Garrigou-Lagrange dropped what Aidan Nichols called the "A-Bomb" of the *nouvelle théologie* controversy. Henri Bouillard had written in *Conversion et grâce chez S. Thomas d'Aquin* (1944) that "a theology that would not be contemporary [*actuelle*] would be a false theology."[29] Garrigou-Lagrange asked the question, "How can '*an immutable truth*' be held if the two notions that are united by the verb *to be* [the subject and the predicate] are *essentially changing*?"[30] He claimed that, promulgating a form of historical relativism, the *nouvelle théologie* was headed straight toward Modernism. For Garrigou-Lagrange as for Labourdette, the first line of defense against Modernism was a Thomistic metaphysics and epistemology that enabled a secure possession of unchanging truth against the backdrop of an ever-changing world.

While these fragmentary examples from Labourdette and Garrigou-Lagrange do not provide a complete picture of the

---

27. See Aidan Nichols, OP, "Thomism and the Nouvelle Théologie," *The Thomist* 64 (2000): 3–4.
28. Richard Peddicord, OP, *The Sacred Monster of Thomism: An Introduction to the Life and Legacy of Reginald Garrigou-Lagrange, OP* (South Bend, IN: St. Augustine's Press, 2004).
29. Reginald Garrigou-Lagrange, OP, "La nouvelle théologie où va-t-elle?," *Angelicum* 23 (1946): 126–45.
30. Ibid. Garrigou-Lagrange's preoccupation with the "unchanging" is illustrated in his unyielding opposition to Henri Bergson, the philosopher of process. Agnès Desmazières, "La nouvelle théologie, prémisse d'une théologie herméneutique? La controverse sur l'analogie de la vérité (1946-1949)," *Revue Thomiste* 104, no. 1/2 (2004): 241–72.

neoscholastic movement, this brief sketch illustrates the allergy to historicity and the desperate anxiety to preserve a metaphysics of unchanging truth within neoscholasticism and antimodernism. The neoscholastics very clearly foresaw a contemporary challenge to Catholicism posed by historicism and attempted desperately to hold on to truth as eternal, unchanging, and readily available to human reason. Their apologetics, epistemology, metaphysics, and dogmatics depended upon a profound dichotomization between historical reality and eternal truth. However, they mistakenly attributed to the writings of the Modernists and of the *nouvelle théologie* a form of relativism rather than a search for a responsible way out of it.

The Return of the Apocalyptic in Roman Catholicism

Although neoscholastics and antimodernist Catholics in the early twentieth century resisted historicity, this doesn't mean that neoscholastics and antimodernist Catholics lacked a consciousness of the movement of history or of themselves as historical actors. The "eternalism" and "essentialism" of the neoscholastic system depended upon a vibrant consciousness of history and of its contingency. Instead, *fin-de-siècle* Roman Catholicism purposefully organized itself against historical consciousness in the attempt to protect eternity from the wages of time. Catholicism's dominant intellectual schools and political organs, namely neoscholasticism and antimodernism, resisted historical consciousness as the primary threat to doctrine, Catholic identity, and social order. Despite the resistance to historical consciousness, the neoscholastic schools and the antimodernist Roman Catholic culture arising during the same period promulgated a keen consciousness of history, an awareness of human beings as historical agents, and an apocalyptic or cataclysmic view of the modern world. Catholics at the turn of the century viewed the contemporary age as one of decadence. A new era, they believed, had emerged through the rupture of the medieval synthesis between faith and reason, church and state, and heaven and earth. Like their secular counterparts, Catholics viewed their time as the end time.

Although Christians had traditionally described struggles with heretics in terms of the ultimate struggle against good and evil, an apocalyptic interpretation of the present times as the "last days" intensified in the late nineteenth century. Even earlier, as Jean Séguy notes, there was an apocalyptic stream in French and Italian Catholicism before, during, and after the French Revolution.[31] As Joseph Komonchak indicates, the French Revolution "was seen as a decisive battle, perhaps the final one, in the great warfare between God and Satan. The three great heroes of the Restoration, de Bonald, Lamennais, and de Maistre, bequeathed to subsequent generations an interpretation of the Revolution as Satanic in root and branch."[32] The French Revolution joined together three elements that are known today as *secularization*: the sociological phenomenon by which religion became less central to people's lives, the rise of the nonsectarian state, and the seizure of church property by the state. Spurred by a profound anxiety of the church's place in the modern world, Roman Catholics manifested what Émile Poulat calls a "cataclysmic eschatology." This cataclysmic eschatology—essentially an apocalyptic interpretation of the present era—formed the narrative around which Roman Catholics understood their place within the modern world.

31. Jean Séguy, "Sur l'apocalyptique catholique," *Archives de sciences sociales des religions*, no. 41 (1976): 165–172. Émile Poulat states, "This Catholic *catastrophism* that seems to surprise us today. . . dominates the whole of the nineteenth century and maintained its vigor for a long time. . . . In its way, the Catholic nineteenth century manifested an acute consciousness of the Reign of God. . . .The religious climate of the time is of a 'tragic ultramontanism.'" Émile Poulat, *L'Église, c'est un monde: L'ecclésiosphère*, Sciences humaines et religions (Paris: Éditions du Cerf, 1986), 255.
32. Komonchak, "Modernity and the Construction of Roman Catholicism," 359–60.

According to Henry Edward Cardinal Manning (1808–1892), the Catholic archbishop of Westminster, secularization's "various features represented the great apostasy which must shortly precede the appearance of the Antichrist."[33] In the Italian annexation of the Papal States in 1870, Catholics witnessed the loss of the "ideal" relationship between religious and civil society—that is, a unity of throne and altar. The political struggle was interpreted as the struggle for the soul of society.

This "catastrophic" eschatology became a dominant stream in Catholicism's self-interpretation within the nineteenth century, especially among the neoscholastics, within papal encyclicals, and popular journals. While the neoscholastics of the nineteenth century promulgated antiapocalyptic theological discourses, they nevertheless disseminated a historical narrative about the modern world that contributed to apocalypticism. Three Jesuits particularly helped link an interpretation of history with the neoscholastic system: Giovanni Perrone, Matteo Liberatore, and Joseph Kleutgen. Giovanni Perrone (1794–1876), one of the founders of neoscholasticism, developed the idea that the recovery of Thomas Aquinas could overcome the division between faith and reason characteristic of the modern age. Matteo Liberatore (1810–1892), who cofounded and edited the popular journal *La Civiltà Cattolica*, connected the political problem to the theological one. For Liberatore, eternal, unchanging principles derived from revelation, and the church must govern civil and political society, not vice versa.[34] The unmooring of civil society from those unchanging principles initially occurred in the Protestant

---

33. Ibid., 358.
34. "Against the view that the church should submit to political authority, Liberatore argues that since the church is a divine and unchanging institution while the state is earthly and changing, the church should not be subject to the state. How can we submit what is eternal to the temporal? Since the eternal cannot submit to the temporal, the church should never submit to the state. Any other view, we are told, is Protestant and therefore wrong." John Inglis, *Spheres of Philosophical Inquiry and the Historiography of Medieval Philosophy* (Leiden: Brill, 1998), 76.

Reformation, the effects of which were being worked out in contemporary life. The recovery of the medieval theological-philosophical synthesis held the promise of overcoming secularization.

Joseph Kleutgen's (1811–1883) *Die Theologie der Vorzeit verteidigt* (1860–1873) and *Die Philosophie der Vorzeit verteidigt* (1878) provided an intellectually robust account of the differences between medieval and modern philosophy. Kleutgen interpreted modern rationalist and empiricist philosophy as a dissolution of a previous medieval epistemological synthesis. According to John Inglis, Joseph Kleutgen and Albert Stöckl "were consciously 'recovering' a philosophical tradition in order to provide an alternative to what they took to be the inherent skepticism and individualism of modern philosophy."[35] They offered an alternative to the histories of philosophy of the eighteenth and nineteenth centuries that interpreted the faith of the medieval period as a detriment to human reasoning. According to Kleutgen, the realist epistemology of the medieval period united the respect for observation of the concrete (in the spirit of modern empiricism) with an emphasis on universals (in concert with modern rationalism).[36] The premise upon which the neoscholastic revival was based was the need for a circumnavigation of a modern separation between philosophy and theology, and between civil society and the church.

The early neoscholastics were generally quite sober in their understanding of history and not very amenable to apocalypticism. However, the neoscholastic narrative concerning modernity—modernity as a perfidious time in which faith and reason are estranged, and the basis for social cohesion is lost—would contribute to an apocalyptic reading of modernity in the papal

35. Ibid., 11.
36. Ibid., 296.

encyclicals and popular journals.[37] The Dogmatic Constitution *Dei Filius* (April 1870) of the First Vatican Council depicted the Protestant Reformation as the beginning of a decline of the faith. Moreover, the Protestant principles of individual interpretation, Scripture alone (*sola scriptura*), faith alone (*sola fide*), and the individualistic rebuke of church authority constituted threats to the ancient faith and to the cohesiveness of human society.

> The abandonment and rejection of the Christian religion, and the denial of God and his Christ, has plunged the minds of many into the abyss of pantheism, materialism and atheism, and the consequence is that they strive to destroy rational nature itself, to deny any criterion of what is right and just, and to overthrow the very foundations of human society.[38]

In short, the fathers of Vatican I could not imagine a social or political unity apart from religious unity.

In July of 1870, the First Vatican Council promulgated *Pastor aeternus*, the dogmatic decree that included the definition of papal infallibility. It highlighted that a definition of papal authority was necessary due to the spiritual warfare that lay behind the struggle over church unity and authority, "since the gates of hell, trying if they can to overthrow the Church, make their assault with a hatred that increases day by day against its divinely laid foundation."[39] *Pastor aeternus* asserted the direct and immediate jurisdiction of the pope

---

37. Liberatore had a popular influence through his journal *Civiltà Cattolica*, which supported a close union of church and state. Kleutgen directly influenced official ecclesial documents. He was a consultant to the first Vatican Council as a theological expert in the writing of *Dei Filius* (1870) and later composed the first draft of Pope Leo XIII's encyclical *Aeterni Patris* (1879), which established scholasticism at the heart of the Roman Catholic Church's intellectual response to modernity.

38. *Dei Filius*, 7 in *Acta Sanctae Sedis* 5 (1869–70), 482–83. *Acta Sanctae Sedis* (hereafter *ASS*) and *Acta Apostolicae Sedis* (hereafter *AAS*) constitute the compendia of Roman Catholic Church documents. While I provide paragraph numbers to the Latin texts, the original documents lack numeration of paragraphs. The numbers were added to a revised edition of the texts in 1931.

39. *Pastor aeternus*, 6 in *ASS* 6 (1870–71), 40–41.

over the entire church and rejected interference by civil authorities into church affairs.

For Catholic antimodernists, *Dei Filius* and *Pastor aeternus* were prophetic documents. Two months after the promulgation of *Pastor aeternus*, the Italian army invaded the Papal States and surrounded the Vatican. As Komonchak states, the loss of the Papal States was felt by many Catholics to be an attack on Christianity's public and social role (not just its political role) and a suppression of the exercise of the faith.[40] For nineteenth-century Catholicism, the church is seen as the spatially and temporally extended outpost of the eternal within time. The pastors of the church administer God's reign over the earth, mediating the conformity of the temporal, social, and political sphere to the eternal. The papal encyclicals treat the many challenges to church authority as incursions into the social space occupied by the church and ultimately as challenges to God's sovereign rule. With the annexation of the Papal States in 1870, that "space" has collapsed: the sociopolitical world that was Catholicism's medium was coming to its end. The prophecies in the documents of Vatican I had swiftly come true. As a result, history was unhinged from eternity, giving an impetus for an already-existing apocalyptic view of the modern age.

Pope Leo XIII's *Aeterni Patris*, written nine years after the annexation of the Papal States, interprets the outward crisis as a spiritual and intellectual crisis: "False conclusions concerning divine and human things, which originated in the schools of philosophy, have now crept into all the orders of the State, and have been accepted by the common consent of the masses."[41] As the intellect guides the will and the will guides public life, the misguided philosophies of the moderns have exercised a deleterious influence on the public order. *Aeterni Patris* presents the restoration of scholastic

40. Komonchak, "Modernity and the Construction of Roman Catholicism," 338–39.
41. Leo XIII, *Aeterni Patris,* 2.

41

thought, with its unity in distinction of philosophy and theology, as the primary intellectual response to this situation. Given the historical context in which *Aeterni Patris* was written, the document is quite measured. While its analysis is incomplete from a contemporary perspective, it does not contain the vitriolic language of subsequent papal encyclicals in reference to modern thought.[42]

Pope Leo XIII, however, freely elaborated a "catastrophic eschatology" elsewhere. The most dramatic of these is the legend that arose surrounding the "Prayer to Saint Michael," which Leo added in 1886 to the "Leonine Prayers" said at the end of the low Mass. These were earlier previous prayers that Leo modified in 1884 to make them into intercessions for the freedom of the church throughout the world. While the prayer may have its inspiration in a mystical experience of Leo, a millenarian legend about the origins of the prayer developed later. A long version of the prayer contains vibrant apocalyptic imagery. It explains that the devil has taken the form of an angel of light and invaded earth, sending wicked people against the Church:

> These most crafty enemies have filled and inebriated the church . . . with gall and bitterness, and have laid impious hands on her most sacred possessions. In the Holy Place itself, where the See of Holy Peter and the Chair of Truth has been set up as the light of the world, they have raised the throne of their abominable impiety, with the iniquitous design that when the Pastor has been struck, the sheep may be.[43]

This prayer's lively apocalyptic images linked recent political events directly to the spiritual warfare between the angels and the devil.

---

42. The document does contain some apocalyptic language: "In these late days, when those dangerous times described by the Apostle are already upon us, when the blasphemers, the proud, and the seducers go from bad to worse, erring themselves and causing others to err, there is surely a very great need of confirming the dogmas of Catholic faith and confuting heresies" (ibid., 14). Leo's language here is a quotation from the sixteenth-century pope, Sixtus V, whose bull *Triumphantis* confirmed the perennial utility of scholastic theology in combating error.

43. *Rituale Romanum,* 6th ed. post typicam (Ratisbon: Pustet, 1898), 163.

The Catholic antimodernism of the early twentieth century only intensified this apocalypticism. In 1907 Pius X promulgated *Pascendi*, the premier document of the antimodernist movement. *Pascendi* suggested that a cataclysmic contest between good and evil was presently occurring and dividing the Catholic Church itself. The church, Pius wrote, has always needed to be vigilant against those who will mislead it. Yet "it must be confessed that the number of the enemies of the cross of Christ has in these last days increased exceedingly. . . . [They are] striving, by new and subtle arts, to destroy the vital energy of the Church, and, if they can, to overthrow utterly Christ's kingdom itself."[44] In his first encyclical, Pius set his pontificate the task of "restoring all things in Christ" with God's grace. Alluding to the French Revolution, Pius condemned the extinction of God in the public and private realm: "There is good reason to fear lest this great perversity may be as it were a foretaste, and perhaps the beginning of those evils which are reserved for the last days; and that there may be already in the world the 'Son of Perdition.'" For St. Paul, he writes, the "distinguishing mark of the Antichrist ... [is that] man has with infinite temerity put himself in the place of God." Pius states that human beings have usurped God's place in the temple.[45] For Pius, the events of the French Revolution, the annexation of the Papal States, and the challenges of the modernists offer an insight into the underlying meaning of modernity and where it is heading. Recent attacks against the Roman Church unveil the revolt of the devil against God and God's church: this age is the site of a cataclysmic contest between good and evil. Furthermore, for Pius, these recent events unveil the ultimate trajectory of the Protestant Reformation, which culminates in the siege against the church. The suppression of the public role of the

---

44. Pope Pius X, *Pascendi Dominici gregis* 1 in *ASS* 40 (1907), 593–94.
45. Pope Pius X, *E Supremi* 5 in *ASS* 36 (1904), 131–32.

Catholic Church in France over the next forty years would deepen the crisis, confirming the anxiety over the disintegration of Christian and European unity.

The apocalyptic mentality of Roman Catholicism complicates any neat division between "classicism" and "historical-mindedness" (in Bernard Lonergan's terminology). On the one hand, neoscholasticism did not successfully integrate the historical consciousness of the age. On the other hand, Roman Catholicism was increasingly organizing itself around a cataclysmic eschatology found in political interventions by lay Catholics, in the messages contained in the alleged appearances of Mary, and in official church pronouncements. The contrast is striking between the serene, rational "eternalism" of neoscholasticism and the apocalypticism of the encyclicals. This apocalypticism functioned as a religious explanation for the church's confrontational relationship with modern thought and politics, as well as a justification for the ecclesial response. Both a classicist neoscholasticism and apocalypticism were joined within Roman Catholicism in a form of historical experience and a manner of interpreting the contemporary world.

Although Roman Catholic apocalypticism and neoscholasticism reinforced each other, they were not theologically integrated with each other. Neoscholasticism had an understated eschatology at best. Within the neoscholastic manuals of the nineteenth to twentieth centuries, eschatology comprised a discrete subject within dogmatic theology. It exclusively focused on the *last things:* death, judgment, heaven, and hell. Not only did neoscholasticism not generally integrate a contemporary apocalyptic sensibility, but scholasticism as a whole resisted millenarian tendencies. In part, this resistance was due to the traditional opposition of the medieval scholastics to the apocalyptic imagination present in the Franciscan Spirituals and other marginal or heretical groups. Ironically, many of the same proponents of the neoscholastic system, including Liberatore and Pope Leo XIII, employed apocalyptic images to make sense of current crises within the church and society. This apocalyptic sensibility envisioned a form of the ultimate drama occurring as a present prelude to the ultimate fight between good and evil. There remained a tension between the apocalyptic sensibilities and eternalism within Roman Catholicism at the *fin de siècle*.

Conclusion

The feeling of being at the end of an era and of the present time as a foretaste of the end had much in common with the growing eschatological consciousness in European modernity. Similar to the conflict over the meaning of time within cultural and literary modernism, Roman Catholicism reflected a preoccupation with time and eternity. One of the cardinal problems of European modernism—how to recognize the eternal in the midst of flux—became a fundamental concern for the Roman Catholic response to modernity, though it was addressed in widely divergent ways. The Catholic apocalyptic response—which envisioned the present moment as a decline of the current temporal order, often the emergence of a new era, and an ultimate battle between good and evil to come—mirrored the responses to modernity found in the Futurist Movement, the Decadent Movement, forms of fascism, and Marxism. While, traditionally, scholasticism rejected all forms of millenarianism, in the late nineteenth century, the "catastrophic eschatology" of Catholic antimodernism began to merge with the serene eternalism of neoscholasticism. A tension between the two still remained. After the First World War, the new situation of Catholicism spurred a reimagining of "social Catholicism" in France. Moreover, beginning in the 1930s, theologians such as Marie-Dominique Chenu, Yves Congar, and Henri de Lubac would seek to reconcile a modern historical consciousness with the doctrinal tradition of Catholicism. The debates before, during, and following the Second World War over the "theology of history" addressed directly the ongoing tensions over history and eternity.

2

Time and Eternity in the *Nouvelle Théologie*

One of the most prominent characteristics of the *nouvelle théologie* authors was that they faced the challenges of a modern historical consciousness, attempting to reconcile it with traditional sources of theological reflection.[1] The *nouveaux théologiens* criticized the then-dominant theological methodology, neoscholasticism, for its poor understanding of the relationship between theology and history. Neoscholastics tended to ignore the diachronic development of doctrine and, moreover, appeared stubbornly wedded to a medieval model of science and Aristotelian categories of thinking. It would be a simplification, however, to merely oppose the *nouvelle théologie* to neoscholasticism. There was significant continuity between them. Most of the *nouveaux théologiens* considered themselves to be followers of St. Thomas Aquinas, the "Angelic Doctor," the premier

---

1. The *nouvelle théologie* had this in common with the so-called Catholic Modernist authors—George Tyrrell, Alfred Loisy, and Friedrich von Hügel—who were part of a previous generation engaged precisely with the issue of the methodological impact of history on the discipline of theology.

scholastic theologian. The *nouvelle théologie*, like neoscholasticism, was a *ressourcement* ("return to the sources") of the Christian intellectual heritage in order to address contemporary problems. Like neoscholastics, the *nouveaux théologiens* had a keen awareness of living in a secular world, a world that was divorced from the ways of thinking of the patristic and medieval period. While theologians like Marie-Dominique Chenu and Jean Daniélou were more open to the spirit of modern thought, they believed that modernity had fallen away from an ideal of Christianity previously attained during the patristic era and the Middle Ages. Originally a movement of reform growing out of a neoscholastic tradition, the *nouvelle théologie* was critical of the lack of historical consciousness in contemporary Catholic theology.

The *nouvelle théologie* sought to make Catholic theology relevant by engaging modern thought, specifically modern historical consciousness. Yves Congar's article "Déficit de la théologie" (1934) in *Sept* magazine was an early instance of the attempt at outlining an historically conscious theology. Congar called for reimagining theological methodology in light of the present human condition. Theology, he explained, had become a "closed domain," cut off from other disciplines and human activity: "As long as we talk about Marxism and Bolshevism in Latin, as I have seen it done in classes and conferences of theologians, Lenin can sleep in peace in his Moscow mausoleum."[2] Congar called for a new theological engagement with the modern intellectual world. Marie-Dominique Chenu's *Une école de théologie: le Salchoir* (1937) proposed a new model of theological education. Theology, he said, should be reorganized around the study of history. Because human beings are in time and history, grace

---

2. Quoted in Jürgen Mettepenningen, *Nouvelle Théologie—New Theology: Inheritor of Modernism, Precursor to Vatican II* (New York: T & T Clark, 2010), 45.

shapes the human intellect within its historical and social conditions. Appealing to the incarnation, Chenu stated that theology takes a historical form. These proposals set the stage for a wide-ranging debate over theological methodology for the contemporary age.

The debate over the "theology of history" (1943–1962) is only one instance of the broader debates over theological methodology. The debate was initiated by Henri-Marie Féret's book, *L'Apocalypse de saint Jean: Vision chrétienne de l'histoire* (1943). After the liberation of France, a flurry of articles in the journals *Dieu vivant, Études,* and *Recherches de science religieuse* responded to this book. The participants included Henri-Marie Féret, OP (1904–1992), Jean Daniélou, SJ (1905–1974), Joseph Huby, SJ (1878–1948), Gaston Fessard, SJ (1897–1978), and Henri de Lubac.[3] De Lubac's contribution to this debate came out in his books on Origen, the history of medieval exegesis, and his two books on the posterity of Joachim of Fiore. Daniélou cited de Lubac's earlier *Catholicism* (1930) as an inspiration for the recovery of a patristic understanding of history.[4]

The debate over the theology of history arose over differences among *nouveaux théologiens* over the interpretation of Scripture and the theological interpretation of human history. If we know God primarily by God's interventions into history that reach their apex in Jesus Christ, then theology seeks primarily an understanding of those interventions. It also seeks knowledge of the consummation of history at the end. The *nouvelle théologie* shared a broad agreement that Christianity is historical and theology must recover an historical

3. Huby, Fessard, and Mouroux are sometimes not included in the usual rosters of the *nouvelle théologie* authors. Huby, who was de Lubac's teacher, was really from a previous generation. Gaston Fessard, though he was caught up in the *nouvelle théologie* controversy of the 1950s, is often not numbered among the "new theologians." For example, Jürgen Mettepenningen hardly mentions Fessard in *Nouvelle Theologie—New Theology*. Jean Mouroux's publications mostly came after the *nouvelle théologie* controversy.

4. Mettepenningen locates the end of this debate as the beginning of the Second Vatican Council, during which history became a prominent theme.

mode of thinking. However, the debate over the theology of history indicated fissures over the "end of history" within the *nouvelle théologie*. Differences among these theologians over how to regard history and its ending affected how they interpreted the events around World War II and how they saw the church's social and political mission.

What follows is an introduction to the historical and political context of the debate over the theology of history. In this debate, Féret, Huby, Fessard, Daniélou, and de Lubac sought a method for the religious interpretation of the events that shaped their world. This debate forms the backdrop for de Lubac's turn to Scripture as a source for a theology of history and his subsequent eschatological synthesis.

The Socio-Political Context of a Debate

In the wake of the loss of the political power, social status, and public role of the Catholic Church in France, Catholics were searching for alternative models of religious witness and social identity. The "Social Catholicism" of the 1930s sought to rediscover the social space of Catholicism in a new secular milieu. In the 1940s, the Catholic resistance to Nazism and the Vichy government appealed to the social meaning of Catholicism against coercive and violent forces. The turn to a theology of history arose in the context of the envisioning of the sociopolitical role of the church in the temporal realm.

At the end of the nineteenth century, the French Republicans sought to eradicate the Catholic Church's public role in France. They tried and succeeded to remove from France the Catholic religious congregations and their hold on public education.[5] Prior to 1879, the religious congregations were permitted to function even if the law heavily circumscribed their activity. From 1879 to 1889, France

5. The Republicans (*Républicains modérés*) gained a majority in the Chamber of Deputies in 1876, replacing a previous majority of monarchist representatives.

began to expel some religious congregations. At the same time, the French government created a system of free, obligatory primary school education without religious instruction. It is at least symbolic that, at a time when there was a concerted effort to remove the public footprint of Catholicism from France, an iconic expression of technical modernity, the Eiffel Tower, was being erected as the most visible structure on the Parisian skyline to celebrate the hundredth anniversary of the French Revolution.

French Catholics positioned themselves in opposition to Republican efforts, leading to the further marginalization of Catholics within French society and government. In 1889, Action française rose as an antirevolutionary movement that advocated the return of the monarchy and the return of the Catholic Church as a state religion in France. Charles Maurras, the principal spokesman for the movement, was an agnostic who wished to capture the power of social cohesion offered by Catholicism for the French state. While Action française attracted many Catholics, others were quite suspicious of the movement. The Dreyfus Affair put Catholics on the defensive yet again.[6] Under the French Concordat of 1801, the church had held a place of privilege and was subsidized by the government. From 1899 to 1914, Catholics were excluded from government and public office. Religious orders, including the Jesuits, were exiled. A 1904 law forbade the religious to teach. In 1904 France broke diplomatic relations with the Holy See because Pope Pius X refused the French government the power to name bishops. In response, French Republicans took away the church budget. In

---

6. Alfred Dreyfus, an army captain of Jewish descent, was condemned to life imprisonment for giving military secrets to the Germans. When it became clear that another man had committed treason and that anti-Semitism was behind his condemnation, his case was reopened in 1899. The case split France as well as French Catholics. Members of the Augustinian religious order joined a rush to condemn him, triggering an anti-Catholic backlash. Yet prominent Catholics were among the Dreyfusards, including Charles Péguy, the devout (though nonpracticing) Catholic poet and essayist.

1905, the Law of Separation allowed the church to organize itself as it pleased, but provided for lay associations for the conservation of church property. Due to the latter provision, Pius X unwisely condemned the Law of Separation. The Catholic Church did not establish associations immediately, so many church properties were given by the state to other organizations.

The aftermath of the Great War put Catholics in a very different situation. Returning from exile abroad, religious served as chaplains, medics, and soldiers; thus they could no longer be seen as the enemy. Foreign affairs and domestic economic problems dominated France, which no longer had a place for anticlerical politics. Religious congregations were allowed to return, though the law banning them remained on the books until 1942. In 1921 France and the Holy See resumed relations. In 1924, a modification of French law allowed the church to own property. An anti-Catholic government was elected in 1924, but fell quickly in 1925. In 1926, Pope Pius XI condemned Action française, occasioning a crisis of conscience for many committed Catholics who generally opposed French Republicanism.[7] The condemnation precipitated the search for new models of Christian involvement in the social and political realm that did not require the return to a Catholic monarchy.

A theological renewal occurred in France in the 1920s and 1930s during a time of political truce between Catholicism and Republicanism. The generation of Catholics following World War I were not as tied to the political establishment as those of the previous generation. They were less inclined to believe that partisan political interests were aligned with spiritual needs. New pastoral initiatives and domestic missionary work outside the institutional church

---

7. See Peter J. Bernardi, *Maurice Blondel, Social Catholicism, and Action Française: The Clash Over the Church's Role in Society during the Modernist Era* (Washington, DC: Catholic University of America Press, 2009), 209–11.

engaged the laity. The reclaiming of the theological virtues, mysticism, and spirituality became a central pastoral task, especially as so many Catholics were disengaged from the morality and sacramental practices of the Church. The amelioration of tensions between the French government and Catholics allowed for this reenvisioning of the relationship between society and the church.

Turn-of-the-century initiatives of Catholic philosophers, theologians, and other writers contributed to seeking new forms of Christian witness and corporate practice, such as "Social Catholicism." The philosopher Maurice Blondel was a prominent participant in the Catholic "social congresses" from the late nineteenth century to the early twentieth century. Under the inspiration of Leo XIII's social vision for Catholicism, Marc Sangnier founded *Le Sillon* [The furrow] in 1894. *Le Sillon* was a progressive Catholic labor movement and political alternative to Marxism. The group was endorsed by the pope until the 1905 law of separation, which *Le Sillon* supported. In 1912 *Le Sillon* was condemned by Pius X. The search for a social form of the faith continued to inspire Catholic social philosophers of the 1920s and 1930s.[8] Henri-Marie Féret was involved in founding three pastoral initiatives just before World War II: *Journées sacerdotales*, retreats for priestly formation; *Cours Saint-Jacques*, a parallel retreat for lay people; and *Groupe évangélique*, a women's bible study. Henri de Lubac and Yves Congar participated in *Semaines sociales*, an annual conference on the social dimensions of Christianity for laity. These numerous pastoral and social initiatives were experiments in Social Catholicism, a vision of the social and political dimensions of the church as the leaven for

---

8. Jean-Yves Calvez names Jacques Maritain, Emmanuel Mounier, Gaston Fessard, Teilhard de Chardin, and Henri de Lubac as the most significant theorists of Social Catholicism. Jean-Yves Calvez, "The French Catholic Contribution to Social and Political Thinking in the 1930s," *Ethical Perspectives: Journal of the European Ethics Network* 7, no. 4 (December 2000): 312–15.

society.[9] Social Catholicism, moreover, constitutes a vision of the church in the temporal realm, the very subject of a "theology of history."

The debate over the theology of history also had roots in the Second World War, specifically in the Catholic resistance to Nazism and the postwar political context. In general, those involved with the debate over the theology of history were active participants in the "spiritual resistance" against the État français, which collaborated with Germany and the German occupiers. The spiritual resistance consisted of acts of nonviolent struggle, including prayer, social organization, and publication. The publications criticized Nazi ideology, provided a Christian interpretation of the contemporary political struggles, and contain elements of the later debate.[10]

The underground journal *Cahiers du Témoignage chrétien* [Christian witness notebooks] is a notable organ of the Catholic spiritual resistance. In 1941, in Lyon, the avant-garde editor and art critic Stanislaus Fumet arranged a meeting between the Jesuits Pierre Chaillet and Gaston Fessard, and Henri Frenay, the head of the *Combat* network of resistance movements.[11] Fumet and Frenay encouraged Chaillet to start a clandestine paper that criticized Nazi ideology from a Christian perspective. The first edition of *Cahiers*

---

9. In the period following World War I, French Catholic literature undertook the task of reimagining the social role of Catholicism. The work of Leon Bloy, François Mauriac, Georges Bernanos, Charles Péguy, Gabriel Marcel, and Paul Claudel had an immense influence on those who would form the *nouvelle théologie*.

10. *Cahiers du Témoignage chrétien* was one of a series of publications that criticized Nazism. *Temps présent,* which became *Temps nouveau,* was shut down by the authorities in 1941. *Sept, Esprit, L'Aube,* and *Semaine religieuse* were all under surveillance by the authorities. See Guy Boissard, *Quelle neutralité face à l'horreur: le courage de Charles Journet* (Saint-Maurice, Switzerland: Éditions Saint-Augustin, 2000), 215.

11. The administrative center of the État français was in Vichy, located a mere 150 kilometers from Lyon. East of Lyon was an area of Italian occupation. The southern zone in general, and Lyon in particular, became a bastion for resistance movements. Many of the contributors to *Cahiers du Témoignage chrétien,* including de Lubac, who were located near Lyon, had a greater freedom of movement and communication than those in Paris, allowing for the publication of the journal.

du Témoignage chrétien appeared under the title *France, prends garde de perdre ton âme* in 1941. From 1941 to 1945, Pierre Chaillet, Gaston Fessard, Stanislaus Fumet, Henri de Lubac, Georges Bernanos, Yves de Montcheuil, and Jean Lacroix were among the authors writing for *Cahiers du Témoignage chrétien*. Jacques Maritain was among the editors. *Cahiers du Témoignage chrétien* presented the fight against Nazism as part of the spiritual battle between the forces of good and evil.

Other journals, such as *Courrier français du Témoignage chrétien* and *Dieu vivant*, interpreted the current struggle against Nazism with a Christian apocalyptic view of history. Yves de Montcheuil, a scholar at Institute catholique de Paris active in the spiritual resistance, exuded an apocalyptic interpretation of the present time. Particularly apocalyptic is "Perspectives," in which he interprets the present totalitarianism in terms of the beasts of Revelation.[12] While ministering to students in the armed resistance movement, *le maquis*, he was captured and killed in 1944.[13] From 1945 to 1955, *Dieu vivant* communicated an eschatological view of Christianity in conversation with contemporary events. Despite the diversity of eschatological perspectives of the authors, *Dieu vivant* presented an "eschatological crisis of conscience" facing humanity in the face of current struggle.[14]

While the writers for *Cahiers du Témoignage chrétien* were united in their opposition to collaboration with Nazism, this unity frayed almost immediately in the postwar period. Maritain and Bernanos had antirevolutionary leanings and ties to Action française, and they

12. Yves de Montcheuil, "Perspectives," *Courrier français du Témoignage chrétien*, no. 9 (1944): 1. Yves de Montcheuil, "Communisme," *Courrier français du Témoignage chrétien*, no. 5 (1943): 2–3. See also David Grumett, "Yves de Montcheuil: Action, Justice and the Kingdom in Spiritual Resistance to Nazism," *Theological Studies* 68, no. 3 (2007): 618–41.

13. Aidan Nichols, OP, "Henri de Lubac: Panorama and Proposal," *New Blackfriars* 93, no. 1043 (January 2012): 20.

14. Etienne Fouilloux, "Une vision eschatologique du christianisme: Dieu vivant (1945–1955)," *Revue d'histoire de l'Église de France* 57, no. 158 (1971): 58.

supported anticommunist regimes.[15] On the other hand, for many French resistors, communism appeared to be a viable political alternative. In 1947, writing in the left-leaning journal *Esprit*, Emmanuel Mounier and Jean Lacroix took a stance against the "fascism come to France" of General de Gaulle. They appealed to nonfascists, including Catholics, to "collaborate" with communists. The contributors to *Cahiers du Témoignage chrétien* had opposing responses to this invitation. Henri de Lubac and Jean Daniélou were more sympathetic to the social and eschatological impulses of communism and sought to understand it in light of a Christian understanding of history. In July 1947, de Lubac's, Mounier's, and Lacroix's joint participation in the *Semaines sociales de France* (an intellectual retreat for Catholic laypeople) contributed to the perception of the emergence of a leftist Catholicism in Lyons. Lyons was home to the Jesuit seminary located at Fourvière from which the *Cahiers du Témoignage chrétien* was launched. It also was the home to the new series Sources Chrétiennes and Théologie, which would come under increasing criticism from neothomists. Mounier and Lacroix, editors of *Esprit,* were also living in Lyons, as was Fumet. In private letters to Henri de Lubac, Gaston Fessard criticized what he saw as a community of thought developing in Lyon that was open to communism. De Lubac denied that his proximity to this group in Lyon played a significant role in his thinking.[16]

The controversy over the theology of history that would unfold was catalyzed by the reflection over the social space of Catholicism in the modern world in the 1920s and 1930s and by the spiritual resistance to fascism in the 1940s. Several of the writers associated

15. Bernanos had supported Franco during the Spanish Civil War, but became disillusioned with the brutality of the war. During and after World War II, he supported Charles de Gaulle.
16. Frédéric Louzeau, "Gaston Fessard et Henri de Lubac: leur différend sur la question du communisme et du progressisme chrétien (1945–1950)," *Revue des sciences religieuses* 84, no. 4 (2010): 531.

with the *Cahiers du Témoignage chrétien* also contributed to this debate. While the *théologie de l'histoire* concerned primarily the understanding of God's interventions in history, the political questions over the response to communism and the remained in the background.

The Book of Revelation as a Theory of History

Henri-Marie Féret earned his doctorate in theology in 1930 at Le Saulchoir, a Cistercian abbey located in Tournai in Belgium, the house of studies for the French Dominican province. After the expulsion of the religious orders from France in 1903, the Dominicans relocated their house of studies there.[17] Féret was appointed as professor of church history at Le Saulchoir upon completion of the doctorate, working with Marie-Dominique Chenu and Yves Congar. Féret, Chenu, and Congar shared a theological vision and proposed a coauthored book aimed at articulating the faith through the study of history.[18] However, they anticipated that a book would not be sufficient and that a broader project, the reorganization of theological studies around the study of history, would be needed. While the book never came to fruition, these three authors contributed in their own way to the broader project. Chenu's *Une école de théologie: le Saulchoir* (1937) and Congar's programmatic long article "Théologie" in *Dictionnaire de théologie chrétienne* (1946) were individual responses to this shared project. The book *L'Apocalypse de saint Jean: Vision chrétienne de l'histoire* was Féret's response. It began as a series of lectures in Paris

---

17. See André Duval, "Aux origines de l' 'Institut historique d'études thomistes' du Saulchoir (1920 et ss): notes et documents," *Revue des sciences philosophiques et théologiques* 75, no. 3 (1991): 423–48.

18. Mettepenningen mentions a seven-page outline of the proposed book coauthored by Congar, Chenu, and Féret. Mettepenningen, *Nouvelle Théologie—New Theology*, 59.

in 1941, the year following the German occupation of France, and was published in 1943, a year before its liberation.[19] The subtitle of his book—*Vision chrétienne de l'histoire* [A Christian vision of history]—suggests more about Féret's intentions. Féret believed that the book of Revelation held the keys to understanding God's action in the present: "Theology of history taught by St John prompts and sustains Christian action in history far more than is possible for any mere philosophy of history."[20] *L'Apocalypse de Saint Jean* advanced an interpretation of history through a biblical and apocalyptic lens, reflected on the methodological implications of history on theology, and gave voice to a powerful religious intuition of the presence of God in history and God's providence over its outcome.

Féret affirmed that the prophet of the Apocalypse illumined the religious future, but could only express it through contemporary religious symbolism: "Even though [St. John] may lift the veil from the future, he never does so except from a foundation of contemporary events which he has personally witnessed. . . . He can only express his prophecy by dressing it in the contemporary concrete mode."[21] While the content of Revelation is "dressed" in symbolism and imagery from the first century, it provides the "concrete details" concerning the development of God's plan in history, particularly with regard to the church. While Féret warned of a crassly literal reading of the prophecies of the book of Revelation, he maintained that Revelation contains prophecies of the future. Revelation concerns both the eschatological end of time and the evolution of God's plan through history. Arrayed in symbol, Revelation contains glimpses into the prophetic future.

---

19. Henri-Marie Féret, *L'Apocalypse de saint Jean: Vision chrétienne de l'histoire* (Paris: Corrêa, 1943); Féret, *The Apocalypse of St. John*, trans. Elizabethe Corathiel (Westminster, MD: The Newman Press, 1958).
20. Féret, *The Apocalypse of St. John*, 224.
21. Ibid., 174.

Féret argued that St. John affirmed a threefold division of church history. First, the Book of Revelation marks a period of persecution by the Roman Empire that ends in the demise of the Empire and the triumph of the church. The second period, our present time, is a time of ongoing struggle between the power of evil in this world and the power of the gospel. Third, a time during which the truth of the gospel rules over the earth. The rule of the gospel (the "last days") has already begun in Christ, but will be completed through the conformity of the world to the gospel. Rejecting the "messianism" of Hegelianism, Marxism, and liberalism, he states that the Christian cannot look to a new revelation or a new age because Christ has already initiated the new age through his death and resurrection.[22] However, an evolution by which the world is conformed to the gospel must occur in the time between the first coming of Christ and the second coming.

Féret saw modern ideologies of history—such as liberalism and Marxism—as false messianisms and false imitations of the gospel. Judiciously, Féret refrained from directly criticizing fascist ideology on the same grounds that he criticized liberalism and Marxism, though he launched his denunciation subtly:

> The progress of truth's victories in history can only be brought about through the co-operation of mankind. Here is perhaps the most profound cleavage between the false messianisms by which the second Beast seeks to lead mankind astray, and the truth by which God saves them. False messianisms mistrust the human personality. They sacrifice whole nations to their shadowy ideologies, and, having led them into this trap, reduce them to a slavery and a spiritual humiliation which are worse than death. We have had many examples of this sort of thing in modern times—messianisms that have demanded the whole lives and the very souls of their dupes, and for what? Christian truth, on the contrary, respects and exalts man, in that it treats him as an indestructible

---

22. Ibid., 216.

individual . . . but still more, it calls for his active co-operation in the work for the redemption of all human values . . . and for the salvation of mankind.[23]

The Beast continues to mislead humanity. Although Christ assures victory, our present history is characterized by the ongoing struggle of the church against the Beast. Féret insisted that the historical victory over evil must happen through the cooperation of human beings with the gospel, in witness and resistance.

The third period of Féret's historical division responds to the book of Revelation's description of an era of peace. In Rev. 20:2–3, the seer tells of the defeat and imprisonment of the devil for a thousand years, during which time the saints and martyrs reign with Christ. According to Féret, this account of the thousand years justifies a millenarian interpretation of history, that is, a belief in the total transformation of society in the future. At the culmination of the last days, the gospel will rule not only over individual human hearts, but within society as a whole. During this era, the fight between good and evil would continue as a struggle within each individual, while religious and civil society would find peace. Roger Auber describes Féret's vision of the last era as a "progressive amelioration of the situation: through numerous difficulties, spiritual and religious values would little by little take the place that they should."[24] Significantly, the victory of the gospel over evil will occur in time, however incompletely, invisibly through the reign of Christ in individuals and visibly through the conformity of our social organization to God's reign. Féret explains, "This long period of triumph for the truth of the gospel in human affairs will in reality be the personal reign of Christ and the saints from heaven on this earth."[25] At the end of this period

23. Ibid., 221–22.
24. Roger Aubert, "Discussions récentes autour de la théologie de l'histoire," *Collectanea Mechliniensia* 33 (1948): 133.
25. Féret, *The Apocalypse of St. John*, 197.

would come a resurgence of evil in the world, followed by the final intervention of God who would destroy evil and bring about a "new heaven and a new earth."

Féret gave voice to a Christian theology of history that could function as an alternative to contemporary philosophies of history in fascism and Marxism. Jürgen Mettepenningen states, "Not only did he [Féret] give an initial impetus to a biblical-theological explanation of the course of history, but also evidently to a theology of history, i.e., a theological reflection on history that took seriously history and endeavored to integrate it to the full."[26] It is significant that *L'Apocalypse de saint Jean* proposes that Christians should hope for the victory over evil, not only in the individual soul or at the end of time, but also *within history*, through the organization of society in conformity to the gospel. "The cause of Christ is assured of triumph, not only on the plane of individuals who arrive in heaven, but on the plane of a humanity, who in this world will experience . . . an organization of the world here below conformed to the truth of the Gospel."[27] As suggested above, Féret's apocalyptic and millenarian interpretation of history in light of the book of Revelation had precedents within magisterial documents of the nineteenth and early twentieth centuries, as well as in the Social Catholicism of the 1920s and 1930s. Féret's social and historical vision sustained a Christian engagement in history and the social sphere during these "last days."

The Exchange Between Féret and Huby

In 1944, a year after the publication of Féret's *L'Apocalypse de saint Jean*, Joseph Huby, SJ (1878–1948), responded to the book in an article, "Apocalypse et histoire," to correct what he believed was

26. Mettepenningen, *Nouvelle Théologie—New Theology*, 59–60.
27. Aubert, "Discussions récentes autour de la théologie de l'histoire," 133.

its specious interpretations of the book of Revelation. Huby, then a professor of Scripture at Lyon-Fourvière, had been a professor of apologetics at Ore Place, Hastings from 1913 to 1917 and of Scripture at Ore Place from 1923 to 1926. As de Lubac's teacher at Ore Place from 1924 to 1926, Huby encouraged de Lubac to begin the body of research that would become *Surnaturel*.

Responding to Féret's millenarianism, "Apocalypse et Histoire" outlined a nonapocalyptic theology of history.[28] Huby explained that the apocalyptic discourse in the book of Revelation is a "succession of visions that reveal the designs of God." Revelation serves to reveal the ultimate meaning of conflicts between the church and the world in the time when it was written and in the present, and then presents a vivid description of the events that culminate in the end of history. According to Huby, these representations of the end of history in the apocalyptic genre are only a "contingent manner by which to represent this end."[29] While the apocalyptic genre represents God's judgment over history as occurring within time, this temporal judgment is "one with the universal judgment at the end of time (or the 'eschatological' judgment)."[30] In other words, the apocalyptic genre employs concrete images of catastrophe, yet these concrete images apply not only to one point in time in the future, but to the whole fabric of human history. The book of Revelation symbolically suggests that we must be torn from our temporal condition to reach our end.

According to Huby, the future eschatology of Féret makes us forget that the book of Revelation is thoroughly christocentric: Revelation does not so much signify the reign of God in the historical future as it reveals the reign of God already intervening in the world

28. From 1941 to 1944, *Construire* replaced the Jesuit-run journal *Etudes* when *Etudes* was suspended during the German occupation.
29. Joseph Huby, "Apocalypse et Histoire," *Construire* 15 (1944): 89.
30. Ibid., 84.

through Christ. "Among the revelations that this book brings us, the most important concern not so much particular events as the person of Christ himself and the reciprocal relationships between Christ and his faithful."[31] While Féret saw an era of persecution in the history of the church, Huby stated that the church, as a sign of contradiction and judgment against the world, will remain in conflict with the world until the end of time. Where Féret saw an historical era of peace in Revelation 20, Huby saw the "glorification of the martyrs" at the "general resurrection" at the end of time.[32] For Huby, the book of Revelation lifts the veil, not on the future, but on the present: "Revelation has as its object a present, contemporary mystery."[33]

While Huby eschewed millenarianism, he envisioned history as an ongoing struggle between the world and God's kingdom until Christ's return and the end of time. The church is presented with a tension between the assurance of God's success in the end and the experience of persecution: "It seems to us that the condition of the Church on earth is at the same time *assured* and *precarious*: assured because it has the promise of Christ that the gates of hell will not prevail against it, that the powers of evil will not have the last word; precarious because it is always, as is Christ, a 'sign of contradiction.'"[34] The reign of God has already been realized in Christ and is already present in the church. Through the church militant on earth, the eschatological church triumphant is already made present. We cannot expect an historical era of peace because, in history and in time, the Gospel always remains a contradiction to the world.

In an article, "Apocalypse, histoire, et eschatologie chrétiennes," Féret clarified and developed his original thesis in response to Huby's "Apocalypse et Histoire." At the outset, Féret distanced himself from

31. Ibid., 95.
32. Ibid., 100.
33. Ibid., 84.
34. Ibid., 99.

any literal millenarian reading of John's Revelation. Instead, he clarified the outlines of a theory of symbol that could support the prophetic, future-oriented message of the Scripture. According to Féret, the realities about which the apocalyptic text speaks "are presented—and without doubt first of all known to the inspired author—only through symbols."[35] The meaning of the text is conveyed through symbols and images—the horsemen, the lamb, the lamp stands, the beasts, the woman—that are polyvalent. These symbols usually refer to a historical reality from the time of the author. In addition, they often possess a prophetic character. Apocalyptic symbols, "save exceptions sufficiently marked by their meaning or contexts, are normally overt about the future or announcing it. . . . We cannot contest that they . . . predict the future."[36] An accurate interpretation of apocalyptic texts will acknowledge that they are intended to reveal something about future events.

Féret located a key difference between his account and Huby's in the hermeneutics of Scripture. Whereas Huby believed that the temporal characteristics of prophetic symbols signified the enduring and permanent conditions of humanity and the church, Féret argued that the temporal characteristics within prophecy themselves are significant. The millennial prophecy (Rev. 20:1–6) symbolically portrays an historical era of peace that would come about in the future. Huby places the era of peace at the end of time. According to Féret, though we lack explicit knowledge of the concrete form that future era will take, we cannot neglect that it points to the historical future. The temporal mode of prophetic expression is itself of importance and should figure into our interpretation of the New

35. Henri-Marie Féret, "Apocalypse, histoire, et eschatologie chrétiennes," *Dieu Vivant* 2 (1945): 119.
36. Ibid., 122–23.

Testament. The prophetic symbols in Scripture prefigure the "aspect of the mystery of the Church in its future evolution," that is, a time in which the church will overcome the systemic forces of evil in the world.[37]

Féret claimed that the biblical apocalyptic looks forward to a future completion. While the Old Testament authors awaited a further completion and looked forward to the coming of the Messiah, the authors of the New Testament recognize that, while the Messiah has come, Christians await his return:

> In faith the Christian lives inseparably by the fulfillment of the ancient promises made by God to his people—a fulfillment inaugurated in the first place by Christ—and in expectation of their fuller blossoming—a blossoming that the parousia or second coming of the same Christ at the end of time will realize. It is on the future that the eschatological fragments of the New Testament project their own light, in their way, according to variable stages.[38]

God's promises have been fulfilled with Christ. Yet those same promises are oriented to a subsequent development into the future, a temporal extension of the fulfillment brought by Christ. Féret's theology of history is one in which the church extends the mission and presence of Christ temporally, transforming human relationships and social structures, eventually overcoming the evil in the world.

Neglect of the "prophetic perspective" (the future-oriented perspective) argued Féret, is "of grave consequence not only for Christian eschatology . . . but already for the prophetic documents [of the Old Testament]."[39] He feared that, by not recognizing the element of prefiguration in Scripture, we would reduce its symbols to "some general atemporal truths."[40] As a result, the content of

37. Ibid., 130.
38. Ibid., 123.
39. Ibid., 125.
40. Ibid., 130.

Christian hope would be an abstraction and would no longer have any bearing on the present church and its current struggles. Ultimately, Féret's concern was pastoral. If the gospel is to retain its meaning, the Christian must hope for a transformation or conversion of the world in history, and not just in eternity.

Huby responded to Féret again in an article entitled "Autour de l'Apocalypse" (1946), which witnesses to the rapprochement between the two authors in their basic understanding of Scripture and to their remaining differences. The point of contention was the manner in which we must interpret the "prophetic," "messianic," or "future" meaning of the Scriptures, particularly John's Apocalypse. Féret had stated that prophetic inspiration really sees something "that appears to touch on the future." Huby agreed that

> any Catholic interpreter would not hesitate to admit with Fr. Féret that, in the Apocalypse as in the messianic prophesies, the "inspired author claims to glimpse and announce, through the symbols which he uses, something of the future." . . . It remains to be determined more accurately what this "something of the future" is and to show how this "something," captured by a mode of knowledge other than that of history, is "really in continuity with another reality accessible to historical knowledge."[41]

The question is not whether the prophetic symbols point to the future. The question is whether this future reality applies simply to a future historical era, or whether it applies to new and analogous situations throughout the history of the church.

According to Huby, some scriptural symbols, like the beasts of Revelation, refer both to the historical context of the author and to future realities. While the human author of Scripture did not foresee the concrete realities in the future, the symbols that represent historical realities in turn bear an analogy to present-day

41. Joseph Huby, "Autour de l'Apocalypse," *Dieu Vivant* 5 (1946): 125.

circumstances. In a sense, the persecutions of the church throughout time are contemporaneous to the persecution occurring in the time of the author.

> I believe that this "contemporaneity" of the Apocalypse to each of the great fights of the church permits one to call the visions of Saint John properly prophetic visions: through a supra-historical view they make him *present* to the spiritual crises that the church would have to cross before its final transformation in the heavenly Jerusalem. It is in this sense that I speak of a *legitimate* application, that is to say, conformed to the intention of the inspired author, of the teachings of the Apocalypse that Christians make to analogous crises of the Church from the persecution of Diocletian, without moreover causing the complete distinction of successive periods, which map in advance the contours of the history of the church, to enter into the Johannine vision.[42]

Huby affirmed two depths of interpretation of scriptural symbols, the historical meaning and the prophetic meaning. He affirmed that the book of Revelation contains a prophetic meaning beyond the "historical plane" that tells us something of the historical future. However, he resisted "the tendency to conceive this prophetic or apocalyptic perspective as a *second plane itself also historical*," that is, a perspective that would single out particular future events as precisely foretold by the Scriptures.[43] The scriptural symbols are analogous to and contemporaneous with events throughout the life of the church.

In summary, Féret and Huby articulated the scriptural and theological grounds for a theological understanding of the historical future. They remained divided on a point of biblical hermeneutics, a point that was implicated in their respective understandings of history. Féret voiced the notion that the Christian must hope for and work toward an era in human history in which society, culture, and human institutions are conformed to the gospel. In this hope for the

42. Ibid., 126.
43. Ibid., 124.

future, Christianity held a response to communist aspirations. Huby suggested that Féret's conceptualization of a future era of history was illusory. While the symbols of Scripture had bearing on the future, they symbolize every future historical period in the church in its warfare against evil. Huby's theology of history spoke to a different prophetic aspect of Scripture: the Gospel always remains transcendent to the structures and social relationships in this world. The eschaton cannot be temporalized.

Gaston Fessard's Dialectic of History

In 1947, Gaston Fessard, SJ, intervened in the debate over the theology of history from the perspective of a philosopher rather than that of a biblical theologian. He was an editor of the Jesuit-run journal *Études*, an expert on the philosophy of Hegel, and had written numerous publications on contemporary European politics and Christianity. His writings from the 1930s and 1940s demonstrate his keen interest in social philosophy and its applicability to international relations, political authority, society, and the crises then enveloping Europe.[44] In Lyon, he openly denounced the Vichy government in 1940 for its collaboration with the Nazis. During the occupation of France he worked on *Cité nouvelle*, a journal dedicated to addressing social issues. In June 1941, François Varillon, SJ (1905–1978) and Jean Daniélou petitioned him to write a tract for the Catholic youth of Lyon warning them of the anti-Christian nature of Nazi ideology.[45] Fessard's collaboration with Pierre

---

44. Gaston Fessard, *"Pax nostra": Examen de conscience international* (Paris: Grasset, 1936); Fessard, *Le Dialogue catholique-communiste est-il possible?* (Paris: Grasset, 1937); Fessard, *Épreuve de force: Réflexions sur la crise internationale* (Paris: Bloud et Gay, 1939); Fessard, *Autorité et bien commun* (Paris: Aubier, 1944); Fessard, *France, prends garde de perdre ta liberté* (Paris: Éditions du Témoignage chrétien, 1946).

45. See Renée Bédarida, *Les Armes de l'Esprit: Témoignage chrétien (1941–1944)* (Paris: Les Éditions Ouvrières, 1977), 48–9.

Chaillet, SJ, would result in the clandestine journal *Cahiers du Témoignage chrétien*. In 1947, Fessard published "Théologie et histoire: à propos du temps de la conversion d'Israël" [Theology and history: concerning the time of the conversion of Israel] in *Dieu Vivant*. This article contained his objection to the apocalyptic interpretations of scripture in Féret, and was the initial articulation of a theology of time that would culminate in a book, *De l'actualité historique*.[46]

Fessard recognized that an apocalyptic view of history, especially that contained in the Apocalypse of John, had a resonance in the contemporary age: "A time of world conflicts and atomic bombs seems to place in question the very existence of humanity and to presage its end under the form of a cosmic drama."[47] There is, he says, a contemporary apocalypticism manifest in the despair at the human condition and a hope for a utopian future. He writes, the "'apocalyptic' Christian . . . knows that the work of the church here below is, like the terrestrial life of Christ, doomed to failure, so that he must live 'under the scope of a rupture of historical time.'"[48] Since this age is destined for war and conflict, the Christian hopes for a future era of peace.

Among Christian theologians, an apocalyptic view of history implies that God's promises—peace, conversion, reconciliation of humanity, and so on—will take place in the future. The subtitle of Fessard's article, "Concerning the Time of the Conversion of Israel," indicates that he was particularly engaging the question of *when*

---

46. Gaston Fessard, "Théologie et histoire: à propos du temps de la conversion d'Israël," *Dieu Vivant* 8 (1947): 37–65; Fessard, *De l'actualité historique* (Paris: Desclée de Brouwer, 1960). See also Michel Sales, *Gaston Fessard, 1897–1978: Genese d'une pensée*, Presences 14 (Brussels: Culture et Vérité, 1997); Michèle Aumont, *Philosophie sociopolitique de Gaston Fessard, S.J.* (Paris: Éditions du Cerf, 2005); Nguyen Hong Giao, *Le Verbe dans l'histoire: la philosophie de l'historicité du Pere Gaston Fessard*, Bibliothèque des Archives de philosophie 17 (Paris: Beauchesne, 1974); Mary Alice Muir, "Gaston Fessard, S.J.: His Work Towards a Theology of History" (M.A., Marquette University, 1970).
47. Fessard, "Théologie et histoire," 39.
48. Ibid., 40.

BETWEEN APOCALYPSE AND ESCHATON

the conversion of the Jews will take place. Fessard was responding specifically to Charles Journet, who argued that according to Romans 11 the conversion or salvation of Israel is an expectation of a *time* in which Jew and Gentile will be united. E. B. Allo, Henri-Marie Féret, and Jacques Maritain supported the opinion of Journet, for whom the prophetic meaning of the Scripture must come to pass within time. Yet the opinion handed down from the church fathers and Thomas Aquinas was that the restoration of Israel would occur at the end of time. "Here then are three or four theologians, philosophers and exegetes, whose affection toward St. Thomas is not in doubt, who do not hesitate to abandon the opinion of their Master, on a secondary matter it is true, in appearance at least."[49] Fessard accuses these theologians of contradicting the traditional Thomistic interpretation of Scripture.[50] The abandonment of the "traditional opinion" on this precise matter illustrates, for Fessard, a more generalized shift toward a hermeneutic that interprets the symbolic language of Scripture as prophesies of future historical events.

The traditional hermeneutic allowed for the "spiritual interpretation" of the literal sense of Scripture: "What distinguishes essentially sacred prophecy from profane divination is that it claims to discover less the superficial and transitory phenomena of history than—if one can say it—its 'noumena,' its intelligible essence, in brief what gives a religious meaning to the event."[51] Fessard explains that if the church fathers

> were not tempted to place [the conversion of Israel] in time, it is also that their conception of history, the foundation of their exegesis, more spiritual than literal, allowed them to perceive in the pagans and the Jews

49. Ibid., 43.
50. Moreover, Journet's belief that the conversion of Israel will occur in the future is potentially antisemitic in its view of history. It points forward to a time in which Israel is superseded by the church.
51. Fessard, "Théologie et histoire," 47.

less the phenomenal realities than "historical categories," of which the opposition clarifies the whole mystery of Christ and of the redemption of the universe.[52]

The "spiritual sense" in the church fathers and Thomas justified recognizing the temporal realities of Scripture as symbols of a more universalized set of meanings or "historical categories." Historical events symbolize the meaning of history in its development and its final state.

According to Fessard, the Pauline prophecy of the conversion of the Jews and gentiles must be understood as a glimpse of the union of all humanity in Christ. In Romans 11, Paul explains his apostolate to the gentiles as something that would contribute to the salvation of Israel itself:

Before Christ, Paul had been the Jew proud of his election in the face of pagans without God and without promise in this world; once seized by Christ, he became the apostle to the idolatrous Gentiles whom he called to conversion, while the Jews were rejected for their incredulity. He unveiled the meaning and the end of the dialectical process in the final unity of "All Israel saved" and of "the mass of Gentiles entered into the Church." Naturally, in the course of this reflection, pagans and Jews who are first phenomenal historical realities, are stylized, so to speak, into "existential attitudes" characterizing the diverse positions of man in the face of God, so that finally "the pagan" and "the Jew" appear as "historical categories" of which the interplay—the function of the *before* and the *after* of Christ—defines the *future-Christian* in each man as in the whole of humanity, by relationship to the second Coming, the end of history.[53]

In Fessard's account, the Jews and pagans are literally historical people. These historical people symbolize the human response to God's revelation. The "pagan" tends toward idolatry, the worship of

52. Ibid., 48.
53. Ibid., 49.

the world rather than God, while the "Jew" is incredulous, refusing to respond to God's authentic word. By the fact that "Jew" and "pagan" represent existential attitudes within humanity they "transcend time" and are present in every epoch.[54]

The tension between Jewish incredulity and pagan idolatry is representative of the fundamental tension between the cataphatic and apophatic responses to God's presence. The cataphatic is the recognition of God's presence in the immanent world. The apophatic dimension is the recognition that God transcends all things and can never be reduced to our categories of thinking or language to describe God. Fessard explains, "The enmity between the two people reveals the truth of human nature, always divided between the need to incarnate the absolute in the sensible—the need that causes pagan idolatry—and the essential requirement of reason to transcend every given—the requirement that causes Jewish incredulity and rejection."[55] On the one hand, we must recognize God's presence in the world. On the other hand, this presence can never be identified with the features of this world or be fully grasped by our intellect. These two existential attitudes require a synthesis that occurs through Christ. In Christ, the enmity between Jew and Gentile, man and woman, slave and free, rich and poor is dissolved. Only at the end of time will all of humanity be fully reconciled in Christ. The pagan and Jew as existential poles within humanity, while already healed in Christ himself, are completely reconciled only at the second coming, when all of humanity is gathered into Christ.[56]

Fessard believed that there were serious theological, as well as exegetical, shortcomings in the contemporary "apocalyptic" interpretations of Scripture that placed the conversion of Israel within

---

54. Ibid., 54.
55. Fessard, *De l'actualité historique*, 107.
56. Fessard, "Théologie et histoire," 52.

time. First, those who project the conversion of Israel and the Gentiles within time—and by extension expect the realization of a perfected Christian state within time—reduce Christianity to a perfection of the natural or social world:

> They have forgotten that one cannot *be* Christian as one is French or English, blond or brunette, intelligent or dull: in other words, that Christian existence [*l'être chrétien*] must never be conceived as a mode of a *natural* reality. For the reason simply that the genesis of this existence is essentially *supernatural*. This is what Kierkegaard meant when he said: one is never—in the full sense of the word—Christian, but it is always something of the future.[57]

For Fessard, "Christian existence" or the "New Man" is something that must always remain in expectation until the end of time, lest we reduce the supernatural life to an aspect of the natural.[58] In the sense that they reduce the supernatural life to an aspect of the natural, the theology of history proposed by Féret and others represented a loss of a genuine Christian eschatology and a close approximation to Marxist and fascist philosophies of history.

Second, apocalyptic interpretations of history impoverish the eschatological meaning of the present. Fessard claimed that the historical-future eschatology of Journet and Féret limited the meaning of scriptural symbols to particular times and eras, thereby losing the sense in which they are applicable universally. Although they wish to avoid the implication that the meaning of scriptural prophecy is a series of abstract and atemporal truths, in reality, Journet and Féret make those prophesies merely "relative" to a particular people or age. To say that there will be a point in history at which the "New Man" is fully established, in other words, when the oppositions that characterize our history are resolved, would be

---

57. Ibid., 53.
58. Fessard consciously contrasted the Marxist "New Man" with the Christian "New Adam."

to vacate the eschatological meaning of the present as the time of existential decision.

For Fessard, "to have a history" means to be actively engaged, through concrete decisions, in crafting the meaning of one's existence. The Christian recognizes that the concrete condition and activities of humanity already conduce to its future eschatological completion. All human beings struggle to reconcile opposing tendencies—the idolatrous "pagan" and the unbelieving "Jew"—within themselves in their concrete lives. Salvation enters into the situation of every person at all times, though it is never fully realized until the end of time. The dialectic of the pagan and the Jew contains a powerful subtext. By interiorizing the Pauline figure of the Jew as a character trait belonging to all human beings, Fessard avoids implying that Judaism is an historical stage that must be superseded in God's plan. His eschatology avoids the supersessionist tendencies present in the writings of Journet and Féret.

According to Fessard, communism and fascism possessed an underlying view of history and human agency as merely a natural or human progress. Lacking transcendence, communism and fascism must establish a new historical order through violence. Following World War II, France was involved an ideological struggle between communist, socialist, and Catholic political factions concerning the future of French identity and political existence.[59] Fessard's articulation of a theology of history implied limits to political or ideological alliances between Catholics and communists in postwar France.

---

59. See Edward Baring, "Humanist Pretensions: Catholics, Communists, and Sartre's Struggle for Existentialism in Postwar France," *Modern Intellectual History* 7, no. 3 (2010): 581–609.

Jean Daniélou's Fulfillment Theology

Jean Daniélou (1905–1974) was a theologian of history par excellence. This younger Jesuit confrere of de Lubac earned a doctorate in theology from the Institut catholique de Paris with a dissertation on Gregory of Nyssa. He served on the editorial board of Sources Chrétiennes, and he edited the first volume of the series, Gregory of Nyssa's *La vie de Moïse* (1942). In 1943 he was appointed as professor at the Institut catholique de Paris and became editor-in-chief of *Études*, an established Jesuit journal. Daniélou's *Sacramentum futuri* (1950) and *Essai sur le mystère de l'histoire* (1953) exemplify his "fulfillment theology," in which the historical events of salvation history are "types" or sacraments of future events that will fulfill them.[60] These essays were given over to an elaboration of a Christian understanding of history that can respond to present-day understandings of progress and evolution.

Two brief articles published in 1947—"Christianisme et histoire" and "À travers les revues: Christianisme et progrès"—exemplify Daniélou's intervention in the debate over the theology of history.[61] His controversial 1946 article "Les orientations présentes de la pensée religieuse," published in *Études*, gave the context for this debate.[62] "Les orientations présentes" argued that contemporary theology (that is, neoscholastic theology) was not sufficient for the authentic needs of living souls and unresponsive to the current intellectual world. Remained fixed in medieval thought forms, scholasticism had lost contact with the movement of philosophy and science. Daniélou was deliberately provocative. Many neoscholastics claimed that

---

60. Mettepenningen, *Nouvelle Théologie—New Theology*, 89; Hans Boersma, *Nouvelle Théologie and Sacramental Ontology: A Return to Mystery* (New York: Oxford University Press, 2009), 168–90.
61. Jean Daniélou, "À travers les revues: Christianisme et progrès," *Études*, no. 255 (1947): 399–402; Jean Daniélou, "Christianisme et histoire," *Études*, no. 254 (1947): 166–84.
62. Daniélou, "Les orientations présentes de la pensée religieuse," *Études*, no. 249 (1946): 5–21

scholasticism integrated the truths of other disciplines into a unified *scientia*. By implying that scholasticism no longer could account for modern science and history, Daniélou was announcing its death.

Daniélou's articles on the theology of history aimed to identify the salient features of modern thought to which Christianity responds, chief of which is an understanding of history that gives meaning to human temporal existence. In "Christianisme et histoire," he argued that developing a Christian account of temporal existence was key to responding to modernity:

> The search for a vision of history that permits an interpretation of reality and gives meaning to human action is, after a century, at the center of the preoccupations of philosophers. It suffices to speak here of the philosophy of history of Hegel, the historical materialism of Karl Marx, the creative evolution of Bergson, the Spenglerian theory of the birth and decline of civilizations, the role of temporality in the anthropology of Heidegger. This is a new dimension that is now overt in thinking. For the old philosophy, the future is the world of illusion and of multiplicity, which is opposed to the world of being. The conception of time as a positive value, of creative duration is an acquisition of modern thought. But modern thought received this conception from Christianity.[63]

The affinity of modern thought with a Christian view of history makes it critical to rediscover and articulate this view in dialogue with the world. Whereas history is critical for modernity, "the notion of history is foreign to Thomism."[64] For Daniélou, it is not just modern philosophy that is affected by a view of history, but also the lives of modern people who hope for a meaningful political and social existence. The recovery of a Christian notion of history goes hand in hand with establishing deeper contact between theology and life. He mentions new pastoral and social initiatives taking place in

---

63. Daniélou, "Christianisme et histoire," 166.
64. Daniélou, "Les orientations présentes de la pensée religieuse," 10.

France—the movements of Action catholique and Jeunesse ouvrière chrétienne (Young Christian Workers)—as well as Emmanuel Mounier, whose work was sometimes associated with leftist movements.[65]

According to Daniélou, the church fathers—he names Gregory of Nyssa, Clement of Alexandria, and Augustine—"are the nourishment most modern for people today." In them we discover a struggle against the Hellenistic and gnostic evacuation of history and the articulation of an authentically Christian understanding of the value of human action, social life, and temporal existence.[66] For the church fathers, Christianity concerns historical events more than abstract doctrine. Through these irrevocable events, God initiates the slow pedagogy that brings humanity from infancy to maturity, in which one dispensation prepares for the next. Each historical dispensation must pass away in order to make way for a new stage of fulfillment. The passage from Judaism to Christianity, as its succession and fulfillment, is analogous to the passage from the temporal to the future age: "Thus this entire world has to pass away, undoubtedly not in its very being but in its form, in order to make way for the future age, which is built here below by the invisible operation of

---

65. Ibid., 18.
66. Daniélou contrasted the first- and second-century Christian theology of history with its competitors, Hellenistic philosophy and Gnosticism. On the one hand, the Hellenistic philosophy of history is characterized by the "eternal return." The divine world is the unmoving world of ideas: "Immutable laws of the cosmos and of the city are the visible reflection of this eternity of the invisible world. Movement itself is an imitation of this immobility. It is conceived, in fact, as cyclical, in the regular movement of the stars as in the eternal return that regulates the movement of history and according to which the same events are eternally reproduced." Daniélou, "Christianisme et histoire," 168. In this scheme, the events of history are merely reflections of the eternal ideas. On the other hand, Gnosticism depended upon a metaphysical dualism between the inferior or evil god of creation and the god of salvation. The god of salvation represented an "irruption . . . of a new world without relationship to the old." Ibid., 169. Hellenism evacuated history entirely, Gnosticism made history entirely discontinuous. Oswald Spengler's *The Decline of the West*, with a "chain of heterogeneous civilizations," is an example of this gnostic tendency.

charity and will be manifest on the last day."[67] The Christian must look forward in hope to the fulfillment of the present.

While Daniélou admits that this understanding of history has analogies in evolutionary systems, these systems lack a key trait of Christianity. "Christianity . . . is not only a progress, but the term of progress." Christianity is eschatological, he states, in three ways. First, history is not just an unending process, but has a definite fulfillment. Second, Christianity *is* that term: "Christ is presented as coming at the end of time and introducing the definitive world. Thus, there is nothing beyond Christianity. It is truly 'eschatos,' 'novissimus,' the last." Third, the end has already arrived in Christ's death and resurrection: "The last things exist already."[68] Christians are now living in the last days, awaiting the transition from the temporal to the eternal. While death and evil have been vanquished in Christ, we nonetheless await the ultimate triumph in the rest of creation. Daniélou describes this period of waiting as analogous to the time between the moment of victory in the war and the victorious entrances into Paris.[69]

For Daniélou, the Christian lives in the tension between the future and past. The eschatological is already present now, albeit in anticipation. "The future age exists already, but in mystery, under the sacrament."[70] Yet, the present is also a culmination of a temporal process. In a rather unclear passage, he explains,

> The Christian is divided between two successive worlds that are found to coexist. The mystery of the present time is in fact that it brings together the presence of a past world, that survives itself, and a future

---

67. Daniélou, "Christianisme et histoire," 172.
68. Ibid., 173.
69. "This moment is the resurrection of Christ. Then will come the *Victory Day* [*Viendra ensuite le Victory Day*], the day when we pass under the arches of triumph." Ibid., 182. He was referring to the parades through the Arc d'Triomphe in Paris following Germany's surrender to the Allies.
70. Ibid., 182.

world that is already existing in an anticipated fashion. This is to say that in fact there is not a present world, or that this world is only a passage. For the Christian, the world of natural life and of science, the world of the temporal city and of economic life is something essentially anachronic. It is radically transcended by the world of the Church, which is the future already present. The world of the Church, in turn, seems, in relationship to political society, "catachronic" in the measure that it appears in the future. Juxtaposition of a past and future, such is the Christian present.[71]

Daniélou's understanding of Christianity is thoroughly eschatological insofar as it awaits a definitive fulfillment yet to come. However, in the "world of the Church" the eschaton exists already. The secular world requires a fulfillment that only the church possesses, though the church possesses that fulfillment in sacramental anticipation of the end of the world. Thus, Christianity appears as the "future" of the political and the social.

Daniélou's theology of history gives rise to his response to the political question. In "Christianisme et histoire," he explains that "human progress is ambiguous."[72] "A travers les revues: Christianisme et progrès" fills out his understanding a little more. He claims that a belief in human progress—he envisions both technological and political advancement—may be an "elementary form of religion," that is, a basic component of religious faith that takes into account humanity's creative role in the temporal. The affirmation of humanity's creative role in forging its existence is something valid in Marxism. However, its presentation of human progress is an "idolatrous pretension" insofar as it awaits the salvation of humanity by human power.[73] The conception of human progress advanced

---

71. Ibid., 183. He defines *catachronique*, an antonym of *anachronique*, as "the anticipation of a reality to come." Ibid., 183n1.
72. Ibid., 183.
73. Daniélou, "À travers les revues: Christianisme et progrès," 400. Daniélou says that Marxist understandings of history betray the "great heresy of the modern world," to believe that by human effort we can save ourselves.

by Marxism is one that lacks transcendence since it seeks an utter transformation of the world by merely human means. In contrast, for the Christian, an authentic transformation requires grace: "The progress of history, according to Christianity, is not a process of continual accumulation, as technological progress. . . . It is ascent."[74]

At the Roots of a Reflection: De Lubac's Engagement with Marxism

Henri de Lubac's intervention into the debate over the theology of history has its roots in his response to the philosophies of history implicit in modern atheism. The final part of Henri de Lubac's *The Drama of Atheist Humanism* contains a chapter entitled "The Search for a New Man," based on a lecture given for the *Semaine sociale* in Paris in 1947, the theme of which was "the Christian idea of man."[75] The lecture defends a Christian account of the vocation of humanity against a Marxist social anthropology summed up in the phrase *The New Man*, a phrase that became ubiquitous in leftist circles following the war. *The New Man* suggested a humanity evolved to a new stage of social, moral, and political development as promised by the Communist revolution. This evolution would result in such a social union and solidarity that the singular *New Man* is an adequate descriptor. At the end of the Second World War, Marxism offered an attractive ideal of social solidarity that sought a structural transformation of the temporal world. Responding to this ideal, de

---

74. Ibid., 401. Quoting from Emmanuel Mounier, *Dieu Vivant* 10 (1947): 10.

75. *Le Drame de l'humanisme athée* was originally published in 1944. The first and third parts were based on studies published in *Cité Nouvelle* in 1941 and 1943. In a later addition de Lubac added a fourth part, entitled "Affrontements mystiques" ("Mystical Confrontations"), which contained the chapter entitled "La Recherche d'un homme nouveau" ("The Search for a New Man"). The chapter was previously published as "L'idée chrétienne de l'homme et la recherche d'un homme nouveau" ("The Christian Idea of Man and the Search for a New Man") *Etudes Religieuses*, though it was based on an earlier lecture given for the *Semaine social* in Paris in 1947. See Henri de Lubac, *The Drama of Atheist Humanism* (San Francisco: Ignatius Press, 1995), 397.

Lubac asked whether Christianity possessed an ideal of social solidarity and the transformation of the temporal: "What solution will [the Christian] offer for this new state of the problem of the relations between the temporal and the eternal? . . . Optimism or pessimism, social action or eschatological expectation."[76] De Lubac sought "a confrontation with the Marxist idea that was seducing a number of minds at that time," contrasting the Christian understanding of the New Man with that of Marxism.

According to de Lubac, the emergence of modernity is animated by the realization that the world is constructed through human agency. Human beings are not merely resigned to the workings of fate or providence, but instead can shape their social reality through science and the "rational organization" of the social world.[77] The late sixteenth to early seventeenth century witnessed the beginnings of this faith in science to shape human beings and human nature. The work of René Descartes exemplifies the optimistic belief that science can improve upon human nature, and even shape it. In the nineteenth century, the Cartesian "dream" was revived in the possibility of shaping human society through the scientific management of industrial and social practices. Not only did it seem that humanity could be transformed through science, but scientific knowledge enabled the "transformation of society" in service of the human good.[78] De Lubac recognized in the work of Henri de Saint-Simon (1760–1825), Auguste Comte (1794–1859), and Pierre-Joseph Proudhon (1809–1865) an attempt to bring about a new social organization through a new scientific grasp of economic and societal mechanics.[79] With this possibility of transforming society, the value

76. Ibid.
77. Ibid., 409. This modern sensibility toward human freedom and action is broadly existentialist.
78. Ibid., 406.
79. De Lubac traced the emergence of a new idea of human agency and social organization in two articles on Proudhon appearing in Cité Nouvelle in 1943, in Le Drame de l'humanisme

of human agency and work was elevated: "The idea of a new value and new significance of human work sprang up everywhere and gradually conquered minds. In this, capitalism and socialism, those two great antagonistic forces, were in agreement: they were like the two faces of the same movement that carried away the entire century."[80] The nineteenth century proclaimed the advancement of a "whole 'technology' of man" in economic, sociological, biological and psychological domains.

Although, de Lubac admitted, faith in scientific and material progress has been impaired in the twentieth century by the experience of evil, the new perception of humanity's role in the world was an advancement within human thinking. Human beings rightly desire material, technological advancement as well as social advancement. Far from rejecting the earnest search for social progress in the name of God's governance over worldly affairs—a false belief that de Lubac entitles "providentialism"—Christianity suggests that human agency in bettering itself is elemental to being in the image of God as a cocreator. He writes, "Let us even say that in this above all consists man's faculty as worker, which thus seems in a way, still in the image of his creator, *causa sui*."[81] While de Lubac acknowledged a distinction between progress in social organization and salvation, he stated that one must affirm both as complementary rather than opposed truths. The modern movement of thought that assigns human beings a role in shaping this world is fundamentally in harmony with the Christian faith.

The problem, however, with Marxism is that it seeks progress in the social realm through the displacement or annihilation of the

athée (1944), "Proudhon contre le 'mythe de la Providence'" in *Les Traditions socialistes françaises* (Neuchâtel, Switzerland: Cahiers du Rhône, 1944), 65–89, and *Proudhon et le Christianisme* (Paris: Éditions du Seuil, 1944).

80. De Lubac, *The Drama of Atheist Humanism*, 106.
81. Ibid., 418.

transcendent.[82] Marxism, as well as modern humanist atheism, participates in what de Lubac called a "Promethean" tendency toward human self-creation. In order to affirm the value of human history, it denies the transcendent. Rather than to "collaborate in the divine work," it organizes the effort of "earthly construction" as a renunciation of dependence on God, providence, or anything beyond the earthly.[83] Quoting Teilhard de Chardin, de Lubac claimed that "the true name of communism should be earthism [terrénisme]."[84] Human beings have tended to recognize signs of the transcendent in the material world. In Marxism, the mystical impulse is reversed: "Instead of seeing in visible and tangible realities so many signs of the invisible kingdom to which he [the modern human being] believed himself destined, he no longer wanted to recognize in any of these conceptions any spiritual order except groundless symbols . . . of the sole reality of this world which science is at last handing over to him."[85] In the model of modern humanist atheism, Marxism looks upon religion as belonging to prescientific explanations of reality, now outdated and needing to be replaced. Religion was a stage in human development toward a scientific view of the world, which now supersedes it. As de Lubac explained, "The essential reproach [the humanist atheist] addresses to the Christian mystery is similar to the one which Origen once addressed in the name of this mystery to the Jewish religion: he reproaches the figure for its refusal to disappear in the face of the truth that fulfills it."[86]

---

82. In contrast with Jean Lacroix, de Lubac's lecture at the *Semaine sociale* claimed that Marxism shared with Christianity a sense of human dignity in history, although it reversed a Christian understanding of the world. De Lubac made reference to Jean Lacroix, *Socialisme?*, Le Forum (Paris: Éditions du Livre Français, 1946).
83. De Lubac, *The Drama of Atheist Humanism*, 421.
84. Ibid., 422–23.
85. Ibid., 422.
86. Ibid. Already, Origen was important for de Lubac, who was considering how early Christian thinking about Judaism became a pattern for atheistic thinking about Christianity. In 1947, the same year as the *Semaine sociale* lecture, he published the introduction to Origène, *Homélies sur*

Only when the transcendent disappears can the work of shaping human society begin.

Marxism, de Lubac stated, is not only a plan for economic or social organization, but a "spiritual phenomenon" that anticipates a transformation of previous society into a perfected society.[87] There is a "family resemblance" between the early Christian anticipation of the body of Christ and the Marxist anticipation of the union of humanity as the New Man: both look forward to the "end of history"; both see a perfection of human unity.

> Only, what the Christian hopes for in another world, at the end of time, the Marxist dreams of for this present world, within our time. What the Christian awaits from a supernatural intervention, the Marxist anticipates as the natural end of a wholly immanent process. A transfiguration of the here and now without the presence of a Beyond! An end of history in the midst of a time that continues to unfold![88]

As de Lubac points out, the Marxist philosophy of history contains a fundamental spiritual contradiction. On the one hand, instead of hoping for the world to come, Marxism awaits an eschatological fulfillment within time, a "temporalization of the kingdom." On the other hand, Marxism promulgates a faith in a "radical utopia," which is "essentially indescribable . . . because radically different from all the relative states through which humanity passes in the course of existence. The end of history could not be made of the same elements of its course."[89] The future state of humanity is wholly other. In sum, Marxism is wedded to historical immanentism—a refusal to see anything beyond the present, historical world—yet wishes to

l'Exode in Sources Chrétiennes. De Lubac only highlighted that the logic of supersessionism is at work in Marxism. Although he had already written extensively against the Nazis, he did not indicate that the supersessionism implied in Origen's statement is also present in Nazism.

87. *The Drama of Atheist Humanism*, 432.
88. Ibid., 435.
89. Ibid., 439.

bring about a new state of humanity that transcends the historical conditions.

De Lubac criticized the Marxists for a fundamental misreading of the Christian understanding of time and history. In "Theses on Feuerbach" (1845), Marx wrote that so far the "philosophers have only interpreted the world in various ways; the point is to change it." Whereas ancient humanity was content to be part of the natural world, imitating and understanding nature, modern humanity now recognizes its responsibility to shape the world. Whereas the ancients "refused" history, constrained by the laws of the gods and by fate, moderns have awakened to its role in shaping the course of history. While de Lubac largely accepts the Marxist characterization of ancient humanity, he suggests that it characterizes non-Christian cultures in premodern society rather than Christianity. Christianity has been falsely charged with not valuing terrestrial existence and envisioning salvation as an escape from the temporal; but rather than refusing history, it offered a revolutionary view of history. Because revelation is God's action within history, the course of history is meaningful. Our participation in God's plan "allows us to 'redeem time,'" that is, to transform the temporal order into an anticipation of eternity.[90]

De Lubac gives insight into a theological understanding of history and eternity that pervades his work:

> The real work of a good God, the world has a real value. It is more than just the milieu in which man must act and be engaged, more than the instrument that he must employ; it is, so to speak, the fabric of the world to come, the material of our eternity. It must not be annihilated but transfigured. Man thus has less to free himself from time than to free himself through time; he does not at all have to escape the world but to take it upon himself. . . . Only, in order to understand time and the world, it is necessary to focus beyond: for it is its relation to eternity

90. Ibid., 423–24.

that gives the world its consistency and that makes of time a real future. Time is not, therefore, as the ancients imagined, the simple projection of an eternal; humanity in time is not enclosed in a circle. But if time has a positive face that constructs rather than destroys, if humanity is really progressing, it is because eternity is carrying them.[91]

On the one hand, the historical world in which we live is meaningful. However, it is not meaningful in the sense that it is only a necessary means for eternal life that one must pass through, then leave behind. The "present life" is not, in the words of Gustavo Gutiérrez, merely a "test."[92] Instead, history is the "material of our eternity" that must be "transfigured." On the other hand, that which gives meaning to time lies beyond it. Only in relation to the eschaton can time be meaningful. At the time of the *Semaine sociale* in 1947, de Lubac was already turning to the sources of an ancient Christian theology of history in scripture and the church fathers that could provide an alternative to Marxism.

Conclusion

The post–World War II debate over the theology of history manifested an intense interest in eschatology and a fragmentation of opinion on Christian eschatology. The backdrop to this debate was the German occupation, the restructuring of French civil and political society after the war, and the French Catholic responses to this restructuring. The controversy over the "theology of history" addressed the question of eschatology directly: *Theologically, what is the relationship between our historical world—experienced in the church and secular history—and its promised consummation?* Around the time of the Second World War, the political and cultural implications of

---

91. Ibid., 428–29.
92. Gustavo Gutiérrez, *A Theology of Liberation: History, Politics, and Salvation* (Maryknoll, NY: Orbis Books, 1973), 150–51.

this question were immense. The nascent *nouvelle théologie* sought a response through a retrieval of an early Christian understanding of history from the Bible and the church fathers. These authors agreed that Christianity is essentially eschatological. Fessard and Daniélou spoke of Christianity as something "to come." For Daniélou, the church is where the future is made present under the sacrament. Fessard spoke of "Christian existence" or, alternatively, the "New Man" as a reality yet to come and not fully present now. Féret suggested that the conformity of the church to the gospel awaits a future completion.

Yet they came to opposing conclusions on two correlate questions. First, *to what extent can the contemporary eschatological and historical consciousness (such as that present in Marxism) be reconciled with a Christian understanding of history?* Fessard opposed Féret's interpretation of the Apocalypse, in part, because he believed that Féret's future eschatology too closely mirrored an understanding of history undergirding both fascism and communism. On the other hand, Féret and, more explicitly, Daniélou believed that an authentic Christian eschatology served as a corrective to both ahistorical neoscholasticism and the dialectical materialism of Marx.

Second, *what form of eschatology preserves the eternal significance of the present moment and the social space of Christianity?* In the period between World War II and Vatican II, the relevance of Christianity to the social world would be addressed in widely varying directions in the work of Gaston Fessard, Jacques Maritain, Marie-Dominique Chenu, and Maurice Montuclard, among others. In the debate over the theology of history, St. Paul and the book of Revelation became touchstones for the understanding of the theological significance of the present and the encounter with God through the concrete realities of social existence. While Féret, Huby, Fessard, and Daniélou agreed that the Scriptures provide a vision of history and its consummation, they disagreed on how the Scriptures provided a theological understanding of the present and future. This disagreement prompted de Lubac to examine the early Christian interpretation of Scripture in the church fathers and medieval Christianity as the source for a theological understanding of history. "Part 2: Temporal Ruptures" examines the development of de Lubac's theology of history and eschatology through the recovery of the spiritual sense of Scripture.

PART II

Temporal Ruptures

De Lubac recognized that all Christian theology hinged on the understanding of history because God's word has intervened into history, changing it irrevocably. De Lubac looked to the patristic period to recover a theological understanding of history for the present day. Yet he chose the most unlikely figure as a model for a Christian understanding of history, namely Origen of Alexandria (185–254 CE). Origen was widely thought to be one of the most Neoplatonic thinkers in the early church. His "allegorical" interpretation of Scripture appeared to be similar to the Neoplatonists, for whom the stories about the gods were merely myths for philosophical truths. The implication was that the events narrated in Scripture were mere mythological representations of philosophical truths. De Lubac, however, discovered a profoundly Christian understanding of history precisely in Origen's allegorical interpretation of Scripture. Origen's interpretation of the Bible constituted an interpretation of ruptures—between the Old and New Testament, and between the New Testament and the eschatological fulfillment—within a continuous history. Moreover, Origen transmitted a method of interpreting Scripture that would be dominant in Christianity until the Middle Ages, a method that preserved a Christian view of history. However, the Middle Ages witnessed the rupture of these patterns of interpretation, resulting in dramatically different streams of eschatological and apocalyptic thinking. One of de Lubac's most important contributions was his tracing the eruption of political messianism in his own day to the unraveling of Origen's historical-eschatological synthesis in the Middle Ages. The unlikely character of Origen became the key for de Lubac's recovery of a theology of history.

Chapter 3, "Scripture and the Structure of History," traces de Lubac's recovery of an early Christian sense of history from Origen of Alexandria and outlines its key components from which de Lubac's theology of history emerged. Chapter 4, "Christ Is the Center of History," examines de Lubac's recovery of Origen for an understanding of the centrality of Christ in history. Chapter 5, "Between Apocalypse and Eschaton," examines de Lubac's genealogy of modern eschatological thinking from the medieval rupture in biblical interpretation.

3

Scripture and the Structure of History

Henri de Lubac devoted more of his writing to the history of the interpretation of Scripture than to any other theological topic, including nature and grace, atheism, and ecclesiology. Composed over several decades, his writings especially focused on the spiritual interpretation of the biblical text. Spiritual interpretation constituted a hermeneutic for interpretation of the Bible in the early church that endured until the modern period, informing both preaching and theology. Spiritual interpretation is, quite simply, the practice of reading the text for more than its literal, face-value meaning. One reads *beyond* or *through* the "letter" to reach the depth dimension of the text. But de Lubac realized that Christian spiritual interpretation of the Bible reflected a theology of history. By turning to the spiritual interpretation of the early church, de Lubac believed that he could recover the roots of an early Christian understanding of history relevant for the contemporary age.

In the introduction to *Catholicism* (1938), voicing the objections of a critic of Christianity, he asks, "'How . . . can a religion which apparently is uninterested in our terrestrial future and in human fellowship offer an ideal which can still attract the men of today?'"[1] People were attracted to the social and historical vision in Marxism. De Lubac asked, what kind of social and historical vision does Christianity proclaim? In *Catholicism*, de Lubac responded to this question by explicating the ideal of social unity and corporate salvation in the writings of the fathers of the church. Christianity, he claimed, held the corrective to two views of human existence, Hellenism and Marxism. On the one hand, Hellenism proposed a circular view of history in which the only salvation is escape from the world and temporality. History itself lacks value. On the other hand, Marxism discovers the value of history, yet this history lacks a transcendent goal. The understanding of history present in the fathers of the church, he believed, united a regard for the value of human social progress in time with the sense of transcendence beyond it. De Lubac's insight concerning the value of history in Christianity formed the basis for a wide-ranging project in which sought to articulate a theology of history for the current day. At the center of this theology of history is Origen, the second- to third-century Egyptian theologian, whose work, de Lubac claimed, systematized and transmitted a Christian understanding of time and eternity.[2]

De Lubac's writings on the Christian exegetical tradition are key to his theology of history and its consummation at the end. First, de Lubac sought to recover the spiritual interpretation of Scripture

---

1. Henri de Lubac, *Catholicism: Christ and the Common Destiny of Man*, trans. Lancelot C. Sheppard and Sister Elizabeth Englund, OCD (San Francisco: Ignatius Press, 1988), 13–14. Originally published as *Catholicisme: les aspects sociaux du dogma*, Coll Unam Sanctam 3 (Paris: Éditions du Cerf, 1938).

2. Henri de Lubac, *Medieval Exegesis: The Four Senses of Scripture*, trans. Mark Sebanc, vol. 1 (Grand Rapids, MI: Eerdmans, 1998), 142. Originally published as *Exégèse médiévale I: Les quatre sens de l'Écriture*, Théologie 41 (Paris: Éditions Montaigne, 1959). De Lubac argued that multiple exegetical traditions of spiritual interpretation of the Middle Ages can be traced back to Origen.

primarily to rediscover an ancient Christian understanding of history, and not as an alternative to modern critical methods of interpreting the Bible. Second, de Lubac believed that early Christian interpretation of Scripture was an antidote to the Hellenistic view of history. Third, de Lubac turned to Origen for a theology of history that unites the value of the historical with transcendence beyond it.

The Spiritual Senses

The exegetical consensus of the premodern Christian tradition is that Scripture contains meanings beyond and beneath the literal sense, that is, the plain meaning of the text. The reading of Scripture should involve a penetration of the text and the text's penetration of the believer, so that she or he might attain to its hidden depths. Various theological formulations of this teaching proliferated during the Middle Ages. De Lubac argued that these formulations generally had a common structure.

A medieval formula summarized this traditional teaching in a short rhyme:

> Littera gesta docet, quid credas allegoria,
> Moralis quid agas, quo tendas anagogia.
> (The letter teaches what took place, allegory what to believe,
> The moral what to do, anagogy what goal to strive for.)

The foundational meaning, upon which the others were based, was the literal sense. De Lubac describes the literal sense as essentially a historical meaning, insofar as the text truthfully conveys what occurred, namely God's interventions in time. The text also reveals a spiritual meaning, which was sometimes divided into multiple spiritual senses. Allegory (often called the "mystical sense") signified the christological meaning of the Scriptures. It suggested that the events narrated in the Scriptures are fulfilled in the Christ event and that this fulfillment extends into the church. The moral sense (often called the tropological meaning) denotes the implication of the historical meaning for the moral and spiritual life of the individual soul and of the church. The anagogical sense denotes the last meaning, the ultimate fulfillment at the end of the world. De Lubac saw the fourfold sense exemplified by the Christian interpretation of the city of Jerusalem.[3] The historical city of Jerusalem is symbolic of the city of God "renewed in Christ," but it also symbolizes the reign of God in the soul, and, ultimately, the historical city of Jerusalem refers to the heavenly city. The Old Testament reference to Jerusalem is assumed into a broader interconnection of scriptural realities and images.

While de Lubac recognized a "terminological anarchy" during the patristic and medieval periods with regard to the meanings of Scripture, he argued that the various terminologies often contained a common structure.[4] The foundational division is a dyad between the "historical sense" (or the letter) and the "spiritual sense" of Scripture. The spiritual sense is subdivided generally as the allegorical, moral, and anagogical senses. The primary division between *letter* and *spirit* expresses the relationship between the Old Testament and the New Testament: the Old Testament is the history of God's actions; the New Testament *is* the spiritual meaning of the Old Testament history. Indeed, the title of his monograph on Origen, *History and*

---

3. *Medieval Exegesis,* 1:108. Henri de Lubac, *Medieval Exegesis: The Four Senses of Scripture,* trans. E. M. Macierowski, vol. 2 (Grand Rapids, MI: Eerdmans, 2000), 199. Originally published as *Exégèse médiévale II: Les quatre sens de l'Écriture,* Théologie 41 (Paris: Éditions Montaigne, 1959). Henri de Lubac, "On an Old Distich: The Doctrine of the 'Fourfold Sense' in Scripture," in *Theological Fragments,* trans. Rebecca Howell Balinski (San Francisco: Ignatius Press, 1989), 115. Originally published as "Sur un vieux distique: La doctrine du 'quadruple sens,'" in *Mélanges offerts au R. P. Fernand Cavallera* (Toulouse: Institut Catholique, 1948), 347–66.

4. The phrase *terminological anarchy* is from Walter Burghardt. See Kevin L. Hughes, "The 'Fourfold Sense:' De Lubac, Blondel and Contemporary Theology," *The Heythrop Journal* 42, no. 4 (2001): 451–52.

Spirit, reflects this distinction. As the first of the spiritual senses, de Lubac often identifies "allegory" with the spiritual sense as a whole, inclusive of the moral and anagorical senses. However, at times, he specifically distinguishes allegory from the other spiritual senses. This various usage is reflective of the diversity within the exegetical tradition. The various formulations of the senses of Scripture reflect the most basic division between history and spirit.

The beginning of the first volume of *Exégèse médiévale* serves to sort out all of the various lists and orderings of the spiritual senses that developed in the patristic and medieval periods. In their most basic forms, de Lubac discovers two orderings of the spiritual senses and two divisions of each ordering. In one ordering, which de Lubac associates with John Cassian, morality directly follows history: history, morality, allegory, (anagogy). Another ordering, associated with Augustine, places allegory right after history: history, allegory, morality, (anagogy).[5] There are examples of threefold or fourfold divisions of each ordering. Thus, the threefold sense (history, allegory, morality) is essentially the same as the fourfold sense (history, allegory, morality, anagogy).

Although there is a great variety of practice with regard to spiritual meanings, de Lubac traces all of the lists to Origen: "These two lists, with the two orders that characterize them, can be found in the same author, the author who dominates the whole of the later tradition: Origen."[6] The importance of Origen for de Lubac cannot be underestimated. Origen is the progenitor of the multiple streams of spiritual interpretation that flow through the patristic and medieval periods. He has an immense historical significance. But because of his historical role, Origen is also theologically significant for de Lubac. Since spiritual interpretation had such a vast impact on the

---

5. De Lubac, *Medieval Exegesis*, 1:114.
6. Ibid., 1:142.

development of Christian theology, it is of immense importance whether Origen's exegesis contained an authentically Christian understanding of history or was the product of an ahistorical Hellenism. According to de Lubac, Origen's spiritual interpretation systematized a Christian understanding of history. This is why Origen is always in the background of de Lubac's exposition of the history of the interpretation of Scripture.

The Recovery of Spiritual Interpretation

De Lubac's publications on spiritual interpretation began in the 1940s. In 1947, de Lubac argued in "Typology and Allegorization" that the patristic allegorization of Scripture constituted a uniquely Christian transformation of the Philonic and Greek modes of interpretation.[7] In 1948, de Lubac published a short article, "On an Old Distich: The Doctrine of the 'Fourfold Sense' in Scripture."[8] This article argued that the "spiritual meanings" embodied in the fourfold sense of Scripture not only influenced a long tradition of Christian interpretation of Scripture, but also that their logic structured the relationship between theological disciplines. De Lubac's groundbreaking *History and Spirit: The Understanding of Scripture according to Origen* was published two years later.[9] It claimed that Origen, the second- and third-century Egyptian catechist and theologian, was largely responsible for systematizing the Christian teaching on the spiritual meaning of Scripture. De Lubac refuted the then-dominant opinion that Origen's practice of spiritual

---

7. Henri de Lubac, "Typology and Allegorization," in *Theological Fragments*, trans. Rebecca Howell Balinski (San Francisco: Ignatius Press, 1989), 129–64. Originally published as Henri de Lubac, "'Typologie' et 'Allégorisme,'" *Recherches de Science Religieuse* 34 (1947): 180–226.
8. De Lubac, "On an Old Distich."
9. Henri de Lubac, *History and Spirit: The Understanding of Scripture according to Origen*, trans. Anne Englund Nash (San Francisco: Ignatius Press, 2007). Originally published as Henri de Lubac, *Histoire et esprit: l'intelligence de l'Écriture d'après Origène*, Théologie 16 (Paris: Aubier, 1950).

interpretation was Hellenistic in character, arguing instead that Origen's spiritual interpretation preserved a Christian understanding of God's intervention into history. De Lubac would emphasize that Origen's treatment of *anagogy,* the final "spiritual sense" of Scripture, united both the eschatological anticipation of the future and the contemplation of the transcendent.

In June of 1950, de Lubac was forbidden to teach by his Jesuit superiors. He was under suspicion for his previous writings, including *Surnaturel* (1946), and his conspicuous advocacy of recovery of the ancient Christian tradition. From the Jesuit house in Lyons, he was "exiled" to the Paris residence of Jesuits on the Rue de Sèvres. Given the tendency of the French to think of Paris as the cultural and intellectual center, the choice of Paris as the site of exile was indeed odd. In August of 1950, Pope Pius XII promulgated the encyclical letter *Humani generis,* which many interpreted to contain a line critical of de Lubac. With his theological writings under suspicion, de Lubac turned to studies on Buddhism from 1951 to 1955.[10] While he did not abandon his interest in the theology of history, it had a significant hiatus. It was only in 1958 that he was officially permitted to teach again.[11] De Lubac returned to the theme of spiritual interpretation in an article entitled "Hellenistic Allegory and Christian Allegory" (1959). Against Jean Pépin, he argued that Christian allegorical interpretation of Scripture, particularly in Origen, constituted the antithesis of Hellenistic allegorization. His monumental multivolume work *Exégèse médiévale* (1959–64), a study of patristic and medieval interpretation of Scripture, is often cited for its recovery or *ressourcement* of the spiritual senses of Scripture.

10. Henri de Lubac, *Aspects du Bouddhisme* (Paris: Éditions du Seuil, 1951); Henri de Lubac, *La rencontre du Bouddhisme et de l'Occident.*, vol. 24, Théologie 24 (Paris: Aubier, 1952); Henri de Lubac, *Amida: aspects du Bouddhisme* (Paris: Éditions du Seuil, 1955).

11. See Rudolf Voderholzer, *Meet Henri de Lubac,* trans. Michael J. Miller (San Francisco: Ignatius Press, 2008), 80.

Exégèse médiévale took a diachronic approach to the spiritual senses, tracing their development from the patristic period to early modernity.

By the time de Lubac initiated his studies on ancient hermeneutics in the late 1940s, Catholic biblical scholars were already rapidly adopting higher criticism. Pope Pius XII in his encyclical letter *Divino afflante Spiritu* (1943) called for new translations of the Bible based on the original languages of the Bible rather than St. Jerome's Latin Vulgate, and the encyclical opened the door for Catholics to employ critical methods in biblical studies. Given the rapid adaptation of Catholic biblical scholars to critical methods, de Lubac's *ressourcement* of patristic and medieval exegesis might appear to be a reaction against it. Indeed, some scholars have interpreted de Lubac's work as an attempt to recover an ancient hermeneutic as an alternative to modern exegesis.[12]

Yet de Lubac suggested that his interests were theological rather than strictly exegetical. He indicated that his studies on ancient exegesis were not for the purpose of establishing it anew: "Does this mean that we would propose returning to it as a guide for today's exegesis and theology? No one would seriously dream of that."[13] While de Lubac originally intended to examine the symbolism within premodern exegesis, he later recognized a much wider application to his studies. He explained that his research on spiritual interpretation in Origen was a window to the recovery of a partially lost vision of reality:

---

12. For example, in an excellent introduction to de Lubac's recovery of ancient exegesis, David M. Williams expresses consternation that de Lubac composed no clear methodology for uniting contemporary scientific exegesis with ancient allegorical methods. See David M. Williams, *Receiving the Bible in Faith: Historical and Theological Exegesis* (Washington, DC: Catholic University of America Press, 2004), 169–73.

13. De Lubac, "On an Old Distich," 124.

The subject I had first envisioned assumed a broader scope in my eyes. ... It was no longer even a matter solely of exegesis. It was a whole manner of thinking, a whole world view that loomed before me. A whole interpretation of Christianity of which Origen, furthermore, despite many of his personal and at times questionable traits, was less the author than the witness. Even more, through this "spiritual understanding" of Scripture, it was Christianity itself that appeared to me as if acquiring a reflective self-awareness. This is the phenomenon, one of the most characteristic of the early Christian period, that, in the final analysis, I sought to grasp.[14]

Spiritual interpretation was both an epiphenomenon of the creed and ethos of the early church and also that by which the church attained a doctrinal "self-awareness." Origen's exegesis belonged not only to biblical interpretation, but to an entire way of looking at reality that was the shared inheritance of the early church.

Building on *History and Spirit*, de Lubac leaves another clue to his intentions in *Exégèse médiévale*: "Now this 'complete act' that is ancient Christian exegesis is a very great thing. . . . It sets up a subtle dialectic of before and after. It defines the relationship between historical reality and spiritual reality, between society and individual, between time and eternity. It contains, as one might say today, a whole theology of history, which is connected with a theology of Scripture."[15] De Lubac had little direct interest in recovering ancient methods of biblical interpretation. Instead, he wanted to understand the mentality, the doctrinal vision, and the sensibilities toward history that supported practices of spiritual interpretation. De Lubac believed that the theology of history underlying spiritual interpretation could respond to modern secular visions of history. Moreover, his recovery of spiritual interpretation was intimately bound with his other

14. De Lubac, *History and Spirit*, 11.
15. De Lubac, *Medieval Exegesis*, 1:xix.

theological projects, including his ecclesiology, sacramental theology, and his understanding of the supernatural.[16]

Allegory and the Hellenization Thesis

Patristic and medieval theologians employed allegorical interpretation (also *spiritual interpretation* and *mystical interpretation*) to read the Old Testament in light of the New Testament. Admittedly, this procedure resulted in extravagant interpretations of the Bible and, in many cases, appeared to have few hermeneutic controls. In the Latin Middle Ages, the predominant use of the Latin text and the distance of medieval culture from the Hebrew, Greek, and Aramaic languages resulted in a loss of the textual criticism developed by some church fathers, including Origen. The rebirth of Hebrew, Greek, and Aramaic studies during the Renaissance and the doctrinal battles of the Reformation and Counter-Reformation led to a renewed focus on the literal meaning of the text. New tools of exegesis developed during the Enlightenment led to critical exegesis and to broad challenges to traditions of spiritual interpretation and allegorization.

Nineteenth-century biblical scholarship, especially the work of Adolf von Harnack (1851–1930), constitutes part of the broad context for de Lubac's studies on spiritual meaning, the fourfold sense, and Origen. Employing the tools of critical exegesis, Harnack developed what is described as the "Hellenization thesis." In *History of Dogma* (*Lehrbuch der Dogmengeschichte*) and in a more popular work *What Is Christianity?* (*Das Wesen des Christentums*), Harnack argued that the

---

16. See Susan K. Wood, *Spiritual Exegesis and the Church in the Theology of Henri de Lubac* (Grand Rapids, MI: Eerdmans, 1998); Bryan C. Hollon, *Everything Is Sacred: Spiritual Exegesis in the Political Theology of Henri de Lubac* (Eugene, OR: Cascade Books, 2009); Bryan C. Hollon, "Ontology, Exegesis, and Culture in the Thought of Henri de Lubac" (PhD diss., Baylor University, 2006); Hans Boersma, *Nouvelle Théologie and Sacramental Ontology: A Return to Mystery* (New York: Oxford University Press, 2009); Hans Boersma, "Sacramental Ontology: Nature and the Supernatural in the Ecclesiology of Henri de Lubac," *New Blackfriars* 88, no. 1015 (2007): 242–73.

early Christian development of dogma was "Hellenistic." Christianity developed away from the gospel through its increasing focus on Greek philosophical truth.[17] In other words, Hellenistic forms of thought infiltrated the Hebraic-Christian forms of thought, overshadowing them from the second century to the time of the Reformation. Thus, he suspected the doctrinal development of the earliest councils—including Trinitarian doctrine, *Logos* Christology, and creedal formulations—of being Greek at their core. Harnack's Hellenization thesis suggested that the major theological developments of patristic thought served to mutate the gospel into a species of Greek philosophy.[18] The allegorization of Scripture reflected a development whereby the Greek philosophical milieu permeated and denatured Christian exegesis of the Scriptures.

Harnack's Hellenization thesis impacted the response of French Catholic theologians and historians, like Aimé Puech, Pierre Batiffol, and Louis Duchesne, to early Christian allegorical interpretation, including that of Origen.[19] According to de Lubac, these historians suggested that Origen refused the historicity of the meaning of Scripture, distancing himself from the literal meaning of the text.[20] Unable to accept the letter of Scripture, he "infused Hellenism

---

17. According to Harnack, Hippolytus and Tertullian contributed to identifying elements of the Christian faith with Greek philosophy, for example, by identifying the *Logos* with the Son of God. Origen (Harnack calls him the "Christian Philo") was responsible for "recasting" Christian faith as a dogma in order to compete with the Neoplatonic systems of his day. He sought to transcend the gospel for the sake of speculation. Adolf von Harnack, *History of Dogma*, vol. 2 (London: Williams and Norgate, 1896), 11.

18. For an overview of Harnack's dichotomization of historical interpretation and metaphysical speculation, see James C. Livingston, *Modern Christian Thought: The Enlightenment and the Nineteenth Century*, 2nd ed. (Minneapolis: Fortress Press, 2006), 287.

19. Alfred Loisy, a Catholic priest and scholar, introduced French Catholics to the writings of Harnack in his *L'Evangile et l'Eglise* (1902), which challenged Harnack's assertions in *What is Christianity?* Although Loisy's resolutions were unacceptable to the French Catholic bishops and to the Holy See (Loisy was excommunicated in 1907), he brought attention to the differences between the historical form of the Scriptures and the metaphysics within dogmatic formulations.

20. De Lubac, *History and Spirit*, 17.

broadly into the biblical tradition and . . . substituted a 'metaphysical truth' received from another source for the 'absurdity of the text taken in its literal sense.'"[21] Indeed, the contemporary scholarly consensus on Origen was that he promulgated a "tool for obtaining a 'timeless superunderstanding' of the Bible," a hermeneutic that saw the events narrated in Scripture as mythical expressions of a philosophical reality.[22] Some scholars imagined that Origen was a Platonist or that he anticipated idealist philosophy. At the very least, Origen had, with much of third-century Christianity, "transformed Christianity into a philosophy."[23]

While de Lubac apparently accepted the now-classic contrast between Greek metaphysics and Judeo-Christian historical thinking, he did not believe that early Christianity in general and Origen in particular followed the pattern of Greek metaphysics. For de Lubac, the debate over the so-called Hellenization of Christian thought turned on one's interpretation of allegory. Was early Christian allegorical interpretation primarily a departure from the core of Judeo-Christian historical thinking or was it a means to preserve it? In both *History and Spirit* and "Hellenistic Allegory and Christian Allegory," de Lubac challenged the assumption that "all Christian allegory is bound to be related, in its origins and characteristics, to

---

21. Ibid., 15.
22. Henri de Lubac, "Hellenistic Allegory and Christian Allegory," 174 in *Theological Fragments*, trans. Rebecca Howell Balinski (San Francisco: Ignatius Press, 1989). Originally published as Henri de Lubac, "A propos de l'allégorie chrétienne," *Recherches de science religieuse* 47 (1959): 5-43.
23. The quotation is taken from Aimé Puech, *Recherches sur le discours aux Grecs de Tatien* (1903) in de Lubac, *History and Spirit*, 93n258. See also *History and Spirit*, 259–61. These scholars, de Lubac argued, misunderstood Origen's allusions to the need to pass to a deeper meaning or a higher teaching. For them, it expressed a gnostic doctrine: that the historical events of redemption, including Christ's sacrifice, were only for beginners; that to advance spiritually, one must pass beyond the external and corporeal events of salvation; that there exists a more profound knowledge—a philosophical, gnostic meaning—for those who are spiritual. De Lubac also mentioned Alain Guy, who stated that allegory derived a "philosophical meaning" from the Bible and used the Bible as a "kind of philosophical code and a springboard for ontological mediation." Henri de Lubac, "Hellenistic Allegory and Christian Allegory," 175.

the doctrines of intellectual paganism that allegorized its myths and to Philo's exegesis."[24] De Lubac did not dispute the profound influence of the Hellenistic milieu on Christian theology or the use of Greek categories by the church fathers. Yet he argued that early Christians developed allegory, not as a repetition of Hellenistic categories, but as a reflection upon the realities expressed in the gospel.

An essential difference between Hellenism and early Christianity was their divergent concepts of history. De Lubac described Greek allegory as an attempt to explain unseemly and irreverent exploits of the gods in Homer and the poets by recasting those stories as allegories or myths for philosophical or scientific truths.[25] This reinterpretation occurred through a denial of the literal meaning and discovery of an esoteric meaning:

> There are two features in the allegorism of the philosophers that appear constantly whatever the text on which their work is based or the system that they deduce from it; whatever purpose guides them or the precise nature of the method they use. For on the one hand they reject as myth what appears as a historical account, and deny to its literal sense what they claim to reveal in its meaning as a mystery: their ὑπόνοια [esoteric meaning] is, in the strictest sense, an ἀλληγορία [allegory]. . . . On the other hand, if they "spiritualize" in this way whatever purports to be historical, it is not for the purpose of a deeper understanding of history. They do not see mythical events as symbols of spiritual happenings; but perceive beneath the historical veil scientific, moral or metaphysical ideas.[26]

---

24. De Lubac, "Hellenistic Allegory and Christian Allegory," 165. De Lubac writes that Philo "develops a timeless allegory that maintains no internal relation with biblical history. This is not at all the case with Origen." De Lubac, *History and Spirit*, 22.

25. "For the philosophers, in all the stories that serve as material for their theories, it is not a question of personal beings or spiritual facts; the tangible individuality of heroes or gods is transformed under their eyes into the nature of things or of the human soul or of divinity diffused everywhere; their 'allegory' (their ὑπόνοια [esoteric meaning]) dissipates all history, all real drama; it makes everything 'vanish into the elements of the world.'" De Lubac, *History and Spirit*, 21.

26. De Lubac, *Catholicism*, 166.

In sum, pagan philosophical allegory, for de Lubac, refused the historical account in favor of discovering the "power of nature," the "harmony of the universe," or "the original matter" in these myths. This form of allegorization influenced Philo of Alexandria, a first-century Jewish philosopher. While Philo did not deny that the events of Scripture occurred, he believed that "they are of no interest save through what they symbolize."[27]

According to de Lubac, Hellenistic allegorical method exemplifies certain presuppositions concerning the meaning of history, which, in *Catholicism,* he attributed to Platonism, Buddhism, certain Indian religions, and Christian heresies such as Manichaeism, Docetism, and Gnosticism.[28] These religions and philosophies envisioned human destiny as an individualist escape from history.[29] This pattern of

27. De Lubac, *Catholicism*, 167. De Lubac cites Jean Pépin, whose studies argue the early Christian tradition adapted a method of biblical interpretation from Stoic philosophy. De Lubac, "Hellenistic Allegory and Christian Allegory," 165–66. Pépin found a kinship among the allegorical interpretation of St. Paul, Origen, Porphyry, and Sallust. De Lubac stated that, according to Pépin, "the essential attitude of Christians toward the Bible was the same as that of the Greeks toward their myths." "Hellenistic Allegory and Christian Allegory," 178n82. Referencing Jean Pépin, *Mythe et allégorie: Les origines grecques et les contestations judéo-chrétiennes*, Philosophie de l'esprit (Paris: Éditions Montaigne, 1958).

28. Susan K. Wood notes this correlation between exegetical methods and philosophies of history. She indicates that de Lubac interprets the fourfold sense as a theology of history. In other words, de Lubac does not treat the fourfold sense for its own sake, but only insofar as it proposes a particular understanding of temporality. See Susan K. Wood, *Spiritual Exegesis and the Church in the Theology of Henri de Lubac* (Grand Rapids, MI: Eerdmans, 1998), 51. The correlation is present early in de Lubac's career in *Catholicism* (a chapter entitled "Christianity and History" directly precedes and corresponds with the one entitled "The Interpretation of Scriptures.") *Catholicism* is significant for two reasons. First, de Lubac's first book anticipates many of the themes that are developed later in his career. Second, it provides a broader perspective on how de Lubac understands the alternatives to a Christian conception of history. His other writings on the history of exegesis often make only glancing allusions to problems that he is attempting to resolve. In contrast, *Catholicism* provides a wider lens for de Lubac's fundamental concerns. It is therefore important to read his writings on exegesis in light of his earlier *Catholicism*.

29. De Lubac, *Catholicism*, 140–41. *Catholicism* identified an opposite stream of thought within contemporary thought, exemplified by Marxism, that envisions a purely historical destiny of a corporate humanity. It made little effort to explicate this second stream of thought or philosophies of historical progress that underlie it. However, the main argument of the book is that Christianity possesses a different view of the social unity of humanity than do philosophies of historical immanentism. The context for *Catholicism* is the balkanization of the Catholic Church amid the rise of totalitarianism and nationalism throughout Europe and the loss of the

conceiving history is circular, dualistic, and phenomenal. Despite their diversity, de Lubac asserts, "running all through these many differences there is always agreement about the basis of the problem and its presuppositions: the world from which escape must be sought is meaningless, and the humanity that must be outstripped is without a history."[30] In this pattern, history is cyclical and what occurs in time will return again ad infinitum.[31] The events of history, themselves phenomenal and unessential, will perpetually recur—de Lubac calls it an "infernal cycle"—without true forward movement.[32] Salvation or fulfillment consists in an escape from materiality and history, a spiritual ascent to the One, or the escape from the desires of this world. The world itself is something from which we require salvation or escape.

Platonic metaphysics in particular supported a phenomenal view of history. It posed a dichotomy between the world of ideas made up of stable and unchanging essences and the world we experience, the world of appearances. Platonic dualism—involving a dichotomy between the sensible and intelligible, temporal and eternal, appearance and reality, illusion and truth—affected its appraisal of history.[33] History, of course, falls on the side of the sensible, temporal, illusion, and appearance. It is not that the events of history are unimportant, but they symbolize in movement what exists eternally. Historical reality is "'this moving image of unmoving eternity,' 'this

---

Church's social cohesion. *Catholicism* was published in 1938, prior to the German invasion. The pressing need was to assert the social and historical dimensions of Catholicism in the face of a growing spiritual individualism. During and after the German occupation, de Lubac more directly emphasized the narratives of history within atheistic humanism. He suggested that those philosophies proposing an escape from history and those proposing a historical immanent human destiny shared certain fundamental tenets.

30. Ibid., 139.

31. "The 'eternal return,' from which nothing may be expected, each of its phases—the Great Year, Mahâkalpa, Jubilee or whatever it is called—the end of one being the beginning of another, with never a forward movement, how overpoweringly monotonous it all is!" Ibid.

32. Ibid., 142.

33. De Lubac, "Hellenistic Allegory and Christian Allegory," 186.

eternal image without end' which is 'unfolded in a circle.'"[34] De Lubac recognized within Hellenistic thought in general, and Platonism specifically, a tendency toward a phenomenal view of historical events, according to which history is always something to be eclipsed.

The Greek philosophical view of mythical narrative reflected this dualism. To attain the intelligible truth, the particularity of history or myth must be stripped away. According to Plotinus, "Myths distribute throughout time and separate from each other beings who are not separated in reality. . . . They cause to be born what was never begun, they divide it, thus teaching what they can and leaving to one who understands the task of recomposition."[35] According to Sallust, "It is not that these things [myths] never happened, because they always exist; but the discourse can express only successively what the understanding sees and grasps at the same time"[36] In other words, Hellenistic religious myth served as a metaphoric vehicle or an allegorization of the truth which has always been.[37]

Ironically, the rejection of early Christian biblical interpretation as a "Hellenistic" distortion of the authentic gospel is supported by a dichotomy between history and metaphysics that is itself Hellenistic in form. G. E. Lessing famously expressed this dichotomy in "On the Proof the Spirit and of Power" as the impossibility of crossing the "broad, ugly ditch" that separates the contingencies of history and necessary metaphysical truths. Commenting on a text from Origen,

---

34. De Lubac, *Catholicism*, 141–42.
35. De Lubac, "Hellenistic Allegory and Christian Allegory," 182. Quoting Plotinus, *Ennead* 3, c. 5, n. 9.
36. Ibid. Quoting Sallust, *On the Gods and the World*, c. 4.
37. De Lubac suggested that the Christian docetist heresy especially bore the mark of a Hellenistic conception of religious myth and history. By dividing the mere human appearance of Jesus from his divinity, Docetism repeated a Hellenistic pattern whereby that which occurs in time is unsubstantial and phenomenal. The events of salvation become mere appearances or a signs that point to a reality that they do not themselves embody. In de Lubac's words, Christianity overturns the "docetist mitigation" of history. De Lubac, *Catholicism*, 141.

Lessing stated that although he accepts that the events narrated by Scripture occurred, those events do not provide sufficient evidence of metaphysical truths. For Loisy and other empirical historians, there is a "drastic division between faith or dogma on the one hand and historical and biblical criticism on the other."[38] The same dichotomy presents itself in the antimetaphysical historians like Ritschl and Harnack. Historical reality cannot itself yield metaphysical truth or, alternatively, faith cannot ultimately be based on the contingencies of history. There remains a neo-Kantian divide between historical reality, envisioned as only a changing phenomenal appearance, and metaphysics, the unchanging noumenal truth.[39] Metaphysical truth must come, de jure, from outside the historical system. The rejection of metaphysics as a Greek imposition on the purity of Christianity operates on the assumption—a very Greek assumption—that metaphysics and history cannot go together.

In sum, de Lubac believed that Hellenistic thought vacated history of its value. Its strict dichotomy between history and eternity led to an interpretation of religious narratives in which the narratives symbolize atemporal truths, whether philosophical, moral, or cosmological. Allegorical interpretation, in its pagan forms, was the tool used to discover a deeper philosophical truth within religious myth. However, de Lubac believed that the allegorical interpretation

---

38. T. M. Schoof, *A Survey of Catholic Theology, 1800–1970* (Glen Rock, NJ: Paulist Newman Press, 1970), 63.

39. One of the major commonalities between the empirical historiography at the turn of the century and Catholic neoscholasticism is that they both tended to see history as merely phenomenal. For many neoscholastics, history can function as the occasion for belief insofar as it can rationally prove the reality of Christ and his miracles. History can command rational assent. But this rational assent is different from faith itself. So although we derive the propositions that make up the content of faith from the historical fact, the historical event is merely an occasion for belief. I agree with Boersma's attribution of a "non-sacramental mindset" to Catholic Modernists and neoscholastics, as long as this attribution is restricted to their tendencies to view history as phenomenal and not to the entirety of their theological output. See Boersma, *Nouvelle Théologie and Sacramental Ontology*, 4–21.

of Scripture in the early church overcame and subverted this Hellenistic view of time.

Christian Allegory as a Subversion of Hellenism

De Lubac wished to elaborate a Christian theology of history that could respond to modern secular philosophies of history. It is strange that his search for a theology of history led him to defend Origen, who was maligned for his ahistorical, Hellenistic, and Platonist thinking. Yet despite superficial similarities with Hellenistic thought, De Lubac argued that early Christian exegetical practices diverged significantly from Hellenism.[40] The allegorical interpretation of Scripture (which, as de Lubac claims, influenced the entire development of Christian theology) was neither a syncretistic melding of Greek philosophy with the Scriptures nor a transformation of the gospel into philosophical categories. In practice, de Lubac claimed, Christian allegory and its conception of history functioned as an antithesis or subversion of Greek allegory. Far from negating the importance of history, as Greek allegory did, Christian allegorical interpretation was the primary tool Christians used to preserve its meaning. Contrasting Greek and Christian allegorical interpretation, de Lubac countered the notion that the Christian doctrinal tradition subverted the Hebrew experience of God with Greek ontological categories. As will be shown, de Lubac's anti-Platonism is evident in the theology of history in his writings on the history of exegesis and is consistently promulgated in his writings on the church, Christ, and revelation.[41]

Despite the strong anti-Platonic bent to de Lubac's writings, recent interpreters suggest that the *nouvelle théologie* in general and de Lubac

---

40. De Lubac, "Hellenistic Allegory and Christian Allegory," 183.
41. Susan K. Wood notes that de Lubac's anti-Platonism is found within his understanding of exegesis and in his ecclesiology. Wood, *Spiritual Exegesis and the Church*, 46 and 100.

in particular espoused a recovery of Neoplatonism, or at least depended upon Neoplatonic ontology. Wayne J. Hankey, John Milbank, David Grumett, Guy Mansini, and Hans Boersma have each, to some extent, attributed a Neoplatonic metaphysics to de Lubac. Wayne Hankey suggests that the ressourcement of the Greek fathers in the *nouvelle théologie* (especially de Lubac and Daniélou) and in the series Sources Chrétiennes was a turn to a Platonic ontology. Referring to the *nouvelle théologie*, he writes, "Those who were seeking an alternative to Thomism, whose scientific divisions of this kind they associated with its Aristotelianism, generally saw Platonism as involving the desired integration for the sake of theology understood as mystical itinerarium."[42] John Milbank's influential interpretation attributes a thoroughly Neoplatonic ontology to de Lubac (and to Thomas Aquinas!).[43] David Grumett argues that de Lubac's denial of the theory of pure nature requires an ontology found within Teilhard de Chardin, which he suggests resembles Neoplatonism.[44] Guy Mansini writes that de Lubac's "properly theological influence consists of the re-Platonizing of theology, a re-Platonizing which has been developed and continued in the post-modern drive to avoid the strictures of Heidegger against onto-theology."[45] These authors appeal to Neoplatonic ontology in order to explain aspects of de Lubac's theology of grace, his theology of the supernatural, or his challenge to the scholastic theory of "pure nature."

---

42. Wayne J. Hankey, "Neoplatonism and Contemporary French Philosophy," *Dionysius* 23 (December 2005): 143.

43. John Milbank, *The Suspended Middle: Henri de Lubac and the Debate Concerning the Supernatural* (Grand Rapids, MI: Eerdmans, 2005), 26.

44. David Grumett, "Eucharist, Matter, and the Supernatural: Why de Lubac Needs Teilhard," *International Journal of Systematic Theology* 10, no. 2 (2008): 165–78.

45. Guy Mansini, "The Abiding Theological Significance of Henri de Lubac's Surnaturel," *The Thomist* 73, no. 4 (2009): 597.

Hans Boersma, in particular, has linked the *nouvelle théologie* with Neoplatonism. Boersma's *Nouvelle Théologie and Sacramental Ontology* associates Neoplatonism with the "unified view of reality" found in the *nouvelle théologie* authors, including de Lubac.[46] This Neoplatonist ontology, according to Boersma, recognizes created realities as sacraments of the divine and eternal. The invisible is made present in the visible; the transcendent is made present in the immanent; the supernatural is made present in the natural; the divine is made present within history.[47] De Lubac's insistence that human beings have a natural desire for God and his rejection of the theory of "pure nature" are explained by his critical adoption of a roughly Christian Neoplatonist ontology derived from the Greek fathers.[48] Boersma recognizes instances where de Lubac strongly distances his own theology from Neoplatonism. He writes, de Lubac's anti-Platonic "comments may seem to make it difficult to look to de Lubac as a resource for the recovery of a more sacramental ontology that relies in part on the Platonic tradition."[49] According to Boersma, de Lubac's anti-Platonist comments constituted an obligatory defense against his critics, who accused him of failing to distinguish between creaturely nature and divine grace. The implication is that de Lubac's theology of grace and sacramental view of the world required

---

46. Boersma, *Nouvelle Théologie and Sacramental Ontology*, 113–14. In *Heavenly Participation*, he doesn't hesitate to find an alliance between Neoplatonism and Christian sacramental thinking. Hans Boersma, *Heavenly Participation: The Weaving of a Sacramental Tapestry* (Grand Rapids, MI: Eerdmans, 2011), 117.

47. By framing the relationship between the historical (visible) and the mystical (invisible) in terms of natural and supernatural, Boersma misses how, for de Lubac, the historical is not merely *natural* because it is the place of God's self-revelation. Indeed, the natural-supernatural distinction is ultimately unsuitable for explicating the relationship between history and revelation. See below, chapter 7.

48. "De Lubac was unyielding on the issue of *desiderium naturale* [natural desire] because it provided an essential theological link with a patristic, more or less Neoplatonic mindset, which had been sacramental in character." Boersma, *Nouvelle Théologie and Sacramental Ontology*, 98.

49. Ibid., 89–90.

something like a Neoplatonic ontology, though de Lubac was somewhat inconsistent in developing this ontology in his writings.

The attribution of Neoplatonism or elements of it to de Lubac is inaccurate on a number of levels. First, the similarities between de Lubac's theology and Neoplatonism are not, strictly speaking, unique to Neoplatonism. There were common mystical tendencies toward discovering mysteries within the world and Scripture in Hebraic thought, Hellenism, Philo, patristic theology, including Origen and Augustine, and many medieval theologians.[50] Second, a sacramental mentality that envisions the sacred present in material reality is something common to a broadly Catholic tradition, including modern neoscholastics, who were enthusiastic defenders of sacramental realism. De Lubac's sacramentalism is not itself an indicator of sympathy with Neoplatonism. Third, de Lubac's theological anthropology is not necessarily Neoplatonic. Those who discover Neoplatonic ontology in de Lubac's writings are primarily looking to his theology of nature, grace, and supernatural finality. For certain, de Lubac drew from the Greek and Latin fathers in order to recover a theological anthropology in which human beings possess a single, supernatural finality. De Lubac's critics have argued that his theological anthropology inadequately preserves the autonomy of nature and the gratuity of grace, reflecting a more or less Platonic ontology. Yet there are clear anti-Platonic themes across his writings, especially those on exegesis and the theology of history.[51] As will be established in chapter 7, de Lubac's conception of human finality

---

50. Speaking of the tendency to discover mysteries within the world and the text, de Lubac stated, "This way of thinking, which Origen shares with Philo as well as others, would more or less be that of the whole patristic age. It would persist as well into medieval theology." De Lubac, *History and Spirit*, 185. However, he states that this way of thinking was not sufficient for understanding the threefold sense, which "had the merit of bringing out Christianity and its interpretation of the Bible in all their originality, especially in contrast to Philo." Ibid.

51. For example, against Daniélou, de Lubac argued that early Christian allegorical interpretation of Scripture was fundamentally distinct from its Hellenistic and Platonic counterparts. See de Lubac, "Typology and Allegorization."

reflects his understanding of finality within the historical order. An adequate assessment of de Lubac's theological anthropology would need to examine his theology of history, in which his anti-Platonism is key.

De Lubac's monograph on Origen, *History and Spirit*, highlights the anti-Platonic intention of his work. It argues that although Origen was indebted to the broader Hellenistic milieu and the scriptural interpretation of the Hellenized Jews of Alexandria, the fundamental spirit of his exegesis is different. De Lubac was quick to point out the "Hellenic factor in the Origenian synthesis." He admitted that Hellenistic and Philonic interpretation had a great influence upon Origen, and in many respects Origen is similar to Philo. Origen lived in the same cultural atmosphere as Philo. Today it is difficult to recognize their profound differences: "Seen from a distance, certain doctrinal groupings or certain patterns might seem closely related because a slight common atmosphere envelops them. There has been much confusion, between the spiritual exegesis of the fathers of the church and the allegorism of the Greek philosophers, of which it is the exact opposite."[52] De Lubac asks us to "perceive, beneath the surface of resemblances, the antagonism of fundamental assertions, and beneath the apparent borrowings, the radical transformations."[53] He argued that while early Christianity distinguished "letter from spirit, or biblical history and the mystery borne by it, or figure and fulfillment, or shadow and truth, they do not in the least draw their inspiration, even indirectly, from the Platonic distinction between opinion and true knowledge."[54] In general, the Christian allegorical and symbolic interpretation of the first centuries overcame a Hellenistic view of history: "As paradoxical

52. De Lubac, *History and Spirit*, 182.
53. Ibid., 22.
54. Henri de Lubac, *Scripture in the Tradition*, trans. Luke O'Neill (New York: Crossroad, 2001), 165. Originally published as *L'Ecriture dans la tradition* (Paris: Aubier-Montaigne, 1967).

as this might appear to a modern mind, was not one of the motives for this symbolism in the Christian thinking of the first centuries, precisely to assure history a meaning that pagan antiquity had denied it?"[55] Rather than transposing Greek categories upon the gospel, this exegesis subverted those very categories to preserve its particular understanding of time, history, and eternity.

Hellenistic allegory is structured around two poles: the sensible and intelligible, the changing and the unchanging, the temporal and the eternal, appearance and reality, or illusion and truth. Similar to Hellenistic allegory, Christian allegory was based on a duality. Yet in early Christian allegory, the duality was no longer between a changing history, on the one hand, and the unchanging atemporal truth, on the other. Instead, it was built upon the duality between two events within history: the events of Old Testament and the Christ event that fulfills them: "Two meanings that make one, or of which the first, very real in itself, must step aside for another from the moment that the creative transfiguring Event takes place, are not at all the same as two meanings that exclude each other in the way that appearance and reality, or 'illusion' and truth do."[56] According to de Lubac, the Christian duality between the letter of Scripture and its spirit was fundamentally a relationship between the Old Testament and New Testament.[57] Christian allegory assumes that God has truly intervened in the events narrated in the Old Testament. The allegorization of that Old Testament history is its interpretation in light of another, more ultimate intervention.

In "Hellenistic Allegory and Christian Allegory," de Lubac characterizes Christian allegorization as the antithesis or reversal of Greek allegory:

55. De Lubac, *History and Spirit*, 9.
56. De Lubac, "Hellenistic Allegory and Christian Allegory," 186.
57. De Lubac, *History and Spirit*, 194. De Lubac adds that the "general relation between the letter and the spirit" is seen by Origen as "a first principle of Christianity." Ibid., 195.

Just as the τυπικά [types] or the συμβολικά [symbols] of the Old Testament or the literal reading of the Gospel is not a misleading appearance, the ἀληθινά [truths] or the νοητά [intelligible things] of the New Testament or the final ends are not some kind of essences or immaterial ideas. Jesus is the "truth," he is "full of truth," because he has made "all shadow and cloud" vanish by putting an end to the literal observance of the law. But the law was no less genuinely historically promulgated and observed . . . . For Christians, the πράγματα [things] of Christian allegory, its "invisible realities," are also "future benefits," eschatological, the participation promised as Christ's legacy. Hence far from being analogous, even vaguely so, to the Greek opposites to which they have been compared, the Christian opposites—letter and spirit, darkness and truth, history and mystery—are their antitheses. The union of the two terms in the distinction, which is also the distinction of the two "Testaments" from each other, reveals a world of thought that philosophers reflection on and refining their myths never suspected might exists. . . . Thus, the very structure of the symbolism used by the two groups is different.[58]

In opposition to Hellenistic allegorization, Christian allegorization of the Old Testament affirms that the Old Testament events are authentic interventions by God in time. Significantly, this allegorization does not interpret the Old Testament as a myth of an atemporal truth. Instead, allegories are the actual events in the Old Testament that contain promises that are fulfilled in the future, the objects of hope and expectation.

According to de Lubac, Christian allegory preserves the notion that the events of history are critical for salvation:

Far from showing that the Christians shared the same idea . . . of "religious philosophy" as the Greeks, far from constituting—following an old polemical expression—a sign of the contamination of the Christian idea by the Greek idea, Christian allegory expresses the inverse idea: the idea of the spiritual significance and consequently the primary importance of the very reality that man experiences in the course of time and of the event itself; the idea that in this reality there are "radical

58. De Lubac, "Hellenistic Allegory and Christian Allegory," 187.

changes, absolute initiatives, veritable interventions," producing a history worthy of its name, a history of mankind's salvation . . . ; the idea, above all, of a more radical change than any other, as extraordinary in the spiritual order as the miracle of the water changed to wine in Cana was in the perceptible one. . . . It was a "conversion," a "transposition," a "transfiguration."[59]

The Christian allegorization of the Old Testament reflects a theology of history that has been shaped at its root by God's intervention into history.

While de Lubac was aware of a great diversity within Christian biblical interpretation, he asserted that a stream of allegory from St. Paul to the medieval period diverged significantly from Hellenism. In *Exégèse médiévale* he argued that Origen systematized and transmitted this Christian form of allegorical interpretation of Scripture that became the inheritance of patristic and medieval thought. Christian allegory preserved a uniquely Christian understanding of God's absolute intervention in, and transformation of, history.

Spiritual Meaning and History

As noted above, de Lubac argued Christian spiritual interpretation constituted an epiphenomenon of a Christian understanding of history. The discovery of a multiplicity of meanings within the Scripture reflected an insight into God's interventions into history. In the traditions of spiritual interpretation, the historical city of Jerusalem symbolized the church and the coming reign of God. The escape of the Israelites through the Red Sea symbolized the sacrament of baptism. Christian spiritual interpretation was essentially a reflection on the historical economy of salvation that read the

---

59. Ibid., 195–96. Quoting Emile Bréhier, *Historie de la philosophie* (Paris: Librairie Félix Alcan, 1928), 1:489.

historical events narrated in the Old Testament through the lens of the realities of the New Testament.

But what makes these spiritual interpretations anything more than the product of ahistorical and often arbitrary associations between biblical texts? According to de Lubac, the relationship between the letter and its spiritual meaning are far from arbitrary. Christian spiritual interpretation was intensely historical in two ways. First, spiritual meaning is the meaning of a historical event described by Scripture—the escape of the Israelites, or the manna in the desert, or the city of Jerusalem. Second, spiritual meaning is itself an historical reality, namely the Christ event. The events of the Old Testament contained a hidden mystery, Christ, who would only be revealed later in time. Christ speaks through the Old Testament because Christ is somehow already interior to the realities narrated in the Old Testament. According to de Lubac, spiritual interpretation is grounded "in the objective realm of realities in a living development. . . . That presence [of Christ in the Old Testament] transcends consciousness and man; it is in the profound logic of events and ideas."[60] As a result, "spiritual meaning" is the meaning of an historical event and is itself an event. In de Lubac's interpretation of the traditions of spiritual exegesis, the underlying rationale for "spiritual meaning" was an ontological relationship among the realities of history themselves: the Old Testament history and its New Testament fulfillment.

As suggested in de Lubac's *Catholicism*, the objective rationale for spiritual interpretation has its basis in the historical form of salvation.[61] Because salvation is realized and progresses historically, de Lubac could no longer think of history as composed of mere facts or

---

60. De Lubac, *History and Spirit*, 465. Quoting Dom Célestin Charlier, "Les thèmes bibliques et leurs transpositions progressives," *Esprit et Vie* (1948).

61. For a description of the historical character of salvation, see de Lubac, *Catholicism*, 141.

occurrences. The facts of history are "no longer phenomena, but events, acts." History, "possesses . . . a certain ontological density and fecundity."[62] Because God acts within history and brings about salvation through history, history contains "ontological density" and depth that it would not otherwise contain:

> God acts in history and reveals himself through history. Or rather, God inserts himself in history and so bestows on it a "religious consecration" which compels us to treat it with due respect. As a consequence historical realities possess a profound sense and are to be understood in a spiritual manner, ἱστορικὰ πνευματικῶς [historical things spiritually]; conversely, spiritual realities appear in a constant state of flux and are understood historically: πνευματικὰ ἱστορικῶς [spiritual things historically].[63]

Because God acts within history, there is an infinite depth to those actions and history possesses symbolic or sacramental dimensions.

According to de Lubac, practices of spiritual interpretation reflected the conviction that historical events themselves contained hidden spiritual mysteries. He explains,

> The Bible brings [the Christian believer] a history that is the history of salvation: "*magnum sacramentum spei ac salutis nostrae a saeculis antiquis depositum*" [a great mystery of our salvation and hope is stored up from the ages of old]. This mysterious history is completely imbued with a profound significance, which is its spiritual or mystical meaning, in turn, allegorical, moral and anagogical.[64]

De Lubac argued that, for the great tradition of Christian exegesis, the "spiritual meaning" found in the texts was not primarily *in the*

---

62. Ibid., 142.
63. Ibid., 165.
64. De Lubac, "On an Old Distich," 122. Although the exegetical tradition extrapolated multiple spiritual senses of Scripture (allegory, tropology, anagogy), these senses initially form a unity. "Each of these meanings," de Lubac claimed, "is at first expressed in the singular." De Lubac, "On an Old Distich," 122. The multiple senses are first the "spiritual sense." De Lubac explained that the spiritual sense represents primarily the inner meaning of the events of salvation.

text. Instead spiritual meaning was primarily within history and reality.[65] Mary Healy sums up de Lubac's understanding of the spiritual sense:

> As de Lubac has demonstrated, the spiritual sense, correctly understood, is not a property of texts but of history. The spiritual sense does not refer to a literary relationship but an ontological relationship. . . . Thus the spiritual sense is not an additional meaning retrospectively superimposed upon the texts in light of new events, but something that was *already hidden* in those things written about in the texts.[66]

For de Lubac, history itself is primarily the bearer of the spiritual meaning: "The spiritual meaning, then, is to be found on all sides, not only or more especially in a book but first and foremost *in reality itself*."[67] De Lubac characterized spiritual meaning in terms of the mystery discovered already within the facts of history: "The mystery is not only announced, prefigured or assured by the facts: the facts themselves have an interior that in diverse ways is already pregnant with the mystery."[68] The mystery is something already interior to the bare event, but not exhausted by its pure materiality.[69]

It is critical to recognize that spiritual meaning is not just a metaphysical *meaning* hidden within an event (e.g. the crossing of the Red Sea). Instead, spiritual meaning itself is primarily a historical

---

65. De Lubac claimed that Origen's spiritual interpretation is primarily concerned with discovering the inner meaning of history. Augustine, echoing this idea, wrote, "In the very fact itself and not only in what is said about the fact we ought to seek the mystery." De Lubac, *Catholicism*, 169n14. Quoting Augustine, *In Psalmum* 68, s. 2, n. 6.

66. Mary Healy, "Inspiration and Incarnation: The Christological Analogy and the Hermeneutics of Faith," *Letter and Spirit* 2 (2006): 34.

67. De Lubac, *Catholicism*, 169. De Lubac similarly explained that "Christian exegesis was *claiming to discover a spiritual meaning in history*." De Lubac, "Hellenistic Allegory and Christian Allegory," 195. See also Wood, *Spiritual Exegesis and the Church*, 36.

68. De Lubac, "On an Old Distich," 117.

69. De Lubac sought to avoid what Maurice Blondel, in his "History and Dogma," called "extrinsicism" and "historicism." See Maurice Blondel, *The Letter on Apologetics and History and Dogma*, trans. Alexander Dru and Illtyd Trethowan (Grand Rapids, MI: Eerdmans, 1995), 224–42.

reality, that is the *"mystery* of salvation" that gradually unfolds in history. De Lubac's description of allegory is helpful here: [what] "allegory gives us is doctrine, the very object of faith. It is the 'mystery' that immediately follows the history."[70] The first spiritual sense, allegory, gives us the *mystery* of Christ as head and his members the church.

Within de Lubac's writings, the term *le mystère* has resonances with the Greek patristic *mysterion* and the Latin patristic *sacramentum*. In Pauline usage, *mysterion* referred to "the sacred plan of God from the unfolding of the history of the world." Among the Greek fathers, *mysterion* essentially meant God's plan of salvation as it develops within history, culminating in Christ. The mystery encompasses both Christ's historical existence and his prefigurations in the Old Testament. *Sacramentum* becomes the standard translation of *mysterion* for the Latin fathers.[71] De Lubac's frequent use of *mystère* almost always denotes "God's design for man, whether as marking the limit of or the means of realizing this destiny."[72] *Mystery* is de Lubac's convention for the "economy of salvation," either salvation itself in its final consummation or the progressive historical stages of this salvation. De Lubac associates the spiritual mystery hidden in the letter with the mystery of God's plan of salvation unfolding historically.[73]

---

70. De Lubac, "On an Old Distich," 114.
71. See John D. Laurance, *Priest as Type of Christ: The Leader of the Eucharist in Salvation History according to Cyprian of Carthage*, American University Studies, VII: Theology and Religion 5 (New York: Peter Lang, 1984), 52–65.
72. Henri de Lubac, *The Church: Paradox and Mystery*, trans. James R. Dunne (Staten Island, NY: Alba House, 1969), 13. Originally published as Henri de Lubac, *Paradoxe et mystère de l'Église* (Paris: Aubier-Montaigne, 1967).
73. As I will argue in chapter 7, de Lubac's use of *mystère* suggests that his writings on nature and grace (including *Le Mystère du surnaturel*) incorporates his understanding of the historical economy of salvation.

In contrast with Hellenistic allegory, spiritual meaning in the Christian tradition is discovered *within*, rather than beyond, historical experience. In de Lubac's account, the perception of a spiritual meaning of Scripture is the perception of Christ in the events of the history of salvation and human historical experience.[74]

The Fourfold Sense as an Ontology of History

The Origenian traditions of spiritual interpretation expanded the duality of letter and spirit into multiple spiritual senses, often into a trichotomy (history, allegory, anagogy) or a quaternity (history, allegory, tropology, anagogy). In the trichotomy and quaternary, the fundamental metaphor shifts from a depth within the letter to a network of symbolic meaning. For example, the crossing of the Red Sea (the historical sense) signifies baptism (the allegorical sense); baptism in turn signifies the conversion of the soul and unity with the body of Christ (the tropological), and, finally, the conversion of all people (the anagogical meaning). According to de Lubac, the plurality of spiritual meanings—allegory, tropology, and anagogy—relate the interconnected realities in the historical economy of salvation. Furthermore, they imply a connection betwen stages of development of the single economy of salvation from its genesis to its eschatological consummation. For de Lubac, Origen's spiritual interpretation is paradigmatic of a Christian understanding of history because it communicated an *ontology of history*. First, the unity of the spiritual senses in Origen implies that history was not a set of disconnected phenomena, but instead contains the progressive unfolding of God's plan. Second, Origen's spiritual interpretation and the tradition that followed highlights the forshadowing and anticipation of the New Testament in the Old Testament. This

74. De Lubac, "Hellenistic Allegory and Christian Allegory," 196.

anticipation depends upon the ontological bond between events within the historical economy of salvation.

First, drawing from Origen, de Lubac argued that the logic that governed the movement from one level of meaning to another—from history to allegory to morality to anagogy—was far from arbitrary. In "On an Old Distich," de Lubac explained that the four levels of meaning comprise an interconnected unity: "These four levels of meaning do not fan out in different directions: they follow each other in a continuous series and form a simple whole."[75] Several images drawn from the fathers illustrated this unity. De Lubac noted Jerome's image of the construction of a building, in which history was the foundation, dogma constituted the walls, morality constituted the furnishings, and anagogy was the roof. He also noted the image of excavation by which deeper and deeper levels are extracted from the *sacra pagina*.[76] Each level of meaning is interlinked, but each subsequent level presupposes the previous as its basis.

Yet the images of excavation and construction were insufficient. De Lubac noted in *Exégèse médiévale* that texts from the medieval period, though employing the fourfold sense, often do not reveal the "secret soul of the theory."[77] The multiple senses of Scripture possess a unitary identity:

> We speak, as indeed we must, of diverse senses. . . . One superimposes them, juxtaposes them, or opposes them; one enumerates them and parades them in succession as if they were so many independent entities. This is an unavoidable flattening arising from language, which did not deceive the ancients—any more than a good Thomist would take the principles of being of which he asserts the real distinction as so many "things." Just as one ancient author says of the four degrees of contemplation, so ought we say of these four senses that they are

75. De Lubac, "On an Old Distich," 116–17.
76. Ibid., 117. Referring to Jerome *Ep.* 108.26 and *Ep.* 129.6 (PL 22:902–3).
77. De Lubac, *Medieval Exegesis*, 2:201.

interlinked like the rings of a priceless chain: *concatenati sunt ad invicem* [linked to one another].[78]

The multiple senses of Scripture constitute a single reality, a single whole. We could speak of the different senses of Scripture as different perspectives on the same reality.

Yet de Lubac also insisted that there is a distinct ordering by which each level of meaning leads to the next as through different stages.

> Each of them possesses a propulsive force such that the one leads to the other "through increments of understanding, as it were by certain steps of the mind." "The word of history" is brought to completion by "the sense of allegory," and, in their turn, "the senses of allegory" of themselves incline "to the exercise of morality." We pass by means of a natural and necessary movement "from history to allegory, and from allegory to morality." Allegory is in truth the truth of history; the latter, just by itself, would be incapable of bringing itself intelligibly to fulfillment, allegory fulfills history by giving it its sense. The mystery that allegory uncovers merely makes it open up a new cycle; in its first season, it is merely an "exordium"; to be fully itself, it must be brought to fulfillment in two ways. First it is interiorized and produces its fruit in the spiritual life, which is treated by tropology; then this spiritual life has to blossom forth in the sun of the kingdom; in this [spiritual life consists] the end of time which constitutes the object of anagogy.[79]

Thus, each stage finds its fulfillment and completion in the next. This is because each meaning brings about the next: "Each sense leads to the other as its end."[80] The senses of Scripture represent a succession from one phase to another. In "On an Old Distich," de Lubac affirms that the multiple senses form a unity within which there is a progressive development: "There is also a dynamic

---

78. Ibid. Quoting Guido the Carthusian, *Scala claustr.*, 7.13 (PL 184:482 C).
79. Ibid., 201–2. Quoting Gregory, *In Ez.*, 1.10.1 (PL 76:886 C) and Philip of Harveng, *In Cant. mor.* (PL 203:550 D).
80. Ibid., 203. Note 49 quotes from Gregory *In Ez.* 6.3.18: "*Per litteram ad allegoriam tendimus*" (we extend to allegory through the letter).

continuity. They truly engender each other in a way that makes their internal connection very strong. . . . they are not just parts of the same whole: the same reality exists in each of them; it is just that its different parts are viewed successively."[81] The meanings of Scripture form more than *parts* of a single whole. Instead, de Lubac explains, "*the same reality*"—which de Lubac calls the *mystery*—"*exists in each of them.*" The unity of diverse senses of Scripture reflects the singularity of the mystery in each stage of its development.

These two characteristics of the senses of Scripture—an organic development whereby one sense of Scripture finds its truth in another, and the unitary reality shared among them—converge on a single point, namely, the unity and coherence of God's actions within history. God's earlier historical acts prefigure and anticipate God's subsequent ones. The development from one meaning to another "is first of all temporal. In time history precedes the mystery; it is 'prefiguration.'"[82] The spiritual senses, therefore, presuppose an evolution of God's plan through time, what de Lubac calls the "mystery":

> In the mystery, nothing suffers separation. Through each of its phases the coming of Christ "is something indivisible." If the traditional understanding of Scripture perfectly assures, within the history of our salvation, this "junction of the event and the sense," which, for every reflective mind, is one of the major preoccupations, it is by Christ and in Christ that the understanding assures that junction at each of its stages. It is always pointing to the mystery of Christ in its indivisibility. This is the selfsame unparalleled mystery which is again the mystery of ourselves and the mystery of our eternity.[83]

---

81. De Lubac, "On an Old Distich," 117. De Lubac employs the phrase *dynamic continuity* in *Medieval Exegesis* 2:201 and *Scripture in the Tradition*, 217.
82. De Lubac, *Medieval Exegesis*, 2:202.
83. Ibid., 2:203.

Each phase of God's plan is a stage of growth, fulfilling the previous and leading to the next. Each phase of history is "indivisible" from the next because each phase of salvation represents a gradual evolution of the mystery of Christ.

De Lubac's description of the unity of the threefold and fourfold sense in *Exégèse médiévale* is essentially a recapitulation of his evolutionary view of history found within *Catholicism*. History itself contains an organic development toward a goal, a development powered principally by the divine initiative. Therefore, earlier stages of salvation possess the seeds, so to say, of what will occur later. The unity of God's plan forges unity among events in history, reflected in the threefold and fourfold sense.

Second, according to de Lubac, the foreshadowing in Scripture (the Old Testament events anticipate the New Testament) that is exploited by Origen and the later traditions of spiritual interpretation is indicative of a real anticipation that occurs in history. Paradigmatic of this anticipation is the relationship between the Old Testament and the New Testament. The Old Testament resembles the New Testament because it will *become* what follows:

> There is only one God, author of both Testaments, faithful to himself throughout both, and it is the same gesture of that God that is manifested by both, each in its own way; it is the same salvation that each announces. For every Christian, the first Testament already contains Christ in a mysterious way, but it is consequently only understood through him.[84]

The traditional symbolic correlations between biblical texts—expressed in the dyads of *figure* and *reality*, *type* and *antitype*, or the triad *shadow*, *image* and *truth*—reflected an integral relationship

---

84. De Lubac, *History and Spirit*, 190.

between events of history. Abraham's sacrifice of Isaac is a *type* of the *antitype*, God's sacrifice of the Son.

The relationships of anticipation in the biblical texts are indicative of the real interconnection between the events in the history of salvation. In *Scripture in the Tradition*, he explains,

> If, for example, the manna is really the figure of the Eucharist, or if the sacrifice of the paschal Lamb really prefigures the redemptive death, the reason for this is not extrinsic resemblance alone, no matter how striking this might be. There is actually an "inherent continuity" and "ontological bond" between the two facts, and this is due to the same divine will which is active in both situations and which, from stage to stage, is pursuing a single Design—the Design which is the real object of the Bible.[85]

The term *ontological bond* is an emphatic affirmation of the interior relationship among the events themselves, and not just the descriptions of those events in Scripture. The bond between historical events is ontological because these historical events are interconnected in reality. As stages of God's ongoing plan for salvation, historical events share a "mystical identity" or interior relationship with further temporal and eschatological fulfillments.

Under de Lubac's interpretation, the traditions of spiritual interpretation derived from Origen were not corruptions of Hebraic historical thinking with Greek metaphysics and psychology. The traditions of the fourfold and threefold senses attempted to articulate God's ongoing intervention in the historical economy of salvation. The "spiritual meaning" is not ahistorical or metaphysical. Instead, "spiritual meaning" represents the evolution of the historical economy and its future fulfillment. As a result, the traditions of spiritual interpretation that derive from Origen are an antidote for the

---

85. De Lubac, *Scripture in the Tradition*, 37. Originally published in de Lubac, *History and Spirit*, 462.

division between history and ontology present in much of modern theology.

Conclusion

Henri de Lubac's theology of history is the organic center of his thought. *Catholicism* outlined the contemporary problem: the present age was a historical age concerned with the unity and fate of humanity. The rejection of the transcendent among atheist humanists served to preserve the dignity of human action in the world. Marxism sought a transfiguration of human existence in time. Although Christianity was charged with being captivated by eternity and therefore uninterested in the fate of humanity, de Lubac argued that Christianity united transcendence with the reverence for history. The major apologetic challenge was the rediscovery in Christianity of the intimate relationship between human life and the supernatural, and between this world and salvation. The theological challenge was the rediscovery of a theology of history that articulated the value of experience and human action within the development of God's historical plan for salvation. De Lubac, like Daniélou, discovered this theology of history in the writings of the church fathers. According to de Lubac, the spiritual interpretation of Scripture brought this theology of history to consciousness in the Christian theological tradition. Early Christian exegesis and spiritual practices—in particular, the threefold and fourfold senses of Scripture—communicated the intimacy between the divine life and human experience through an understanding of God's saving activity in time. History is itself the milieu of salvation and that very reality that must be transformed into eternity. History, rightly understood, anticipates the eschatological glory. De Lubac's emphasis on spiritual interpretation reflected his concern that our culture has lost the "sense of the sacred" and fails to recognize the mystical depths of everyday experience.

De Lubac's recovery of a Christian understanding of history from the Greek and Latin fathers, particularly Origen, was not a subscription to Platonism. It was critical to de Lubac's theological project that he defended spiritual interpretation and allegorization as expressions of a profoundly Christian experience rather than as poor imitations of Hellenistic philosophy. Origen—purportedly a Neoplatonist to the core—was responsible for systematizing and communicating to subsequent theological traditions a profoundly anti-Platonic and anti-Hellenistic theology of history, precisely through his exegesis of Scripture. Origen's exegesis preserved a coincidence of historical event and ultimate meaning inconceivable by Greek thought. Moreover, Origen's exegesis expressed a profoundly Christian tension between continuity and transcendence. The unity of the senses of Scripture preserved the continuity and evolution of the mystery through redemptive history. Thus, historical events are not discrete, separate moments, but instead are interconnected realities within the evolution of God's plan in history. The next chapter examines de Lubac's understanding of Christ as the center of the historical economy of salvation who brings about the rupture and transfiguration of history.

4

———

Christ is the Center of History

The spiritual interpretation of the fathers is based ultimately on a view of history as a dynamic, organic process. The theologians of the Tübingen School—particularly Johann Sebastian von Drey and Johann Adam Möhler—had pioneered the recovery of this patristic sense of history during the nineteenth century. The Romantic sense for history in the Tübingen School became the inheritance of the *nouvelle théologie* in the twentieth century. De Lubac's recovery of this understanding of history as a unified—one might say *evolutionary*—process from Origen had to be distinguished from its competitors, chiefly the dialectical materialism of Marx. Marxism articulated history as a necessary social process in which humanity progresses in stages toward a better world. For the Marxist, humanity has progressed through infancy and is on the verge of attaining "The New Man." De Lubac critiques Marxists for their faith that we can bring about a qualitatively different future using only the tools that we have always had. The fundamental problem is the Marxist denial of the transcendent and the attempt to bring about a consummation of history in history. According to de Lubac, Origen articulated a uniquely Christian understanding of history: "Neither does he have the sense of history in the way a post-Hegelian can have it. But that does not prevent him from really possessing and bringing out that sense of history which is one of the essential traits of Christian thought."[1] Origen's theology represented, for de Lubac, the correction or antidote to the loss of the transcendent and an ancient alternative to modern dialectical materialism. Origen's exegetical principles suggested to de Lubac not only an organic development of the historical economy of salvation but also that the transcendent has entered and transformed the historical order.

De Lubac's theology of history is thoroughly Origenian in form. De Lubac defends the Christian allegorization of Scripture (interpreted in light of Origen's theology) for its affirmation that, through Christ, the transcendent has entered history. Allegory communicates the key to a Christian understanding of history because it represents the rupture and total transfiguration of history by Christ. De Lubac, furthermore, interpreted history through an Origenian lens: Origen's leitmotif, "the newness of the Gospel," expressed the transcendence of the Christ event; Origen's "historical exemplarism" presents the historical life of Christ as the unsurpassable reality to which all signs point; and Origen believed that the Christ event permanently transformed the course and meaning of history. De Lubac's recovery of Origen shaped his emphasis on the historicity of revelation and salvation, and its completeness in the actions of Jesus of Nazareth.

---

1. Henri de Lubac, *History and Spirit: The Understanding of Scripture according to Origen*, trans. Anne Englund Nash (San Francisco: Ignatius Press, 2007), 320. Originally published as Henri de Lubac, *Histoire et esprit: l'intelligence de l'Ecriture d'apres Origene*, Theologie 16 (Paris: Aubier, 1950).

Allegory and Typology

De Lubac's work in 1947 represented the confluence of several streams of his thinking about the historical economy of salvation. He delivered the lecture "The Search for a New Man" at the *Semaine sociale* in Paris, which was basically a confrontation with Marxist understandings of history and eschatology. *Origène: Homélies sur l'Exode*, to which de Lubac wrote the introduction, was published around the same time. In the same year, he published an article entitled "Typology and Allegorization," a defense of allegorical interpretation against Jean Pépin and, in part, Jean Daniélou. Marxism proposed a powerful vision of human agency and historical action. The early church proposed another, one that was embedded in the practice of the spiritual interpretation of Scripture. De Lubac suggested that spiritual interpretation was not just a hermeneutic for reading Scripture, but also a hermeneutic for reading the world. He wrote in his introduction to *Homélies sur l'Exode*, "'Whether one reads scripture or the intelligent hierarchy of creatures, one sees the same Light of the Word shining.' The scripture is like another world, built on the model of the first [created world], and if 'it is a composite of things visible and invisible', it is because the [created world] is also."[2] De Lubac was convinced that Origen's allegorical methods of reading the Bible interpreted the spiritual meaning of history, a history in which humanity was still engaged. It is this same history in which Christ remains the center.

Yet Origen was a strange partner for the defense of a Christian view of history. Origen's allegorization was under fire as a form of ahistorical symbolism. Jean Daniélou, especially, contrasted symbolism with pedagogical preparation or, as he called it, "allegory" with "typology," respectively.[3] Daniélou argued that whereas

2. De Lubac, "Introduction," in *Origène: Homélies sur l'Exode* (Paris: Éditions du Cerf, 1947), 73.

allegorization within the Alexandrian fathers tended to mimic an ahistorical Hellenistic allegorization, typology tended to preserve the relationship between preparatory event and fulfillment. The difference consisted in how the church fathers interpreted the symbols and figures of the Old Testament. On the one hand, there was an allegorical mode of interpretation, epitomized by Alexandrian exegetical traditions, that emphasized that Old Testament figures were symbols of the truth found in the New Testament. On the other hand, church fathers such as Irenaeus emphasized that the Old Testament was a pedagogical preparation for the New.[4] This historical and supposedly Hebraic mode of thought emphasized a

3. Daniélou's research grew out of his collaboration with Sources Chrétiennes, a series of publications and translations into French of early Christian writings. The first volume was a translation of Gregory of Nyssa's *The Life of Moses (1942)*, for which Daniélou wrote the editorial introduction. Daniélou wrote that Gregory of Nyssa, like Origen, integrated elements from Philo's symbolism with a more historical mode of interpretation derived from the New Testament. He discerned a contamination of Greek allegory in the symbolism of the Alexandrian theologians. In a series of studies, Daniélou suggested that Origen followed Philo's exegesis too closely. He proceeded to further oppose Origen's allegory to a Christian mode of interpretation, which he called *typology* and that depended more closely on historical *events.* Jean Daniélou, "Traversée de la Mer Rouge et baptême aux premiers siècles," *Recherches de science religieuse* 33 (1946): 492–30; Daniélou, "La typologie d'Isaac dans le christianisme primitif," *Biblica* 28 (1947): 363–93; Daniélou, "Les divers sens de l'Écriture dans la tradition chrétienne primitive," *Ephemerides Theologicae Lovanienses* 24 (1948): 119–26; Daniélou, *Origène* (Paris: Éditions de la Table Ronde, 1948). In studies that followed, he sought to distinguish an authentically Christian view of history. Daniélou, "Christianisme et histoire," *Études*, no. 254 (1947): 166–84; Daniélou, *Sacramentum futuri: Études sur les origines de la typologie biblique,* Études de théologie historique (Paris: Beauchesne, 1950); Daniélou, *Essai sur le mystère de l'histoire* (Paris: Éditions du Seuil, 1953). Daniélou's recovery of a patristic understanding of biblical interpretation was linked to his constructive development of a theology of history. He sought to discern a Christian theology of history within patristic exegesis in order use it to address the historical awareness within the contemporary age, especially as exhibited by Marxist thought. See Jean Daniélou, "Les orientations présentes de la pensée religieuse," *Études*, no. 249 (1946): 5–21.

4. See de Lubac, "Typology and Allegorization," in *Theological Fragments*, trans. Rebecca Howell Balinski (San Francisco: Ignatius Press, 1989), 129n1 and *History and Spirit: The Understanding of Scripture according to Origen*, trans. Anne Englund Nash (San Francisco: Ignatius Press, 2007), 284–85. Contemporary scholarship remains divided on whether the distinction between "allegory" and "typology" adequately describes differences between patristic authors. See Peter W. Martens, "Revisiting the Allegory/Typology Distinction: The Case of Origen," *Journal of Early Christian Studies* 16, no. 3 (Fall 2008): 283–317.

progressive economy where biblical types pointed forward to their antitypes. The term *typology* derives from St. Paul's reference to *type* (τύποι): Adam is the "type of the one to who was to come" (Rom. 5:14 NABRE); the punishments of the Israelites in the Old Testament "happened as examples (τύποι) for us" (1 Cor. 10:6 NABRE). Typology, as Daniélou conceived it, was the discernment of a series of analogical correspondences between events and persons within salvation history. A type bears a likeness to the future reality that it signifies, which prepares for this future reality, without itself being that reality.[5] Typology discovers a really existing pattern joining the events of history and the sacramental life of the church.

In a 1947 article, de Lubac challenged Daniélou's opposition to "allegory" in favor of "typology" and Daniélou's interpretation of Origen.[6] De Lubac departed from Daniélou on several matters of historical interpretation: first, he argued that "typology" is a modern idea and was not distinct from "allegory" in the first centuries; second, the term *allegory*, despite the problems it often caused, was dominant in traditional modes of exegesis; third, Christian allegory developed by Origen was fundamentally different from that of Philo and Hellenism. Whereas Daniélou sought to separate out the "typological" from the "allegorical" in order to distinguish a Christian understanding of history from what was a foreign import, de Lubac argued that Origen's allegorization itself preserved a Christian understanding of history.

De Lubac believed that Daniélou, to some extent, bought into a false dichotomy between a historical and an allegorical exegesis persistent within contemporary early Christian studies. The choice

---

5. See Hans Boersma, *Nouvelle Théologie and Sacramental Ontology: A Return to Mystery* (New York: Oxford University Press, 2009), 174.

6. One should not overemphasize the division between Daniélou and de Lubac. As cofounders of Sources Chrétiennes, they had a shared theological project. Despite their scholarly disagreements, de Lubac's intentions and historical methods were similar to Daniélou's.

between Irenaeus, whose theology was that of a historical pedagogy, and Origen, whose theology saw the Old Testament as a symbol for heavenly realities, was specious:

> This schema also lacks nuances. It is based on a false *a priori* that does not seem to be essential rather than on the study of the texts. . . . Why would the preparation for a coming reality not be symbolic of that reality? And why would the symbol have no pedagogical value? One whole modern school, as we know, has wished to see in supernatural beliefs both a stage toward adult humanism and its anticipated symbol. In Proudhon's eyes, Catholicism as a whole symbolized socialism, which was to complete it by eliminating it. Christian antiquity, in any case, never seems to have perceived any opposition between an explanation of the ancient religion of Israel by symbolism and an explanation by divine "condescension" and the development of revelation.[7]

Not only was this dichotomy false, but Origen himself combined historical preparation and symbolism within his allegory. The mutual opposition between allegory and gradual pedagogy (or symbolism and history) was a thoroughly modern one, driven by a modern dichotomization of history and metaphysics.[8] De Lubac's preference for Origen's theology and its lack of a dichotomy between historical development and allegory reflects his refusal to oppose history and metaphysics to each other.

Although de Lubac agreed that the term *allegory* led to misunderstandings, he insisted against Daniélou that allegory preserved an idea essential for a Christian interpretation of history: the transcendence of Christ in relationship to his anterior anticipations. De Lubac claimed that allegory preserved the "worth

---

7. De Lubac, *History and Spirit*, 285.

8. De Lubac indicates that the modern opposition between history and metaphysics is thoroughly Hellenistic in form. He compares the ancient interpreters of myth (Heraclides, Sallust, Proclus) with modern ones (Julius Wellhausen, D. F. Strauss, G. L. Bauer). Like the Greeks, who make religious stories into a myth symbolizing metaphysical truth, the modern historians interpret biblical narratives as myths indicative of some moral or "cosmological knowledge." Henri de Lubac, "Hellenistic Allegory and Christian Allegory," in *Theological Fragments*, 194–95.

of facts . . . endowed them with a sublime significance, in view of magnifying still another Fact."[9] This Fact is the historical life of Christ, which categorically transcends his anticipations. Christian allegorization preserved a radical difference between the "letter" and the "spiritual meaning," between figure and fulfillment. While maintaining the inner ontological bond between a historical figure and its fulfillment, "allegory" served to also maintain their ontological difference.

Christian Newness and Transcendence

De Lubac defended Origen's allegorical interpretation especially because it preserved two elements in harmony. On the one hand, it maintained the ontological bond between historical realities (for example, Israel and the church) that reflected a development of salvation through time. On the other hand, allegory preserved the categorical difference between those realities (for example, the heavenly Jerusalem is different in kind from its figure, the city of Jerusalem). De Lubac's *History and Spirit*, *Exégèse médiévale,* and *Scripture in the Tradition* each developed the notion that allegory implies a categorical difference—de Lubac used the term *ontological difference*—between the Old Testament figure and its New Testament fulfillment. The Origenian language of *newness* articulated this total difference.

Origen's concept of transcendence is the model for de Lubac: "Newness of the spirit," "newness of life," "newness of Christ," and "newness of Christianity."[10] *Newness* encapsulates the idea that the

---

9. Ibid., 194.
10. De Lubac entitled the final chapter of *Scripture in the Tradition* "The Christian Newness." The idea of the newness of Christianity is found earlier in *Catholicism*. See Henri de Lubac, *Catholicism: Christ and the Common Destiny of Man*, trans. Lancelot C. Sheppard and Sister Elizabeth Englund, OCD (San Francisco: Ignatius Press, 1988), 177, 269–70, 391.

coming of Christ is something unprecedented in a long history of preparations. To speak of the *newness* of Christ, or the *New Testament*, is an ontological claim as much as a temporal claim. It is new not because it comes later. The New Testament is *new*—that is, categorically different from the Old—because it speaks of a fundamentally new situation between humanity and God. Allegory, therefore, communicates the absolute difference of the "act of Christ" in relation to previous figures.

While *newness* denotes the categorical difference in the stages of history embraced by allegory, de Lubac employs another term—*transcendence*—to describe the same phenomenon in his writings on Christology, nature and grace, and apologetics. In "The Light of Christ," de Lubac described a chimerical notion of transcendence that emphasizes the supernatural origin of Christianity by ignoring the human and historical conditions of its development.[11] He said that this transcendence can also be called "exteriority."[12] On the other hand, he writes,

> There is another transcendence, a true transcendence, of which the first was only, at best, the naïve transcription. An intrinsic transcendence, in virtue of which a given reality, considered as a synthesis, in what comprises its own being, surpasses essentially the realities of the same kind that surround it. . . . Any true synthesis is always more than synthesis. A certain recasting is much more than a new combination, a certain "revival from within" transforms everything. It is, in a phenomenal continuity, the passage to a new, higher, incomparable order.[13]

11. Henri de Lubac, "The Light of Christ," in *Theology in History*, trans. Anne Englund Nash (San Francisco: Ignatius Press, 1996), 201–20. Originally published in *Affrontements mystiques* (Paris: Éditions du Témoignage chrétien, 1949), 185–213.

12. "The Light of Christ," 204. De Lubac's exposition of exterior transcendence has resonances with Blondel's critique of extrinsicism in his *Letter on Apologetics*.

13. "The Light of Christ," 205. De Lubac quotes from Sertillanges: "It is a rather widespread error . . . to believe that continuity and transcendence are opposed to one another, as if in the analysis of a single phenomenon the one were exclusive of the other. The truth is that continuity and

While de Lubac is describing the transcendence of grace with regard to "natural" human life, his notion of transcendence here closely aligns with his understanding of allegory. Authentic transcendence is transformation of the original and a passage to a new order without the loss of its identity. Grace elevates nature, but does not destroy it. Similarly, allegory recognizes the continuity between the historical city of Jerusalem and the Heavenly Jerusalem in Scripture, while suggesting a radical difference and transformation from one to the other.

De Lubac describes this radical difference—newness or transcendence—as an ontological difference. This transcendence is that of the New Testament in relationship to the Old Testament, brought about by Christ. As de Lubac explains, allegorical meaning is possible only because of a new principle brought about by Christ:

> [The Christian] relationship of "allegory" to "history" is primarily, as we know, a relationship of "after" to "before." But . . . it is not this alone. It not only makes us pass, as St. Augustine says, "*ex illis quae facta sunt usque ad ista quae fiunt*" [from past facts to present facts], but also, and by the same movement, makes us pass from things "*quae sub umbra legis historialiter accidisse leguntur*" [which one reads as having occurred historically under the shadow of the law] to those which "*spiritualiter eveniunt in populo Dei tempore gratiae*" [occur spiritually in the people of God in the age of grace]. Thus, it is also in the qualitative order.[14]

The christic interpretive principle of the facts belongs to a different order of reality than the facts themselves, protecting the difference between history and allegory.[15] The truth of the literal meaning, he stated, "does not, even from an entirely formal point of view,

transcendence are on two different planes and do not impede each other in any way." Antonin Sertillanges, *L'Idée de création et ses retentissements en philosophie* (Paris: Aubier, 1945), 153–54n4.

14. Henri de Lubac, *Scripture in the Tradition*, trans. Luke O'Neill (New York: Crossroad, 2001), 159.

15. Henri de Lubac, *Medieval Exegesis: The Four Senses of Scripture*, trans. E. M. Macierowski, vol. 2 (Grand Rapids, MI: Eerdmans, 2000), 117.

correspond to the truth" of its spiritual, that is allegorical, meaning.[16] De Lubac made it even more explicit: "An infinite ontological difference" and "an infinite qualitative difference" distinguishes anticipation and fulfillment.[17]

We commonly think of a radical difference as a break or disruption. A likeness between one thing and another depends upon a shared quality or characteristic that places the two things within the same category. Growth of an organism requires a continuity of identity with a change in characteristics (height, weight, age). For it to change into something completely different would be for it to cease to exist or lose its identity. The principle at work within de Lubac's understanding of allegory is different. According to de Lubac, the "infinite qualitative difference" between history and its allegorical fulfillment in a later event establishes rather than destroys continuity.

Concretely, the perennial problem of supersessionism within Christian thought illustrates the importance and dangers of emphasizing a qualitative difference between the Old Covenant and the New Covenant. The Christian emphasis on the absolute uniqueness and transcendence of Christ in relation to the Old Testament may risk negating the validity of the Old Covenant. The first-century theologian Marcion, for example, endorsed an extreme disjunction between the Old and New Testaments and ended by rejecting the validity of the Old Testament. A radical difference between anticipation and its christological fulfillment in Scripture could conceivably support an idea that the New Covenant replaces

16. Ibid., 2:103. Susan K. Wood observes something similar in de Lubac's Christology: "De Lubac's sense of the transcendent quality of grace and the radical rupture and newness achieved in Christ enable him to maintain the distinction between the two orders [of grace and nature]." Susan K. Wood, "The Nature-Grace Problematic within Henri de Lubac's Christological Paradox," *Communio* 19, no. 3 (1992): 401.

17. De Lubac, *Medieval Exegesis*, 2:98; De Lubac, *Scripture in the Tradition*, 159.

and invalidates God's covenant with the Jews. This kind of supersessionism has been a perennial temptation for Christians.

However, de Lubac suggested that the opposite is true: the qualitative difference between the New and Old preserves the Old. Origen, he explains, "appealed to spiritual interpretation in order to defend that Old Testament against adversaries that rejected it."[18] By interpreting the New Testament as the allegory or "spiritual meaning" of the Old, Origen was able to defend the validity of the New Testament against the Jews and the validity of the Old Testament against the gnostics and Marcionites. The spiritual meaning transcends the letter. As a result, the spiritual meaning does not compete on the same ontological or interpretive plane. A mere replacement of the Old by the New would "make out of the allegorical sense, which is a *spiritual* sense, a new literal sense."[19] A correct understanding of transcendence actually preserves Christianity from a crude supersessionism. In orthodox Christianity, exemplified by Origen, the emphasis on the "transcendence" and "newness" of the gospel preserved a twofold awareness: first, that Christ's work is unprecedented; second, that his work is in continuity with God's work in the Old Testament. Following Origen, de Lubac affirmed an "infinite ontological difference," which allowed him to develop his understanding of the symbolic relationship between historical events and their later fulfillment in a historical reality that transcends them.[20]

18. De Lubac, *History and Spirit*, 57. See 54–58.
19. De Lubac, *Medieval Exegesis*, 2:99.
20. The relationship between de Lubac's theology of history and his response to antisemitism is beyond the scope of my research. However, the role of the Jews in God's plan of salvation was clearly important in the post–World War II debate over the theology of history.

Origen's (Historical) Exemplarism

Origen's work was certainly an odd choice for a model of a theology of history, but it is from there that de Lubac mounted a defense of a Christian understanding of history. According to interpretations contemporary to de Lubac, Alexandrian allegorical and symbolic theology was an imitation of Platonic exemplarism in which empirical, earthly realities are imperfect imitations of divine realities. Platonic cosmology contrasted the intelligible world (*kosmos noetos*) with the sensible world (*kosmos aisthetos*). The *eidos* (idea/form) in the intelligible world was the exemplar that was the sufficient cause of empirical things in the sensible world; empirical things were imitations of the *eidos*. In the Alexandrian theologians, like Clement of Alexandria (c. 150–c. 215) and Origen, the letter of Scripture symbolized the spiritual sense, just as sensible realities symbolized the intelligible ideas. The Alexandrian drive to transcend the sensible world seemed to put at risk the value of the concrete and historical.

De Lubac disputed this dominant interpretation of the Alexandrians, arguing that Origen's allegory constituted a subversion of Platonic exemplarism. It is true that Origen himself drew a dichotomy between the "sensible" and the "intelligible" to describe the relationship between history and its spiritual meaning. De Lubac admitted, "The opposition that he places between the αἰσθητά (objects of sense) and the νοητά (intelligible realities) is at times disturbing. His anagogical vocabulary has been judged suspect."[21] However, de Lubac argued that rather than copying Platonic exemplarity, Origen reversed and baptized it. More precisely, Origen expanded upon a transformation of exemplarism already present within Paul and the Letter to the Hebrews. St. Paul's Letter to the Romans contained a division between the visibility of God's works

21. De Lubac, *History and Spirit*, 325.

and "his invisible attributes of eternal power and divinity" (Rom. 1:20 NABRE). The Letter to the Hebrews construed Jewish worship as "a copy and shadow of the heavenly sanctuary" (Heb. 8:5 NABRE). Origen drew from both Paul and Hebrews as a justification for a dichotomy between the sensible world and the intelligible. Speaking of the church fathers' use of Hellenistic categories, de Lubac writes, "Exemplarist thinking and allegorical processes would be borrowed from the ambient culture and profoundly transformed."[22] In the case of Origen, de Lubac preferred to speak of a "Christian transposition" of Platonism rather than a "Platonic transposition" of Christianity.[23] Origen's division between sensible and intelligible is, at its root, biblical rather than Platonic.

In Origen, the dichotomy between sensible reality and intelligible reality took on a new dimension precisely due to its integration into a historical schema. In Origen, the Platonic dichotomy between the sensible and intelligible became a trichotomy—shadow, image, truth—that reflected the historical division of the Old Testament, the New Testament, and heaven. His schema reflects his threefold division of the meaning of Scripture: history, allegory, and anagogy. The Old Testament (history) is a figure for the New Testament (allegory), which in turn is a figure for the heavenly reality (anagogy). Although Origen continued to employ a language of "sensible" and "intelligible," the meaning had shifted significantly. This is because, unlike the Platonic exemplarism, the "sensible" Old Testament symbolizes its "intelligible" exemplar, the New Testament, which occurs *within* history.

As a result, the intelligible realities are not "pure essences" or ideas or "abstractions."[24] Instead, they are a *future* fulfillment. The

22. Ibid., 469.
23. Ibid., 326.
24. Ibid., 327.

literal meaning of the Old Testament "designates also 'something else' the very reality of which (not merely the manifestation of it) is to come."[25] Old Testament figures are both prophetic ("προφητικα σύμβολα [prophetic symbols]: a declaration, a foreshadowing, προτύπωσεις") and a preparation.[26] They are not inadequate images of a prior transhistorical reality.[27] Instead, they invoke a fulfillment of a future reality.

> These "heavenly things" toward which he has us raise our eyes are for him, as for the Letter to the Hebrews, to be taken in their fullness, future realities in relation to the signs of them contained in the Bible. . . . They are "the mysteries of the age to come." . . . They are always related to a future situation, and they always presuppose the Mystery of Christ.[28]

Old Testament figures point to and prepare for a future reality. But this future reality is, at the same time, a transcendent event. Allegory, he explained,

> goes from history to history. It relates the unique facts with another unique fact, divine interventions that have already taken place with another divine intervention, equally real and incomparably more profound. It does so in such a way that everything culminates in a great fact, which in its completely unique singularity is the carrier of all spiritual fecundity. Thus, its result is simultaneously completely "historical," "mystical," and "celestial." It is, we repeat, the fact of Christ, both unique and universal.[29]

25. De Lubac, *Catholicism*, 172.

26. Ibid.

27. "The events of Jewish history clearly continue to herald the future Jerusalem. There is no 'reversal' that would make of them 'the image of an earlier and higher history, the reflection and the result of a past celestial history instead of being the prefiguration of a celestial history to come.'" De Lubac, *History and Spirit*, 331. Quoting Jean Daniélou, *Origène* (Paris: Éditions de la Table Ronde, 1948), 195.

28. *History and Spirit*, 327–28. De Lubac notes that there is some ambiguity in whether these Old Testament figures are related to the first coming or the second coming of Christ.

29. De Lubac, "Hellenistic Allegory and Christian Allegory," 195.

The events and symbols of which Scripture speaks point to and culminate in a *future* event that utterly transcends what occurred before.

The principles of allegory drawn from Origen are consequential for de Lubac's view of history. For de Lubac, Christ becomes the *historical* exemplar of Old Testament history:

> The whole Christian fact is summed up in Christ—as the Messiah who was to come . . . who had to be prepared for in history, just as a masterpiece is preceded by a series of rough sketches; but as the "image of the Invisible God" and the "first born of all creation" he is the universal Exemplar. . . . Christ, in so far as transcendent and existing before all things, is anterior to his figures, yet as a historical being, coming in the flesh, he appears after them. . . . This living synthesis of the eternal and temporal is one in its duality: Christ existing before all things cannot be separated from Christ born of the woman, who died and rose again.[30]

Allegorical interpretation becomes the vehicle to express a paradox that could not fit into the Hellenistic pagan world view. The concrete life and death of a human being is the transcendent eternal mystery prefigured in time.

This represents, for de Lubac, a reversal of Platonic exemplarism.[31] It is the particular Christ event that becomes the exemplar of previous historical realities. The "spiritual fecundity" of history, laid out by the practice of spiritual interpretation, is less a universal law of which Christ is an example than a consequence of Christ himself. Rather than the universal constituting the sufficient reason for the historical particular, the historical particular (the Christ event) becomes the sufficient reason for the universal pattern in which all things find a fulfillment in Christ. This pattern, for de Lubac, is characteristic

---

30. De Lubac, *Catholicism*, 174.
31. "The body follows its shadow, the exemplar its 'type.' . . . The rough sketch is the preparation for the archetype, the imitation (μίμημα) comes before the model." Ibid., 172.

of Christianity itself: philosophical knowledge anticipates Christian revelation; non-Christian religions anticipate their completion in Christ event; creation anticipates redemption.[32] De Lubac's understanding of salvation, religious epistemology, and the finality of the created order each exhibit an underlying pattern traceable to or exemplified by Origen.

The Word in History

If Origen preserved a Christian concept of history by making Jesus of Nazareth the historical exemplar, he also preserved a sense in which all of history has been transformed by the life of Jesus. The entrance of the Word into history impacts the fundamental meaning of history. In the traditions of spiritual interpretation, the impact of the Word is communicated by the relationships established between history, allegory, morality, and anagogy. The Word's assumption of humanity is the eternal entering into history and transforming it. By assuming it, he made it into an anticipation of himself. The structure of history itself is changed. The Old Testament is made into an anticipation of a future fulfillment. According to de Lubac, history itself is irrevocably shaped by the incarnation, death, and resurrection of the Son.

---

32. Susan K. Wood notes this very principle within de Lubac's ecclesiology and in his defense of Teilhard de Chardin's Mariology. She writes, "In spite of the strong exemplarism in Teilhard, the most Christian element in his thought here may be the principle that the universal exists because of the particular. Specifically, the ideal universalized as feminine exists in its unitive and spiritually receptive function because a particular, concrete, historical woman embodied such perfection in her own being. This transforms Platonic exemplarism into its mirror image, in which all is reversed. The real is not dehistoricized so that the particular is only an imperfect image of an ideal and perfect reality, but the universal exists because it has been achieved in historical particularity. The concrete is not a symbol of the universal, but the universal is a symbol of the concrete." Wood, *Spiritual Exegesis and the Church in the Theology of Henri de Lubac* (Grand Rapids, MI: Eerdmans, 1998), 100. I would only add that within de Lubac's understanding of biblical exegesis and the fourfold sense, rather than the "universal" being a symbol of the concrete, it is prior events of salvation that become symbols of the concrete event. Historical particulars symbolize the "exemplar," the historical life of Christ.

Some patristic and medieval theologians found an explanation for allegorization in mystical psychology. The Old Testament authors, these theologians said, had a privileged insight into Christ, and when they spoke they were also vaguely speaking of Christ. The prophets were privy to a mystical vision of Christ in advance.[33] De Lubac noted that it may be possible to affirm a kind of "implicit knowledge," grounded in the "dynamism" of the spirit, by which the rites of the Old Covenant carried out in faith were joined to those of the New Covenant.[34] However, he wished to ground the Old Testament anticipation of Christ in the objective features of history.

According to de Lubac, the Christ event did not confirm an already-existing spiritual meaning; instead the Christ event is *creative* of that meaning. Because the coming of Christ event inserts a new, transcendent principle into time, the nature of the course of time itself is transformed. The Old Testament possesses a spiritual meaning by virtue of a new principle:

> This exegesis is aware of being developed by virtue of a creative, or more precisely a transfiguring, principle, but it does not posit this principle. It merely draws from this principle the infinite consequences, by using the tools which each age offers it. Christian exegesis believes in Jesus Christ, who bestows this meaning on the Scriptures. It believes in Jesus Christ, who has transformed all things and renewed all things. In him the ancient Scripture is "converted."[35]

Christ transfigures the Scriptures, "bestows meaning" on the Scriptures, brings about a "transcendence," brings all newness, and effects the bond between the Old and New Testament.

De Lubac emphasizes that, for Origen, the Christ event does not merely bring about the understanding of the depths of the Old

---

33. De Lubac, *History and Spirit*, 464n110.
34. Ibid., 464n108.
35. De Lubac, *Scripture in the Tradition*, 147.

Testament. Instead, the entrance of Christ into history effects the meaning of the Old Testament events themselves because it provides a new context for their existence:

> Through this Christian event the Old Law has become spiritual. Which does not mean only that we can now, thanks to the light of Christ, finally see the spirit that was in this law; rather, it means that this very spirit is a creation, a radiation from the Christian event. This event alone makes, not so much our understanding, as, first of all, the things themselves pass from the "obsolescence of the letter," where we could have stagnated indefinitely, to those "heights of spiritual newness" that transform the whole horizon. To tell the truth, Jesus Christ, therefore, does not come to *show* the profound meaning of the Scriptures like a teacher who has no part in the things he explains. He comes, actually, to *create* it, through an act of his omnipotence.[36]

This creative act of omnipotence is "none other than [Christ's] death on the Cross, followed by his Resurrection."[37] Christ, so to say, objectively reorients anterior realities, refounding them, making them new, making them anticipations of himself. Since Christ himself is the absolute fullness of what God wishes to communicate to humanity, previous prophetic figures and types receive their "total fulfillment" in him.

Rather than entirely dismissing the Old Testament anticipation of the New Testament or justifying it by appeal to a prescient mystical knowledge, de Lubac sees it as the result of an interior relation between events brought about by Christ:

> Is this to say that, outside of a kind of wholly implicit knowledge that we have just defined, no ray ever filtered, under the Old Law, of that light which was to shine in Jesus? Assuredly not. But these rays, like those of the dawn, were already from the coming Sun. We could just as well call them a shadow, as Origen did. They thus did not constitute a

36. De Lubac, *History and Spirit*, 310.
37. Ibid.

146

stage that was in itself independent from the stages that were to follow. The important fact in this order, the one that permits us to say that the Old Testament anticipates the New, was not a present spiritualization of the earlier history or institutions of Israel. It was not even absolutely the eschatological orientation of Israel's reflection on its great memories. It was the proclamation of a future spiritualization thanks to the insertion of a Principle that would be given from above, the proclamation of a total and definitive renewal.[38]

Intitially, de Lubac employs the metaphor of the sun casting its light to describe the relationship between the anticipatory figure and the reality that fulfills it. At dawn, one can see the rays of sun peeking over the horizon. They are the anticipation of the sun that will soon arrive. Christ is the new principle that creates his own anticipation in the Old Testament. The objective basis for the Old Testament's anticipation of the New Testament is the retroactive causality of Christ.[39] By assimilating Old Testament events to himself, he *became* its spiritual meaning. As a result, the glory of the Christ event casts its shadow backward in history, causing the Old Testament to symbolize and anticipate him.

De Lubac argued that the categories of spiritual exegesis in Origen reflected an acute awareness of the Incarnate Word's assumption of Old Testament realities. In *History and Spirit*, de Lubac explained,

Even in the very consciousness of Jesus—if we may cast a human glance even into this sanctuary—the Old Testament was like the matrix of the New or the instrument of its creation. That means much more than external preparation. The categories in which Jesus expresses himself

38. "Christ, in so far as transcendent and existing before all things, is anterior to his figures, yet as a historical being, coming in the flesh, he appears after them. Late in historic time, but prior in priority to all time, Christ appears to us preceded by the shadows and the figures which he himself had cast on Jewish history." Ibid., 466–67.

39. De Lubac's notion that Christ effects an ontological anticipation in the Old Testament is the basis for his affirmation of Origen's exemplarism. The historical exemplar will be important for de Lubac's understanding of the symbolic structure of reality insofar as it indicates that the universal depends on particular and that symbols are now directed to a particular historical realization.

about himself are the old biblical categories. He explodes them, or, if you prefer, he sublimates and unifies them, by making them converge on himself. But they are in some way necessary to him, and, on the other hand, in this renewed use, they do not become various abstract categories, nor do they serve as incidental images. They preserve all their value and their flavor as allusions to precise facts, to singular realities. These realities in relation to which Jesus situates himself and which he, by that very fact, transforms, are those that fill the history of Israel or that constitute the object of its hope.[40]

De Lubac suggests that Jesus, in his humanity, internalizes the Old Testament in his own consciousness and through his personal action. He assumes the Old Testament to himself and unites it in his person.[41] In this sense, he *is* personally the "spiritual interpretation" of Scripture.

For de Lubac, the practices of spiritual interpretation are profound reflections on the impact of the Word in history. Origen's exemplarism, employing Neoplatonic thought forms, captures the profoundly historical nature of Christian thought. All of human history now draws its meaning from the concrete life of Jesus of Nazareth. His life illuminates everything that came before and everything that will follow. As shown in the next chapter, the glory of Christ radiates into the historical future too. The moral or tropological and the anagogical senses describe the effect of Christ's presence in the historical future.

In sum, the spiritual sense, for de Lubac, reflected a meaning given to history by a new and transcendent principle inserted into it. According to de Lubac, Jesus' life, death, and resurrection is that principle. Jesus *creates* the spiritual meaning of Scripture, introducing

40. De Lubac, *History and Spirit*, 434.
41. The messianic consciousness of Christ ties together the Old and New: "He is conscious of fulfilling and transfiguring at the same time, of fulfilling by transfiguring. He is carrying out the oracles of the prophets, but he knows that he is doing still more: he takes, in his supreme act, a wholly prophetic religion and reveals in its absolute essence, or rather completes its reality, the great divine Gesture, which up until then had been wholly symbolic." Ibid., 465–66.

a new reality at the heart of history. Better yet, Jesus *is* the spiritual meaning. De Lubac sees the divine kenosis in Christ as the locus and concentration of both salvation and revelation. Christ's life, death, and resurrection is, therefore, the event that unifies and transcends all previous revelatory events.

Conclusion

De Lubac defended a Christian exegetical tradition of allegorization that discovered the Old Testament as a prophetic anticipation of the New Testament. Although Origen's exegesis was commonly interpreted as inattentive to history, de Lubac argues that Origen's allegory is radically historical. For Origen, the "allegory" is the concrete and historical life of Christ that fulfills the prophecies of the Old Testament. Christ is the historical exemplar in whom all historical events find fulfillment and to whom they are oriented.

Three interrelated characteristics of Origen's spiritual interpretation became critical for de Lubac's theological understanding of history: historicity, christocentrism, and transcendence. First, de Lubac characterized history and salvation in radically historical terms. De Lubac emphasized that God's self-disclosure is radically historical. It occurs through the historical life of Jesus Christ, culminating in his kenotic death and resurrection. Through his kenotic self-gift, salvation and revelation are united, manifest visibly in time.

Second, Christ is the center of history. The entrance of the Word into history is the assumption of the Old Testament and transformation of it. De Lubac suggests that Christ becomes the historical exemplar in whom all temporal realities have their fulfillment. The historical actions of Jesus take on a comprehensive scope: unveiling the meaning of human history, fulfilling all things, bringing unity to all reality, and uniting all revelation in himself.

De Lubac unites the historicity of revelation in Jesus of Nazareth with the cosmic breadth of the Colossians Christ hymn: "For in him the fullness of God was pleased to dwell, and through him God was pleased to reconcile to himself all things, whether on earth or in heaven, by making peace through the blood of his cross" (Col. 1:19–20 NRSV).

Third, Origen's phrase *the newness of Christ* correlates directly with de Lubac's understanding of transcendence. Transcendence is not the displacement or supplanting of the current order, but a transformation of it from within that causes it to be what it is most authentically. Christ transcends the Old Covenant, not by displacing it, but by assuming it to his own life. This notion of transcendence is significant for de Lubac's understanding of nature and the supernatural and for his mystical theology. Moreover, as will be indicated in chapter 6, de Lubac believes that the transcendence wrought by Christ has already brought about the end of history. Our time exists as the "end time," the interim between the first and second comings of Christ. As a result, we live in a time of sacramental anticipation of eternity.

The recovery of spiritual exegesis through Origen was significant to de Lubac's attempt to save history from immanentism, particularly from the dialectical materialism of Marx. De Lubac realized that Marxism was not only an historical theory, but also a way of reading one's own life as meaningful. De Lubac's turn to Origen provided a response. It was foundation for an understanding of history in which the historical present participates in the ongoing drama of salvation, in which the transcendent has entered, and in which the mystery of Christ remains present.

5

Between Apocalypse and Eschaton

Henri de Lubac never developed a discrete eschatology. The array of themes traditional to eschatology—death, the resurrection of the body, judgment, heaven, hell, purgatory, the fulfillment of God's promises, the end of history, the final coming of Christ, the unity of the cosmos with God, the beatific vision—are not gathered in a single place in de Lubac's work or treated systematically. This is due, in part, to his tendency to view eschatology through corporate and communal lenses instead of prioritizing the fate of the individual soul. Eschatology concerns primarily the completion and resolution of God's plan for the universe. While de Lubac does not develop a systematic exposition of eschatology, it forms the backdrop for many of his writings.

In eschatology as in the theology of history, Origen is a significant figure in de Lubac's historical interpretation and theological construction. In *Exégèse médiévale*, de Lubac identified Origen as the primary patristic source of both the threefold and the fourfold senses of Scripture, which governed the shape of Christian theology for a millennium. *History and Spirit* defended Origen's "spiritual interpretation" of Scripture as a transformation of Greek allegorization that preserved a Christian understanding of history. With some caveats, Origen became the norm against which de Lubac adjudicated the subsequent exegetical tradition.[1] The Word of God, by entering into time, bestows a new meaning to temporal existence and establishes an ontological relationship to the past (the Old Testament) and also to the future (the eschaton). Origen's *allegory* represents symbolically the relationship between the Old Testament and Christ. *Anagogy*, the last spiritual sense of Scripture, represents the relationship between the actions of the Word in history and their eschatological fulfillment at the end of time.

De Lubac depended upon Origen's anagogy in two ways. First, de Lubac retrieved it as the fundamental structure of his eschatological thinking. According to de Lubac, Origen's anagogy is not the mystical contemplation of ahistorical essences or the contemplative desertion of this world. Instead it is the mystical participation (in the present) in the eschaton (in the future). Anagogy suggests that our temporal experience is a participation in advance, or foretaste, of the future eschatological completion. Origen's anagogy conveyed a sacramental understanding of time in which the eternal enters into history, drawing toward the eschatological consummation. For de Lubac, anagogy represented a way of seeing the transcendent in the midst of the world that could overcome the modern loss of the "sense of the sacred."

Second, de Lubac interpreted the diachronic development of Christian eschatology from the patristic period to the modern period using Origen as the baseline. Origen's final sense of Scripture,

---

1. For an overview of de Lubac's reading of Origen, see Michel Fédou, "Henri de Lubac, lecteur d'Origène: l'hospitalité de la théologie et sa source mystique," *Revue des sciences religieuses* 77, no. 2 (April 2003): 133–46.

anagogy, systematized a pattern of understanding the end that influenced Christian thinking for a millennium. Anagogy began to rupture into two different streams in the Middle Ages. A medieval theological tradition inspired by Pseudo-Dionysius the Areopagite (fifth to sixth century) effectively lost its foundation in the history of salvation. Coincident with this development, a countertradition launched by Joachim of Fiore (1135–1202), emphasized history to the detriment of transcendence. In the Dionysian tradition, anagogy became a vertical mystical ascent to "higher realities"; in the tradition inspired by Joachim, it became the horizontal expectation of a utopian future. According to de Lubac, modernity inherited both of these developments: on the one hand, a spiritual individualism that seeks to transcend the world by escaping from it; on the other hand, an apocalyptic mysticism that seeks total transformation of the world yet refuses the transcendent.

Anagogy and Anagogies

In *Exégèse médiévale,* de Lubac explained that the term *anagogy* was borrowed from Greek paganism but was given a new meaning within a Christian context. The Latin *anagogia* is a transliteration of the Greek *anagōgē,* meaning "ascent." Its ending *ia* followed the pattern of *historia, allegoria,* and *tropologia.* As de Lubac noted, some authors explained the etymology of *anagogia* as the confluence of *ana* (upward) and *agōgē* (leading), Greek words equivalent to the Latin *sursumductio.*[2] Anagogy became the sense "which leads the thought of the exegete 'upwards.'"[3]

---

2. Henri de Lubac, *Medieval Exegesis: The Four Senses of Scripture,* trans. E. M. Macierowski, vol. 2 (Grand Rapids, MI: Eerdmans, 2000), 179–80. Originally published as *Exégèse médiévale, 2: Les quatre sense de l'Écriture* (Paris: Éditions Montaigne, 1959).
3. *Medieval Exegesis,* 2:180.

De Lubac does not identify the precise origin of anagogy's association with the meanings of Scripture. He noted that in the first few centuries of Christianity, Origen, Gregory of Nyssa, Didymus the Blind, and Jerome employed anagogy as "one of the names of the spiritual sense in general."[4] For these authors anagogy had not yet acquired the specialized meaning that we find in Pseudo-Dionysius, that of intellectual contemplation. However, de Lubac suggests that in John Cassian anagogy became more specialized and that Cassian's anagogy was a step toward that of Pseudo-Dionysius. De Lubac's central point in this part of *Exégèse médiévale* is that the early tradition had not yet made anagogy a specialized term. It united several elements that would later be distinguished and separated. Using a series of quotations from Aelred of Rievaulx, Hugh of Saint Victor, Venerable Bede, Robert of Melun, John Cassian, and Augustine, de Lubac compiled a set of definitions of anagogy:

> Anagogy is first off . . . "a sense of the things above." It leads the mind's consideration "from things visible to those invisible," or from things below "to things above," i.e. to "the divine things." It is this sort of allegory "which lifts the understanding of the mind through visible things to the invisible," or "through which speech is borne over to the invisible things to come." More concretely, this will be the sense that lets one see in the realities of the earthly Jerusalem those of the heavenly Jerusalem: "for a certain part of the earthly city has been made an image of the heavenly city." Although these things no longer belong to time, nevertheless, for us who trudge and toil through time, they are things yet to come, objects of desire and of hope.[5]

Anagogy is a spiritual movement, the movement of the mind or spirit from the visible to the invisible; it is a manner of seeing *through*

---

4. Ibid.
5. Ibid., 2:180–81. Quoting Aelred, *Sermo* 10 (PL 195:205 D), Hugh of St. Victor, *Spec. Eccl.* 8 (PL 177:375 B), Venerable Bede, *In Hex.* 4 (PL 91:168 B, C), Robert of Melun, *Sent.* 1.1.4, John Cassian, *Collationes* 14.8 (PL 49:965 A), and Augustine, *Civ. Dei*, 15.2 (PL 41:439).

visible and present realities to those of heaven. But it is also associated with the virtue of hope because these heavenly realities are future for us. According to de Lubac there are three chief characteristics of anagogy as it derives from Origen:

1. *Objective Anagogy*: Anagogy describes objectively the transcendent or heavenly realities
2. *Subjective Anagogy*: As the ascent of the mind to the transcendent or heavenly realities, anagogy also describes a spiritual journey as the personal process of ascent.
3. *Transcendent/Future Anagogy*: Although anagogy is the contemplation of the transcendent, those transcendent realities consist of what will come to pass at the end.

The Anagogical Dialectic in Origen

We should note that Origen often does not neatly distinguish anagogy from the spiritual sense as a whole. The two aspects that de Lubac ascribes to anagogy in *Exégèse médiéval*—objective and subjective—are found in Origen as characteristics of "spiritual understanding" generally, inclusive of the anagogical sense.[6] Describing Origen's hermeneutics, de Lubac explains, "The spiritual sense, understood as the figurative or mystical sense, is the sense that, objectively, ends in the realities of the spiritual life and that at the same time, subjectively, can be given only as the fruit of a spiritual life. . . . The Christian mystery, in fact, is not to be contemplated with curiosity as a pure object of science; rather it must be interiorized and lived. It finds its fullness in coming to

---

6. De Lubac indicated that Origen, as well as much of patristic thought, lacked rigid systematization of terminology. He associates anagogy with the spiritual sense as a whole: "For some then, the spiritual sense is entirely anagogy: 'mystic anagogy,' Origen used to say, or again: 'the allegories according to anagogy,' or simply: 'according to anagogy.'" *Medieval Exegesis*, 2:35.

completion in souls."[7] Objectively, the spiritual understanding attains the mystery (*le Mystère*). Subjectively, Christians know the mystery only by entering into it and living within it: "The whole process of spiritual understanding is identical, in principle, to the process of conversion. It is its luminous aspect. '*Intellectus spiritualis credentem salvum facit*' (the spiritual understanding saves the believer)."[8] In Origen, the objective reality attained through spiritual understanding, at its base, is the same as the process of conversion to it.

In de Lubac's interpretation, Origen's spiritual understanding consists of an unending process of assimilating oneself to God's mystery. The understanding of Scripture participates in both prayer and conversion. The ultimate meaning of Scripture is both objective and subjective because the Christian's appropriation and interiorization of the mystery is a component of that ultimate mystery itself:

> The sacred text is truly understood, insofar as it is given us to understand it, only in a perpetual effort of transcendence, in a "flight," in a never-completed movement of *anagogy*. This anagogical movement is also an interiorizing movement. And in this respect, too, it is without end. . . . For the understanding of Scripture is at the same time the vital assimilation of its mystery. . . . It does not consist in ideas, but it communicates the very reality of the One whose riches are unfathomable. It can grow indefinitely, because it expands to the measure of the mind's capacity to receive it.[9]

7. Henri de Lubac, *History and Spirit: The Understanding of Scripture according to Origen*, trans. Anne Englund Nash (San Francisco: Ignatius Press, 2007), 446. Originally published as Henri de Lubac, *Histoire et esprit: l'intelligence de l'Écriture d'après Origène*, Théologie 16 (Paris: Aubier, 1950).

8. Ibid., 466. Quoting Augustine, *In psalmum* 33.1.7 (PL 36:305). "There is a reciprocal causality between that conversion to Christ and the understanding of the Scriptures." Ibid., 447.

9. Ibid., 382.

The anagogical meaning consists of the transcendent realities signified in the Scriptures, but these transcendent realities include the believer herself in union with the transcendent: "The Word of God, a living and efficacious word, reaches its real fulfillment and its full meaning only by the transformation that it works in one who receives it."[10] The anagogical meaning of Scripture is not an entirely objectified and discrete intellectual content. As the personal reception and conversion to a personal God, the anagogical movement of the soul more closely approximates what Thomas Aquinas calls the *intellectus* (the simple and intuitive intellectual gaze) rather than the *ratio* (the discursive reason). "It is a matter of attaining, with 'the eyes of the soul' an *intellectus simplicior*."[11]

According to de Lubac, Origen identifies spiritual understanding with one of his most controversial teachings, the notion of the final restoration of all things (*apocatastasis*). De Lubac underplayed the controversial aspects of Origen's teaching on the *apocatastasis*—namely, the conversion of all created intellectual beings to God, including the damned and the devil, and the links between *apocatastasis* and Neoplatonic and Stoic cosmology. Instead, he contended that spiritual understanding "is itself this 'apocatastasis' in which God does not appear as a distant third part with whom we could discourse or as the object of an impersonal contemplation; rather he presents himself to the soul in view of a dialogue of love."[12] *Apocatastasis* is, for Origen, a synonym for the conversion of all to God and for the conversion of the church to Christ. The final stage of the movement of spiritual understanding is then, ultimately, both a transformative conversion and a definitive ecclesial–cosmic fulfillment.

10. Ibid., 447.
11. Ibid., 383.
12. Ibid., 384.

As a result, the coextensive growth of spiritual understanding and conversion is not an individualistic process. The spiritual interpretation of Scriptures is the end and means of an ongoing spiritual dialectic of which the church as a whole is the subject.

> It is a unique movement, which, beginning with initial incredulity, is raised by faith to the summits of a spiritual life whose end is not here on earth. Its unfurling is coextensive with the gift of the Spirit, with the progress of charity. The whole Christian experience, with its various phases, is thus contained in it in principle. The newness of the understanding is correlative with the "newness of life." To pass on to the spiritual understanding is thus to pass on to the "new man," who never ceases to be renewed *de claritate in claritatem* (from glory to glory).[13]

The dialectic of spiritual understanding is the same as the process of conversion and the growth of charity. De Lubac suggests that spiritual understanding is coextensive with the historical dialectic, the growth of the church as a spiritual organism and its passage on to the "new man." Therefore, anagogy, as another name for spiritual understanding, designates the process, and the final phase of the process, of conversion whereby the church as a whole is transformed by charity and united with Christ.

The Objective and Subjective Anagogies

Origen was the source for different traditions of spiritual exegesis in the patristic and medieval periods, including the fourfold and threefold senses of Scripture. In subsequent traditions, the threefold and fourfold methods of interpretation each emphasized a different perspective by which anagogy was understood. As a result, there were two formulations of anagogy: "The one which fulfills the doctrinal formulation of the fourfold sense; the other, which fulfills the spiritual formulation of the threefold sense."[14] The fourfold sense

---

13. Ibid., 448.

constituted the "doctrinal formulation": history (the Old Testament), allegory (the New Testament/Christ), tropology (the moral meaning for the individual), anagogy (the ultimate eschatological meaning). The fourfold sense was doctrinal because the allegory directly follows history, emphasizing the central role of Christ.[15] The threefold sense was the "spiritual formulation": history, allegory, anagogy or, alternatively, history, tropology, allegory/anagogy (the variant inspired by Philo). The threefold sense is the "spiritual formulation" because the three levels of meaning were often correlated with a tripartite anthropology: body, soul, and spirit. So, the threefold sense emphasizes that passages from Scripture possess three meanings according to a process of spiritual ascent: the lowest meaning corresponding to the body, the next meaning corresponding to the soul, and the final meaning corresponding to the spirit.

For de Lubac, these two formulations of anagogy are complementary: "The standpoint of the first anagogy is objective and doctrinal; that of the second pertains to subjective realization; in other words, the one is defined by its object, and the other by the manner of apprehending it."[16] He explains that "the first '*declares* the sacraments of the future age,' or 'disputes about the life to come,' whereas the second leads 'to *beholding* the mysteries of the age to come,' 'to *contemplating* the heavenly mysteries.'"[17]

---

14. De Lubac, *Medieval Exegesis*, 2:181.
15. See Henri de Lubac, *Medieval Exegesis: The Four Senses of Scripture*, trans. Mark Sebanc, vol. 1 (Grand Rapids, MI: William B. Eerdmans, 1998), 146–7. Originally published as *Exégèse médiévale, 1: Les quatre sense de l'Écriture* (Paris: Éditions Montaigne, 1959).
16. De Lubac, *Medieval Exegesis*, 2:181.
17. Ibid. Matthew Gerlach perceptively describes anagogy as containing a double perspective: (a) the things above and transcendent and (b) that which is not yet. Matthew T. Gerlach, "Lex Orandi, Lex Legendi: A Correlation of the Roman Canon and the Fourfold Sense of Scripture" (PhD diss., Marquette University, 2011), 339–40. This double perspective, I will argue, is at the center of de Lubac's eschatological thinking. To be precise, however, de Lubac's quotations from Cassiodorus, Bede, Origen, and Aimon, indicates that both anagogies include a future-oriented element: "future age," "life to come," "age to come." Here, the primary distinction is between the objective (disputes, declares) and the subjective (beholds, contemplates).

We over-emphasize the opposition; but, as we shall see, it is justified. Let us say that the first of the two anagogies teaches that part of Christian dogmatics called "eschatology"—which itself is further subdivided into two parts, according as the ultimate end of each person or that of the universe as a whole is concerned. As to the second anagogy, it introduces us here and now into the mystic life; at the terminus of its movement, it fulfills that "theology" which is made etymologically the equivalent of "theoria" and which is the contemplation of God. In modern terms, the one is speculative; the other, contemplative.[18]

The principal distinction is between the objective and the subjective, between the transcendent reality that is the future object of hope and the contemplation of that reality happening right now.

According to de Lubac, the first, the doctrinal and objective anagogy, was a Christian modification of a thoroughly eschatological Jewish prophetic tradition. Leading up to the time of Jesus, Jewish prophecy conceived the fulfillment of God's promises, brought about by the Messiah, as a heavenly dwelling and a heavenly temple. The coming of the Messiah would closely coincide with the end of time.[19] When Christ came, however, time did not come to an end. The Christian expectation of an imminent end of the world was slowly transformed in the consciousness that Christians now live in the *interim*: "A gap opened up between the first and the last coming. In that gap the Church would unfold its existence for an indeterminate period."[20] Christ introduced a division in time that would require a reconception of the present with regard to the future: "It would seem necessary, then, to conceive the New Testament as truth in respect to the Old, but as a mere 'image' with respect to the ultimate reality still to come."[21] The present time is a "pledge" and "exemplar" of what is to come; the church is a "forerunner" of the "age to come."

18. De Lubac, *Medieval Exegesis*, 2:181.
19. Ibid., 2:182.
20. Ibid.
21. Ibid.

From the very beginnings, a tension marked the shape of Christian eschatological hope. Christ constituted the salvation offered by God, and the Christian now possesses it. However, time has not yet come to an end, and this salvation is not yet possessed in its fullest intensity and luminosity:

> Notwithstanding the gap opened by the first coming and the still unchanged conditions of our knowledge, notwithstanding the sorely felt distance between the *nunc* [now] of the earth and the *tunc* [then] of eternity, it is in fact the very reality of salvation which henceforth is inserted into history and immediately offered to us. By faith, the believer . . . can paradoxically say "night is illuminated as day." He already holds "the substance of the things that he hopes for"; he has already, albeit still secretly, penetrated into the kingdom. The primitive Christian community . . . from the first instant . . . had "an intense awareness of being at once the Israel of God and the heavenly kingdom anticipated on earth."[22]

Because Christ has already come, we have already received God's promised gift. But because Christ has not returned, we still await the consummation of God's promsies. We possess grace, but await glory. The doctrinal formulation of anagogy is founded on an inner identity between the present state and the future state, the church militant and the church triumphant, grace and glory. We could call this a sacramental relationship, in which the present church is an effective sign of the church to come.

The second anagogy is subjective, completing "the movement of mystical tropology."[23] De Lubac describes no longer the object of contemplation, but the act. It is contemplative rather than speculative.

---

22. Ibid., 2:183.
23. Ibid., 2:188. There is some ambiguity in de Lubac's account. De Lubac earlier spoke of this second anagogy as that which fulfills the "spiritual formulation of the threefold sense" (i.e. history, allegory, *anagogy*.) Ibid., 2:181. However, he later calls it the completion of the movement of mystical tropology enumerated within the fourfold sense (i.e. history, allegory, tropology, *anagogy*.) Ibid., 2:188.

By Gregory the Great, anagogy is associated with the "*volatus*: flight, impulse, no longer intellectual representation but spiritual movement, anagogy."[24] For Richard and Hugo of Saint Victor, anagogy is a "real ascent of the soul."[25] Subjective anagogy is not an intellectual method, but a spiritual flight of the mystic or poet, who not only speculates about the heavenly mysteries but is united with them. De Lubac explains that "the fully concrete anagogy, total anagogy, is reserved for the 'fatherland.' Mystical contemplation is not yet vision. So however high anagogy leads, it always leaves something to look for and always with greater fervor, because it still doesn't uncover the Face of God."[26] For Origen as for Gregory of Nyssa, the anagogical movement of the soul is not arrested even in heaven, since God always remains a mystery and the human being must always seek a deeper realization of the mystery.

De Lubac speaks of a unity of the objective (doctrinal) and subjective (mystical) dimensions of anagogy:

> Anagogy realizes the perfection of both allegory and of tropology, achieving their synthesis. It is neither "objective" like the first nor "subjective" like the second. Above and beyond this division, it realizes their unity. It integrates the whole and final meaning. It sees, in eternity, the fusion of the mystery and the mystic. In other words, the eschatological reality attained by anagogy is the eternal reality within which every other has its consummation.[27]

Ideally, these different dimensions are united within anagogy. The perspective of Origen, as transmitted to a broad tradition, was that the mystical contemplation of the heavenly was not entirely distinct from the heavenly reality itself. Contemplation is a participation in

24. Ibid., 2:193.
25. Ibid., 2:190.
26. Ibid., 2:194.
27. Ibid., 2:184.

the heavenly reality, which is constituted by the union of the subject (in the entire church) with God.

De Lubac's description of the two anagogies in *Exégèse médiévale* anticipates the late medieval period, during which anagogy would no longer be strictly associated with biblical exegesis. The objective anagogy developed into a theological discipline concerning the last things and the end of time, while the subjective anagogy developed into a distinct discipline of mysticism or spirituality.

Heavenly and Future Anagogy

De Lubac also emphasized that, for Origen and subsequent tradition, the object of anagogy is both a heavenly reality and a future realization. The anagogical ascent of the soul represents the progress through history toward an ultimate fulfillment at the end of time or beyond time. It is a fulfillment of the world that transforms this world and that is yet to pass.

The structure of Origen's exegesis illumines the meaning of anagogy as heavenly and future. The threefold sense consists of the letter, the allegory, and the anagogy. These three levels of meaning correspond respectively to three stages of historical development: Israel, the church, and the assembly of the kingdom; or, alternatively, the Old Testament, the New Testament, and eschatological heaven. The historical division reflects a tripartite and progressive symbolic structure: "shadow," "image," "truth."[28] The Old Testament contains symbolic prefigurations of the New Testament realities. In turn, the New Testament symbolizes a future, final fulfillment. For Origen, the Old is a mere shadow of the coming truth, that is, the final eschatological reality. The New Testament is its image. Each stage prepares for and prefigures the next. The Old Testament is oriented

---

28. De Lubac, *History and Spirit*, 250.

toward its fulfillment in the New. But the New Testament is oriented to a future fulfillment as well: "It is the whole New Testament, understood as the complete progress of the Christian economy up to the last day, that also appears to him to be oriented toward a more profound, absolutely and solely definite reality; a reality that it has the duty to make known by preparing for it, serving thus as intermediary between the Old Law and the 'eternal gospel.'"[29] Thus, for Origen, the New Testament itself contains symbolic prefigurations of a promised fulfillment.

The prominent Origenian theme, the *eternal gospel*, suggests that just as the Old Testament anticipated the coming of Christ, so does Christ anticipate the coming of the heavenly kingdom. For Origen, "the eternal gospel" (Rev. 14:6) reveals the mysteries of which Christ's actions and words were the figure. Christ announces the realities of the kingdom, not yet fully manifest. "Thus, just as each object from the Old Testament was a sign announcing the New, so each object of the New is in turn a sign whose reality is found 'in the ages to come.'"[30] As the book of Revelation presents itself as a vision into a heavenly drama, it announces the eternal gospel of which the words of Revelation are a sign. Just as the adherents of God's law in the Old Testament awaited its fulfillment in Christ, the Christian awaits a further, subsequent fulfillment of the eternal gospel in the future age.

Origen's formulation could invite the notion that the gospel given by Christ and transmitted by the apostles must be superseded by another, just as the gospel supersedes the Old Testament law. As a result, the Christian would have to await another gospel more definitive than the one delivered by Jesus Christ. This supersessionist positon is represented by Joachim of Fiore, the twelfth-century monk who foretold of an "eternal gospel" that would supplant the gospel

29. Ibid., 248.
30. Ibid.

of Jesus Christ. De Lubac contrasted Origen's interpretation of the eternal gospel with that of Joachim: "There is not really anything more in common between Origen and Joachim of Fiore than this name, eternal gospel—but this is a biblical title drawn from the Apocalypse—and the idea that this eternal gospel consists in the thorough spiritual interpretation of the Gospel—but they completely disagree on the nature and time of this interpretation."[31] Although they both employ the same terminology to describe the final state, Origen and Joachim disagree about *when* the eternal gospel occurs and *what* is it.

The time of the eternal gospel is different: Joachim awaits the eternal gospel and a future spiritual society "in time"; Origen's eternal gospel is no longer in time.[32] De Lubac writes, Origen's "eternal gospel is the antithesis and anticipated antidote of that of the Calabrian monk [Joachim of Fiore]. It is no less opposed to that arbitrary and unhealthy problem which, ever since the time of Montanus has so often reappeared in the history of the Church. In brief, it is completely eschatological."[33] For Origen, the eternal gospel is the supratemporal fulfillment of the gospel of Jesus Christ. For Joachim, the eternal gospel is temporal, a new gospel that commends new forms of life.[34] Second, the nature of the eternal gospel is different in Origen and Joachim. Origen's eternal gospel shares an identity with the gospel of Jesus Christ. A tripartite theology of history—Old Testament/gospel of Jesus Christ/eternal gospel—frames Origen's use of the phrase *eternal gospel*. However, de Lubac added, "this trichotomy tends to be resolved into a dichotomy":[35] Although

---

31. Ibid., 251–52.
32. Ibid., 252.
33. Ibid. Montanus (late second century) preached a revelation that came directly from the Holy Spirit and which superceded the revelation through Jesus Christ.
34. I will elaborate on Joachim's theology later in this chapter.
35. De Lubac, *History and Spirit*, 253.

the gospel of Jesus Christ is a fulfillment of a different order from the Old Testament, the eternal gospel shares an identity with the gospel of Jesus Christ [Old Testament → gospel/eternal gospel (or shadow → image/truth)]. Origen's "eternal gospel remains in close relation to the Gospel that was proclaimed to us. It constitutes another state of it, not something added to it."[36] The eternal gospel is the future state of the present gospel, at which point the mysteries revealed in figures will be unveiled in truth.

Origen's exegesis exemplifies an understanding of history in which the New Testament mediates the passage beyond history to eternity. The Old Testament is the *shadow* of the New Testament. The New Testament is, in turn, the *image* of the eschatological truth:

> In its turn then, in order to be understood as it must be, in its newness, which is to say, in its spirit, in order to merit its name as New Testament, the content of this second Scripture must give way to a perpetual movement of transcendence. The spirit is discovered only through *anagogy*: τήν ἐπί τά πνευματικὰ ἄπταιστον ἀναγωγή (the uninterrupted anagogical ascent to spiritual realities). We must consequently always ἀνάγειν τήν ἱστορίαν (ascend above the history).[37]

Anagogy completes the movement from the historical figures of the New Testament to the transcendent realities that they prefigure.[38] The New Testament history plays a mediatory role. The realities recounted in the gospel have solely the function of drawing us into the gospel in its final state. The gospel, both historical and spiritual, is a preparation for and figure of its future state, which is completely spiritual.

36. Ibid., 252.
37. Ibid., 323.
38. For de Lubac, *anagogy* is a synonym for transcendence. Transcendence is a particularly modern term, imported into the Catholic vocabulary with the help of the Roman Catholic Modernists. De Lubac's use of the term reflects his dependence upon Blondel and his familiarity with the Modernists.

Drawing from Origen, de Lubac emphasizes that history exists only in order to pass beyond itself into an eternal fulfillment. Because God has entered history, history has been drawn into the movement of ascent to God, in a movement that transcends history:

> Linked to the mystery of the Incarnation of the Logos, history, if it is in fact mediatory, must not hold us indiscriminately. Its whole role, on the contrary, is to *pass on*. History, in any case, is essentially what passes on. Thus the events recounted in the Bible . . . all exhausted, so to speak, their historical role at the same time as their factual reality, so as no longer to survive today except as signs and mysteries. Thus, in its entirety, up to its final event, history is a preparation for something else. To deny that is to deny it. The truth to which it introduces us is no longer [of] the order of history.[39]

The relationship between the gospel of Jesus Christ and the eternal gospel in Origen's theology of history reflects the paradox of Christian eschatology. On the one hand, the gospel of Jesus Christ and the eternal gospel share a profound identity, between the present economy of salvation and its final fulfillment. The veil must only be removed from our eyes for us to experience the splendor of God's salvation given to us now. On the other hand, the present order will pass away, existing only to transfer us to eternity. We exist in a time of waiting.[40]

It is difficult to reconcile de Lubac's insistence on the "transcendence" or "newness" of the gospel with the idea that the

---

39. De Lubac, *History and Spirit*, 322–23.

40. De Lubac suggested that this tension is present in Origen, who in different places emphasizes the Old Testament as a symbol for eternity, the New Testament identified with its celestial fulfillment, or the eternal as something yet awaited: "whether the mediating term is omitted, the spirit being elevated from an earthly bond of Israel to 'supra-celestial places,' from the sacrifices of Israel to the Sacrifice that is consummated in the Temple on high—or whether the last two terms are fused together into one by the awareness of their profound identity, since it is a matter of the same Priest, the same Sacrifice, the same Victim, of the same Master of Truth whose 'words do not pass away'—or whether, finally, the third term is less expressed than intended, through a movement of 'transcendence' or 'anagogy' that is not completed, for 'insofar as the Son has not returned in his glory,' the depth of his mysteries cannot be explored." Ibid., 253.

historical features of the gospel exist only to pass away. By emphasizing that the temporal gospel shares an identity with the eternal gospel, the present economy of salvation is united with its final fulfillment as part of a single process. At the same time, the present economy of salvation exists only to lead us to the eternal. This historical-eschatological tension runs throughout de Lubac's writings. It presents Christianity as primarily a history of God's interactions with God's people, the consummation of which will no longer be *in* history.

It is critical that the object of Origen's anagogy is understood as being both heavenly and future. Anagogy treats the *mysteria futuri saeculi*, "mysteries of the age to come."[41] The "things above" are also the "last things." De Lubac explains: "These 'heavenly things' toward which he has us raise our eyes are for him, future realities in relation to the signs of them contained in the Bible. They form this 'intelligible world' that can be seen only by pure hearts. They are the 'mysteries of the age to come.'"[42] Even if, for Origen, anagogy is a movement beyond history, de Lubac claims that the realities of which it speaks are to be fulfilled in the future. In essence, the anagogical is the future orientation of the present. It is the future state of God's plan for creation. It therefore remains an object of hope rather than something already complete or already simply existent on a higher plane.

Although Origen's anagogy is a mystical ascent of the soul, it possesses social and ecclesial dimensions. The terms *spirituality* or *mysticism* do not often connote corporate dimensions; we do not often imagine using them when we speak of the church's corporate

---

41. Ibid., 478. See also ibid., 326–28, 422–23; Henri de Lubac, *Scripture in the Tradition* (New York: Crossroad, 2001), 52. *Scripture in the Tradition* was originally published as *L'Écriture dans la tradition* (Paris: Aubier-Montaigne, 1966).
42. De Lubac, *History and Spirit*, 327.

dimensions and social action. Origen's anagogy disrupts those divisions because is both the journey of the soul and also the union of the soul in the church. Anagogy is the process of personal assimilation of the mystery of Christ in its social and ecclesial dimensions. The objective historical dialectic of the church, its earthly pilgrimage toward its eternal destination, is also a dialectic of interior conversion and of mystical ascent. Because this process is social, it is lived out in the temporal realm as a common ecclesial life. However, de Lubac insisted that this social and ecclesial process of assimilation to Christ is as yet incomplete. It anticipates the total unification of the body of Christ that can only occur at the completion of history. Anagogy concerns the "mysteries of the age to come."

The Narrowing of the Spiritual Senses

De Lubac's exposition of the spiritual senses is diachronic. It examines multiple traditions of spiritual interpretation in their development across time, from Origen through the Middle Ages to modernity. *Exégèse médiévale* traced developments in patristic and medieval thought that obscured the logic of the hermeneutic of the fourfold and threefold senses. Over time, the spiritual senses of Scripture—allegory, tropology, and anagogy—became more narrowly focused and became specialized disciplines. Allegory, once closely associated with the mystery of Christ, became a narrowly tailored discipline focused on the exposition of doctrine. Tropology, once understood as the interiorization of mystery of Christ by the believer, evolved into the exposition of an external moral code. Anagogy, originally the proleptic participation in the mystery, later became a specialized discipline focused on special mystical experiences and unconnected to dogmatics or the economy of salvation. In sum, de Lubac's diachronic exposition of spiritual interpretation traces its evolution into specialized, quasi-independent disciplines in theology (biblical studies, dogmatics, moral theology, and spirituality) as they developed in modernity. It is also a genealogy of the intellectual traditions that now shape modernity.

At the heart of de Lubac's narrative is the radical transformation of mysticism. In St. Paul, the mystery is the "plan of God" that is unfolded in history. In Origen, all the spiritual senses of Scripture are mystical senses, because mysticism is intimately connected with the mystery of the economy of salvation. De Lubac observed a process whereby there was a gradual shift in association of the *mystical* meaning of Scripture from the allegorical, to the tropological, and finally to the anagogical. This shift in association points to a gradual shift in meaning of mystery. *Mystery*, no longer the plan of God developing in time, would be reduced to a static contemplation of "invisible" realities. Mysticism becomes dehistoricized and abstracted from the economy of salvation. Anagogy became the carrier of this dehistoricized mysticism. To explain this process, however, we must provide a rough exposition of, first, how allegory became narrowly associated with doctrine and, second, how tropology became narrowly focused on morality, and both were dissociated from the "mystical."

In early Christianity, spiritual interpretation functioned as both a spirituality and an apologetic, evolving as a response to both paganism and Judaism. Paul used it to defend Christianity against the Jewish rejection of the New Testament. The gnostics, however, claimed to possess a deeper, spiritual meaning that would supersede all biblical revelation. Origen "saved the unity of biblical revelation" by claiming the New Testament was the deeper spiritual meaning of the Old Testament.[43] He defended a spiritual interpretation "through an explanation taken from Scriptures, for the needs of the spiritual

43. Ibid., 59.

life they [the heretics] claimed to satisfy."[44] In Origenian thought, "apologetics continued in spirituality, and the doctrine of the 'spiritual sense' saw its field of application grow indefinitely."[45] As a result, de Lubac claimed, patristic thought associated the mystical meaning of Scripture with allegory in particular:

> The mystical understanding of Scripture counted among the essential components of theology; to be more precise, particularly of that part of theology which, at the time of the Fathers, was called the "economy." From that time forward, the so-called mystical or allegorical sense was always considered to be the doctrinal sense par excellence, the one that sets forth the mysteries relating to Christ and the Church.[46]

Thus, the "allegorical" sense and the "mystical" sense designated the same reality. The allegorical sense was also the doctrinal (theological) sense because allegory interpreted the mystery present within the historical meaning of Scripture, which mystery *is* Christ and his fulfillment of the Old Testament.

However, de Lubac claimed, during the early Middle Ages, a change in context for spiritual interpretation occurred. The apologetic context for the spiritual sense was lost, in part, because of the loss of a constant contact with a living tradition of paganism, which until the medieval period was alive in the Christian consciousness. The idea that there was a fundamental difference between Christian and pagan allegory was no longer an issue. Christian allegory had won out. As a result, there was not much interest in the apologetic criticism of pagan allegory as nonhistorical or in the corollary defense of Christian allegory as faithful to history. More importantly, the key to patristic allegory—that the New Testament is the spiritual depth of the Old Testament—was no longer

44. Ibid., 60.
45. Ibid.
46. Ibid., 474.

as critical to the medieval practitioners of allegory. Thus, during the Middle Ages, the connection between the exegetical procedure of allegorization and the progressive economy of salvation was obscured.

As a result, "mystical" meaning was gradually detached from the doctrinal meaning of Scripture. Allegory in Origen was simultaneously doctrinal and spiritual because the interpreter of Scripture examines the words for their depth, their spiritual meaning. This spiritual meaning *is* doctrine.

> As doctrine appeared more settled even in its least details, moreover, the sense relating to the spiritual life thus acquired a kind of independence. They [Gregory of Nyssa and John Cassian] crossed through the obscure layer of "allegories" more rapidly in order to penetrate the "secret delights" of which they were the promise. Mystical exegesis was no longer of great help for reflection on the mystery: from this point of view, its active role was past; but it remained a marvelous springboard for the inner impulse. The spiritual sense of Scripture became particularly the sense of the contemplative.[47]

After the great doctrinal debates of the patristic period and the ecumenical councils, the fundamental doctrine of the faith appeared more secure. The practice of searching the depths of Scripture was not as essentially tied to doctrinal understanding. As a result, spiritual interpretation continued but became associated with more contemplative practices and took on a more subjective and interior flavor.

Like the allegorical sense of Scripture, tropological sense of Scripture underwent an evolution within monastic culture whereby it described spiritual experiences or regulated external activity. Tropology, the moral sense of Scripture, originally denoted the personal implications of the biblical story for the believer. It "is not

---

47. Ibid.

entirely a 'doctrine of interior illumination.' It is the doctrine of the interiorization of the biblical datum: its history and its mystery. Neither this history nor this mystery is denied or forsaken, as it would at least be possible to believe among those who speak of a birth of the *Word* only within the contemplative soul."[48] Although tropology is an "interiorization" of the mystery, it is not individualistic. Instead, it implicates a reciprocal relationship between individual spirituality and the church.[49] Tropology constitutes dramatic interiorization of the mystery of Christ in the life of the church as a whole, inclusive of the individual.

Connected to the fate of allegory, tropology also underwent an evolution that would separate spirituality from the doctrinal (that is, allegorical) meaning of Scripture. Monastic exegesis especially contributed to a narrowing of tropology. Although monasticism made salubrious contributions to a profound Christian awareness of the meaning of the Scriptures for the individual, it also generated excesses. Christian monasticism centered itself on *lectio divina*, the reading of, and meditation on, the biblical word. It extended patristic mystical tropology, applying it to a particular mode of religious life. A hallmark of monastic culture—the distinction between the laity and the monks, between actives and contemplatives, in sum, between degrees of being Christian—affected its biblical interpretation. As an example of the spirit that animated monasticism, de Lubac described its idea of "conversion." Conversion describes a new orientation to Christ. To convert is to renounce the world for Christ. In the monastic culture, "A 'convert' is no longer a man that has come from error to the truth, from paganism or Judaism to the Gospel: it is the one who renounces the 'world' for the 'cloister.' The day of his entry into religion is the day of his 'conversion.'"[50] Texts traditionally

48. De Lubac, *Medieval Exegesis*, 2:139.
49. Ibid., 2:136.

interpreted as referring to the church as a whole were transposed to the monastery. The city of Jerusalem, commonly interpreted as representing the church, becomes a symbol for the abbey of Citeaux. On the one hand, these transpositions from church to monastery manifested a creative application of traditional themes; on the other, they contributed to a spiritual elitism.[51]

In monastic culture, tropology became narrowly associated with the intense "delight" of contemplation. The word of God contains a spiritual sweetness underneath its letter. The sweetness of honey is extracted from the comb as the spiritual understanding is extracted from the letter. Originally applied to the spiritual understanding as a whole, in the twelfth century the Cistercians described the extraction of the sweetness of Scripture as the interiorization of the mystery in the soul. It indicated the need not only to know the mystery in an intellectual sense, but also to understand the mystery by "experiencing" or "tasting." Outside of the Cistercian order, this theme was transferred from the spiritual sense in general to tropology in particular.[52] This delight of mystical contemplation would be interpreted as the particular prerogative of the monks and directed toward individual experience. While de Lubac claimed the vast majority of monks did not succumb to elitism, he believed that monasticism betrayed the tendency to focus on the experience of the monk as a more intense form of "spiritual nourishment."[53]

Monastic practices were in continuity with a wide-ranging tendency in medieval theology that led tropology to be placed in the service of an increasingly specialized "spirituality."

---

50. Ibid., 2:145.
51. Ibid., 2:150.
52. See the section of *Medieval Exegesis* 2 entitled *Doctor mellifluous*, on the "sweetness" of Scripture. Ibid., 2:174.
53. Ibid., 2:150.

A trend is taking shape toward the beginning of the twelfth century, which tends more and more to put usefulness—and charm—on the side of tropology. With the organization of the ecclesiastical studies and the differentiation of the disciplines, allegory became more theoretical, more impersonal, in a certain way drier, and tropology, on the contrary, more practical, looking more to regulate external activity than to nourish the interior life. In our present categories, we would say that the first becomes the object of theological speculation, whilst the second tends to monopolize preaching.[54]

By the High Middle Ages, both the allegorical and tropological senses became more specialized: allegory was associated with a more objective and technical theoretical discipline of theology, while tropology was employed for interior edification. De Lubac called the shift in focus of tropology a "refinement and gratuitousness."[55] The Scriptures become a mere springboard or "occasion" for spiritual self-edification and for spiritual experiences.[56] "Connections with the doctrinal meaning that formerly, even implicitly, still governed spiritual developments are, in practice, severed. Or else the Bible primarily provides a framework."[57]

De Lubac's history of exegesis argues that, as a whole, medieval practices of biblical interpretation, mediation, and preaching led spirituality to make itself independent from biblical exegesis. "Following dogmatic theology, spirituality was little by little detached, methodologically, from exegesis, in order to follow its own ways."[58] The development of tropology as "practical" and interior, despite some positive development within medieval mysticism, tended to forget the connection of tropology with God's actions within the economy of salvation.

54. Ibid., 2:176.
55. De Lubac, *History and Spirit*, 479.
56. Ibid.
57. Ibid., 497.
58. Henri de Lubac, *Exégèse médiévale: Les quatre sens de l'écriture*, vol. 4, Théologie 59 (Aubier: Éditions Montaigne, 1964), 487.

175

The Rise of Scholasticism

It is common to speak of a "renaissance" in the twelfth century during which radical changes affected medieval culture and thought. Like his Thomist contemporaries Étienne Gilson and Marie-Dominique Chenu, de Lubac traced significant changes in methods and institutions of Christian theology to the twelfth century.[59] In the Middle Ages, centers for theology shifted from monastic schools to the city schools and universities. Scholastic methods arose as powerful intellectual tools for all the sciences. The twelfth century witnessed the rise of the "summa"—a compendium of topically organized theological knowledge—which would eventually replace the biblical commentary as the dominant theological genre. During this period, scholasticism reflected and contributed to a theological methodology in which development and growth of economy of salvation did not fit. As a result, both doctrine (allegory) and mysticism (anagogy) were detatched from history.

The methodological separation between the first two senses of Scripture, history and allegory, contributed to the fundamental shift in metaphor for describing what theology is. The divine *plan* of the patristic period became a *work* of divine wisdom during the medieval. *Plan* suggests that God's intentions are unfolding and built up historically toward an eschatological fulfillment in the future. *Work* of wisdom, on the other hand, suggests God's eternal wisdom, of which the created world and the Bible are manifestations. This difference, however slight, is indicative of an increasing separation

---

59. Étienne Gilson, *The Spirit of Medieval Philosophy* (Notre Dame, IN: University of Notre Dame Press, 1991). Originally published as *L'Esprit de la philosophie médiévale* (Paris: J. Vrin, 1932). See also Marie-Dominique Chenu, *Nature, Man, and Society in the Twelfth Century: Essays on New Theological Perspectives in the Latin West* (Toronto: University of Toronto Press, 1997). Originally published as Marie-Dominique Chenu, *La Théologie au douzième siècle*, vol. 45, Études de philosophie médiévale 45 (Paris: J. Vrin, 1957).

between economy and theology that manifested itself in late medieval theology, which attended more to philosophical problems than to the history of God's manifestation. In de Lubac's account, methodological changes point to an underlying shift in the model of human knowledge in which a linear history of salvation and an eschatological perspective no longer fit.[60]

Two schools of thought that are opposed on the surface—the Victorines and twelfth-century scholasticism—colluded in generating this new model of theological knowledge. The Victorines contributed to a separation of spirituality from doctrine, while the scholastics developed a scientific theology in which mystical knowledge had only a tenuous place. Hugh of Saint Victor (1096–1133), in particular, contributed to a methodological separation between history and allegory. In an essentially conservative attempt to secure allegorization, Hugh divided theology into "two detached pieces"—history and allegory—that were "destined to become, in fact, quite independent of each other."[61] De Lubac explained that the trajectory on which the Victorines set theology gave rise to a division. History would become "historical and literal exegesis," then "positive scholarship," and eventually "criticism."[62] Allegory would loosen its ties to exegesis and become an autonomous system: "It will progress in rationality and in abstraction,

---

60. Several factors that de Lubac examines are worth mentioning for their contribution to a new model of knowledge in the twelfth century. First, dialectical reasoning in theology was not as attuned to historical development or "concrete history." Henri de Lubac, *Medieval Exegesis: The Four Senses of Scripture*, trans. E. M. Macierowski, vol. 3 (Grand Rapids, MI: Eerdmans, 2009), 254. Originally published as *Exégèse médiévale, 3: Les quatre sens de l'écriture* (Paris: Éditions Montaigne, 1961). Second, there was a "resurgence of·the Platonic ideal." *Medieval Exegesis*, 3:254. Third, the "enthusiastic discovery of Nature" in the twelfth century threatened to overtake previous models of theological knowledge. Adelard of Bath, Bernard Silvestris, and William of Conches particularly adopted the categories of Aristotle and Platonism for the advancement of physical science as a universal model of knowledge. Ibid. Fourth, nominalist logic posed a threat to the historical "*dispensatio.*" Ibid., 3:255.
61. Ibid., 3:313.
62. Ibid.

to become the majestic edifice of the Summas of the great epoch."[63]
De Lubac states that Hugh of Saint Victor cannot be blamed for
the widening division that was occurring between exegesis and
speculative theology. Although his own theological synthesis resisted
the dehistorization of Christian theology in his time, his work is
symptomatic of a methodological division that would become
standard in the wider milieu.[64]

Richard of Saint Victor (d. 1173) contributed to the
methodological separation of mystical theology (constituted by
tropology and anagogy) from doctrinal theology (constituted by
history and allegory). According to de Lubac, Richard of Saint Victor
created a new genre of mystical literature that was detached from the
literal and allegorical senses.

> Thus a genre of spiritual literature begins to be established . . . which
> will finally no longer have any visible organic attachment, as has been
> said before, either with exegesis or with theology properly so called. He
> continues in principle to tie the explication of scripture to contemplative
> process, and his mysticism is always chock full of doctrine. On the other
> hand, if we take his work as a whole, we recognize that the influence
> of Pseudo-Dionysius in him, as in Hugh, is allied with that of Saint
> Gregory, which remains very strong. But after him, the evolution rushes
> headlong, To an extent never previously attained, Saint Gregory gives
> way to "divine Dionysius," whose anagogy was, as we have seen, not
> very scriptural. Origen and Saint Augustine alike back away before
> him.[65]

Tropology and anagogy would be "detached from the first two
parts, so as to be constituted as a body of spiritual doctrine rather
remote from its biblical foundations and from the newly constructed
theology."[66] The division between mysticism and theology would

63. De Lubac, *Exégèse médiévale*, 4:314.
64. De Lubac, *Medieval Exegesis*, 3:254, 217.
65. Ibid., 3:321.
66. Ibid., 3:315.

have disastrous consequences down the line. De Lubac explained that "this sort of split . . . intervenes between a theology, once it has become purely 'speculative,' and a spirituality where feeling and imagination are dominant—and which may secretly draw its principles from some non-Christian source."[67] The roots of this division, he argued, is in the exegesis and the loss of "the historical foundation" in theological inquiry.

Scholasticism exacerbated and hardened the shift of theological methodology in early medieval thought.[68] Scholastic theology, by definition, was a theology of the "schools." With the establishment of cathedral schools during Carolingian Renaissance in the ninth century, the centers of theological erudition began a shift away from the monasteries. Scholasticism would make its home in the universities in the late eleventh century. Theology would complete a shift from the "school of contemplation" to the "school of disputation," in part, through a graduation from reading (*lectio*) to disputation (*disputatio*). The monastic practice of *lectio* focused on reading and meditation, which was essentially in the form of an exegesis of Scripture. While this "took on a contemplative aspect," the scholastic *lectio* concerned argumentation.[69] It eventually will become the "dialectical disputation," the argument over a particular question. The *quaestio* called upon students to debate the theological question posed, defending a response of yes or no. Although the traditional links between theology and meditative practices were preserved, the medieval *disputatio* would change the characteristics of the theological discipline. Its contemporary critics believed that

---

67. Ibid.
68. In perhaps an ironic jab at contemporary neoscholasticism, de Lubac described scholasticism as "a new theology with new methods" that arrived on the scene. While de Lubac and other French theologians were accused of inventing a "new theology" (i.e., untraditional and modern), de Lubac indicated that Scholasticism in fact was new.
69. De Lubac, *Medieval Exegesis*, 1:61.

dialectical thought "called upon the mystery 'to be reduced into categories that had already been constituted in their entirety.'"[70] The genre of the *quaestio* shifted the content from an explication of the depths of the text to answering a series of disputed questions. Significantly, the dialectical method worked under the assumption that the disputation could be resolved on the level of the "letter" without appeal to the mystical depths of the text.[71] The contemplative-mystical *lectio* became something additional to but not an essential component of this new mode of speculative theology. The twelfth-century change of theological genre therefore constituted a significant change in mentality.[72]

Later Scholasticism emphasized theology as a "scientific" discipline subject to proofs. The new emphasis on proof effectively dismantled the interconnection between theology and mysticism. Proofs were primarily drawn from Scripture and increasingly focused on its literal sense. A proof could not depend upon a tenuous and uncertain "mystical interpretation." As John of Paris claimed, "*Mystica theologia non est argumentativa*" (mystical theology does not furnish proofs).[73] The field of dogmatics had to depend upon an interpretation of the literal sense of Scripture. Demonstration using the literal sense became the new ideal for theological knowledge. Scholasticism's new

---

70. Ibid., 1:63. Quoting Louis Boyer, *Du protestantisme à l'Église* (Paris: Éditions du Cerf, 1955), 175. See Henri de Lubac, *Corpus Mysticum: The Eucharist and the Church in the Middle Ages*, trans. Gemma Simmonds, CJ, Faith in Reason (Notre Dame, IN: University of Notre Dame Press, 2007), 229. Originally published as Henri de Lubac, *Corpus mysticum: l'eucharistie et l'Église au Moyen âge. Étude historique*, Théologie 3 (Paris: Aubier, 1944).

71. While, in the twelfth century, de Lubac claims, the *quaestio* was not the "well-defined, technical genre" that it would later become, it already influenced the shape of theological reflection. See, *Medieval Exegesis*, 1:67. By the thirteenth century, "the leap is thus made. The break has taken place. 'Dialectic' and its 'questions' have won the day, and the change in methodology is found to have been accelerated by the inroads of an entirely new set of contents, that of the philosophy of Aristotle. Teaching no longer has as its framework the triple or quadruple explication of the biblical text." Ibid., 1:73.

72. Ibid., 1:60.

73. De Lubac, *History and Spirit*, 482.

ideal appropriated the older categories of spiritual exegesis, but at the same time changed them. The great thirteenth century scholastics, including Albert the Great, Bonaventure, and Thomas Aquinas, embedded "spiritual understanding" and the three spiritual senses within a new model for theological inquiry. After the thirteenth century, the "exposition of the fourfold sense remains an obligatory theme for the scholastic." However, it was becoming "merely an empty repetition of an old theory. The application is entirely mechanical."[74] In the new ideal for theology that took root in the twelfth century, "mystical knowledge" held an ambiguous place. The tropological and anagogical senses of Scripture were, to a certain extent, placed outside of the realm of theology properly so called. As a result, the essential interconnection between mysticism and theology could no longer be assumed.

The change of methodology, however, does not imply that medieval scholasticism entirely lost an understanding of sacred history. Bonaventure melded scholastic method with a profound and original reflection on history in response to Joachimite thought among the Franciscan Spirituals. In Thomas Aquinas, though less explicitly historical, theology and Scripture remain united within *Scientia scripturae*. De Lubac claimed, following Congar, Spicq, and Chenu, that Thomas was doing nothing but putting to systematic use the traditional categories of exegesis.[75]

In de Lubac's interpretation, at the close of the twelfth century, the connection between the exegetical process and the historical economy of salvation was becoming attenuated. For Origen,

74. De Lubac, *Exégèse médiévale*, 4:3103.
75. Ibid., 4:310. See de Lubac, *Medieval Exegesis*, 3:315; Henri de Lubac, "Joachim de Flore jugé par saint Bonaventure et saint Thomas," in *Pluralisme et œcuménisme en recherches théologiques: Mélanges offerts au R.P. Dockx, OP*, Bibliotheca Ephemeridum Theologicarum Lovaniensium 43 (Leuven: Peeters, 1976), 34; Henri de Lubac, "On an Old Distich: The Doctrine of the 'Fourfold Sense' in Scripture," in *Theological Fragments* (San Francisco: Ignatius Press, 1989), 109–28.

anagogy is a mysticism that moves from the sensible to the intelligible and that moves toward the end point of the economy of salvation. It incorporates the *vertical* mystical ascent with the *horizontal* journey of the church toward the end of time, the eschaton. By the twelfth century, the last sense of Scripture was no longer viewed as the endpoint of the progression of the historical economy toward its goal, but instead placed in the service of a mysticism disengaged from that economy. De Lubac described a corollary loss of the eschatological association of the anagogical sense of Scripture. This change resulted in

an obscuring of the social and eschatological perspective. In the classical distinction between the four senses, the fourth was concerned with realities that were both heavenly and future, *mysteria futuri saeculi* [mysteries of the age to come]. In Origen himself, as we have seen, anagogy united these two characteristics; it contained the hope of the Church in progress. Now an exegesis essentially attentive to things of the interior life did not have to treat what we call today the "end of history." Centered on the individual soul, it did not have to speak explicitly of the Church triumphant any more than it did of the Church militant. That was a legitimate specialization, from the moment that mysticism thus disengaged remained based on mystery. But this habitual preterition was perhaps not without leading in the end to a certain narrowing of hope.[76]

De Lubac's concern was with the trajectory of developments within exegesis whereby the anagogical sense would stripped of its social and eschatological reference, becoming more narrowly focused on the individual mystical ascent to invisible realities.

Anagogy as Mystical Ascent: The Pseudo-Dionysian Legacy

One of the most significant factors in the shift of the meaning of anagogy within medieval Christian theology was the influence of

76. De Lubac, *History and Spirit*, 478.

the fifth- to sixth-century pseudepigraphal writings of Dionysius the Areopagite. Dionysius's compositions melded a spiritual tradition stemming from Origen with Neoplatonic mystical traditions, resulting in an influential body of teaching concerning the mystical ascent to God and deification.[77] John Scotus Eriugena (ca. 815–ca. 877) translated Pseudo-Dionysius into Latin, making these writings available to early medieval monastic circles. According to de Lubac, although Pseudo-Dionysius was read from the ninth century on, his influence proliferated in the twelfth century: "Just as the march of the mind had passed through Aristotle, so will it pass through Dionysius."[78] De Lubac noted that the popularity of these writings was due, in part, to their false attribution to the disciple of Paul in Acts 17.[79]

Dionysian mysticism is characterized by an anagogical ascent to God that, beginning from material and symbolic representations, rises beyond them. The mystical ascent is composed of three stages: symbolism, affirmation, and negation. Symbols are the divine manifestations, which participate in the "emanation" of God. They are the material representations of the divinity, including those found in Scripture. The second and third stages comprise a dialectic of affirmation (*kataphasis*) and negation (*apophasis*). Symbols are interpreted though this dialectic, by which what we affirm of God within the symbols must be subsequently negated to maintain the transcendence of God. For Dionysius, "God is described as invisible, infinite, ungraspable, and other things which show not what he is but what in fact he is not."[80] Positive representations of the Godhead—word, mind, being—are less fitting than the negative

---

77. Jaroslav Pelikan, *The Emergence of the Catholic Tradition (100—600)*, vol. 1, *The Christian Tradition: A History of the Development of Doctrine* (Chicago: University of Chicago Press, 1971), 344–49.
78. De Lubac, *Medieval Exegesis*, 3:321.
79. Ibid., 3:322.

modes of representation—invisible, infinite. In reality, Dionysius defends biblical imagistic representations of God since, like their philosophical counterparts, they point to rather than comprehend the divinity. Biblical images "[provoke the mind] to get behind the material show, to get accustomed to the idea of going beyond appearances to those upliftings which are not of this world."[81] Yet the anagogical flight to God must rise above images and representations.

For de Lubac, Dionysian mysticism contained a destructive individualism and ahistoricism.[82] He suggests that Dionysius is partly responsible for a transition from an earlier spiritual theology characterized by communally oriented mystical practices to a modern mysticism focused on individual interior states.[83] For instance, *The Mystical Theology* of Dionysius envisioned an individual's ascent through the sensuous realm to the intelligible realm, to the Godhead. In this ascent, the individual soul transcends the historical order. De Lubac's reservation concerning Dionysius has been convincingly disputed by recent theologians who have produced more positive, and perhaps fairer, interpretations.[84] Responding to the charge of individualism, Mark A. McIntosh argues that "the mystical depth encountered by the spiritual seeker is not found by a purely interior ascent of the soul, but rather that such a Neoplatonic itinerary has

80. *The Celestial Hierarchy*, 2:3, in Pseudo-Dionysius the Areopagite, *Pseudo-Dionysius: The Complete Works*, ed. Colm Luibhéid, trans. Paul Rorem, The Classics of Western Spirituality (Mawah, NJ: Paulist Press, 1987), 150–51.

81. *The Celestial Hierarchy* 2:5 in ibid., 153.

82. It should be noted, however, that de Lubac's *Sur les Chemins de Dieu* contains positive comments and quotations from Dionysius. De Lubac, *The Discovery of God*, trans. Alexander Dru (Grand Rapids, MI: Eerdmans, 1996), 87n1, 125, 125n23.

83. See Mark A. McIntosh, *Mystical Theology: The Integrity of Spirituality and Theology*, Challenges in Contemporary Theology (Malden, MA: Wiley-Blackwell, 1998), 44.

84. Hans Urs von Balthasar, *The Glory of the Lord: A Theological Aesthetics, Clerical Styles*, vol. 2 (San Francisco: Ignatius Press, 1984), 144–210; McIntosh, *Mystical Theology*, 44–56; Tamsin Jones, "Dionysius in Hans Urs von Balthasar and Jean-Luc Marion," in *Re-Thinking Dionysius the Areopagite*, ed. Sarah Coakley and Charles M. Stang (Malden, MA: Wiley-Blackwell, 2009), 213–24.

been re-contextualized in the sacramental life of the community." The corporate and ecclesial aspects of Dionysius's mystical theology resist divisions between individualistic spirituality and ecclesial faith.[85]

De Lubac's other charge against Dionysius—that Dionysius loses the historical and eschatological dimensions of salvation—is more difficult to shake. The Dionysian dichotomy between God's invisible reality and the ultimately inadequate scriptural forms of representation make the latter, even the narratives concerning God's historical interaction with humanity, akin to myths. Dionysius's apophatic theology construed the material, historical, and symbolic realities narrated by Scripture as suited to an inferior stage of contemplation. Like the Greek myth, they are springboards for the mind to ascend to the atemporal truth. As Balthasar stated, "What was once historical, temporally conditioned reality becomes for Denys a means for expressing an utterly universal theological content. The dimension of history and of Church history interests him not at all; only the eternal, only the divine interests him."[86] Although Dionysius recognized the value of concrete symbols for the mind's ascent to the divine—and as a result, his mysticism is not entirely divorced from history—these symbols are valuable only for their divine, nontemporal content.[87]

Although de Lubac drew from Dionysius in his apologetic work, *The Discovery of God*, his assessment of Dionysius in *Exégèse médiévale* is particularly negative. De Lubac does not evaluate the merits of Dionysius the theologian. Instead, his concern was for the enthusiastic reception of Dionysius in a new theological climate in the twelfth century and the subsequent legacy of Dionysian thought. The twelfth-century reception of Dionysius exacerbated theological

---

85. McIntosh, *Mystical Theology*, 45.
86. Balthasar, *The Glory of the Lord*, 2:152.
87. Ibid., 2:178–9.

trajectories already in place toward eternalism and a prioritization of interior experience. Eternalism is the tendency to regard only the universal and unchanging as dignified of divinity, thereby relegating the particularity of the actions and events of the history of salvation to the unessential. If the divine is associated only with the universal and unchanging, then mysticism tends to be interiorized and oriented toward pure contemplation of the divine, unmediated by external realities or histories. De Lubac indicates that Dionysian thought contributed to a process whereby the earlier mystical tradition represented by Origen, Augustine, and Gregory was supplanted with what would be a modern form of mysticism. He writes that there was a "transition from mystical understanding to speculative mysticism—to wit, from Scripture to Dionysius."[88]

However, the most alarming development mentioned above is the loss of the eschatological. De Lubac explained,

> When, laden with an insufficiently transformed Neoplatonism, the thought of Dionysius was introduced into the West, the risk of a disturbance in equilibrium arose, at the expense of supernatural historicity and of the eschatological component. This risk came to a head in the work of John Scotus. It was reinforced by the second Dionysian wave in the course of the twelfth century. This Dionysian anagogy, whereby one passes from the order of visions to that of pure contemplation or from symbolic theology to mystical theology, is neither first nor foremost in the end time of an exegesis: it is, as it were, the last spurt of a sort of cosmic energy raising each nature according to its hierarchic order in the graduated series of illuminations. It makes the mind, as Hugh of Saint Victor says commenting on the *Celestial Hierarchy*, penetrate "into the contemplation of higher things," but these "higher things" would at the same time scarcely appear any longer as the "last things." By anagogy, said Cassian, "speech is carried over to the invisible things to come." This was, as we have seen, the language of the Epistle to the Hebrews and that of Origen; it was also to be that of many others. In the tradition influenced by Dionysius, however, a dissociation

---

88. De Lubac, *Medieval Exegesis*, 3:322.

tended to develop between the *invisibilia* and the *futura,* as between the mystic life and the mediation on Scripture. No longer aware of a certain order of personal intimacy between the two liberties, the divine and the human, the mysticism formed by Dionysius spontaneously tended toward the "edification of the holy Church." When these traits came to dominate, they profoundly differentiated the mysticism of Dionysius from that of Origen, Augustine, or Gregory. The history of the struggles for influence and of attempts at synthesis between these two mystical traditions would be extremely interesting to untangle. Here let us simply recall the explanations that Garnier of Rochefort soon gave us about the purification of the understanding which empties itself of every image so as to climb back to its "superessential" original. They [Garnier of Rochefort's explanations] no longer have any more than a very loose connection with Scripture. Now, try as they might to appeal to the authority of the *Soliloquiae,* they in fact came straight from Dionysius.[89]

The fracturing of the *invisibilia* (invisible things) from the *futura* (future things) within Christian eschatology is the key to the transition to modern mysticism. Dionysian anagogy was insufficiently oriented to a future realization. The "higher" reality of Dionysian thought helped to establish the object of anagogy as the atemporal, ahistorical divine reality, whether contemplated through the visible or contemplated directly after the use of signs and images is left behind. As a result, anagogy no longer comprehended the future realities that constituted the fulfillment of God's plan of salvation.

Twelfth-century definitions of anagogy, de Lubac tells us, give evidence of these underlying dissociations between the future and the invisible. For Peter Comestor (d. ca. 1178), anagogy "'deals with God and the things above the heavens,' as if it were a question of intemporal objects."[90] Rupert of Deutz (1075–1129) writes that with Scripture "we can weigh carefully at any time, not what or how God is, but what he is not, and that God is to be likened to no

89. De Lubac, *Medieval Exegesis,* 2:194–95.
90. Ibid., 2:195.

creature."[91] Garnier of Rochefort (d. ca. 1199), described anagogy as the vision "whereby it [the mind] strives to contemplate the most holy heavenly one as he is by the mind's climbing up and going out in nakedness and purity and without covering."[92] By the end of the twelfth century, the connection between the anagogical ascent of the mind and the last sense of Scripture was becoming tenuous. For William of Ockham (ca. 1288–ca. 1348), it is "an explanation whereby the invisible things of God are seen to be understood through those that have been made."[93] In the case of Meister Eckhart the history of salvation was "transposed dangerously in dialectical stages" of the ascent of the soul.[94]

The Lubacian optic concerns what happens to biblical narrative under the strain of Dionysian thought. According to de Lubac, Dionysius influences a widespread transformation of eschatological thinking within the church and the wider culture.

> After the thirteenth century, Denys invades everything: cosmology, metaphysics, ecclesiology, even politics, spirituality. But it is a multiform Denys. The Denys of Albert the Great and of the Thomists is not entirely the one of Thomas of Verceil, of Hugh of Balma, of Robert Grosseteste, and of the Franciscan community; their Denys is not the one of which the secular Guillaume de Saint-Amour had invoked the authority. In the time of Boniface VIII, the pontifical theologians, with a Giles of Rome, had constructed their teaching on a kind of amalgamation of Aristotle and Denys, and this same amalgamation is found a century later in the work of their successor John of Torquemada. However, all the spiritual currents are more or less Dionysian.[95]

91. Ibid., 2:196.
92. Ibid.
93. Ibid., 2:195. "In the same way, the 'sapientia anagogica' which authors like Hugh of Balma define especially according to Dionysius, will no longer be presented as the last moment of an exegesis; it will rather be the high point of a contemplation arising from the 'plane of history,' the 'planities historiae': he will allow it to be opposed to 'any speculative wisdom,' as that which comes from God and not men." *Medieval Exegesis*, 3:316.
94. De Lubac, *Exégèse médiévale*, 4:489.
95. Ibid., 4:494.

Losing the unity of the *futura* and *invisibilia* that it possessed in Origen, anagogy was transformed into speculative mysticism, contemplation, and ascent of the mind. It becomes the contemplation of invisible, transcendent truths. Under the influence of Dionysius, it was losing its connection to the eschaton, the conquest of good over evil, the historical fulfillment of God's plan, and the object of *hope*. Borrowing a line from Yves Congar, de Lubac states that scholasticism exhibited a "lack of the eschatological sense."[96] By tracing the ruptures in scriptural hermeneutics in the medieval period, de Lubac identified the root methodological causes of the loss of historical and eschatological consciousness within Catholic theology during his own day.

Anagogy as Revolution: The Legacy of Joachim of Fiore

A medieval stream of anagogical thinking ran opposite to the Dionysian. According to de Lubac, Joachim of Fiore (ca. 1132–1202) was a voice of protest against the Dionysian traditions dominating the medieval landscape. Joachim reacted against protorationalist tendencies within medieval thought in general and nascent scholasticism in particular. He creatively synthesized the categories of an ancient exegesis into a new, powerful apocalyptic vision that projected Christian hope into the terrestrial future. Yet Joachim's eschatology depended upon the same dichotomy between the future and the invisible that governed Dionysian thought:

> Two deviations threaten spiritual understanding at its peak. Spiritual understanding can forget that Christianity is eschatological and, effectively, suppress hope—at least the specifically Christian hope. On the other hand, by an inverse dissociation of the *invisibilia* and the *futura*, it can also conceive an eschatology upon earth and thereby transform

96. De Lubac, *Medieval Exegesis*, 2:195. Quoting Yves Congar, "La Purgatorie," in *Le Mystère de la mort et sa célébration*, vol. 12, Lex Orandi (Paris: Éditions du Cerf, 1951), 312.

hope—at least a primary phase of hope—into utopia. Some signs of the first tendency, due in part to the influence of Pseudo-Dionysius, had appeared for us with respect to anagogy and we have just picked up its trail once again. It remains to explore the second in its most illustrious instance: that of Joachim of Flora.[97]

The first deviation is a *theologia* (knowledge of God) divorced from *oeconomia* (God's actions in history); the second is *oeconomia* fulfilled within history. The object of Dionysian anagogy was exclusively the *invisibilia Dei*; the object of Joachim's eschatology was a future historical state. Though opposed, Dionysian mysticism and Joachimite prophecy shared the same dissociation between the future and the invisible.

De Lubac wrote more on Joachim (and his legacy) than on any other historical figure, except Origen (and his legacy). De Lubac's earliest significant treatment of Joachim of Fiore appeared in 1950 in *History and Spirit,* in an extended contrast between Origen's and Joachim's use of the term *the eternal gospel.* De Lubac's *Catholicism* only referred to Joachim once, and not in the context of Joachim's exegesis or eschatology.[98] Joachim went unmentioned in *Le Drame de l'humanisme athée* (1944) and *Sur les chemins de Dieu* (1956). Joachim's exegesis and the Joachimite tradition of biblical interpretation appeared in *Medieval Exegesis* 3 (1961) and *Exégèse médiévale* 4 (1964).[99] *Exégèse médiévale* examined the "exegetical posterity" of Joachim, namely those who followed his exegetical methods. This posterity consists of those who interpret prophecies of Scripture literally and historically. Three years later, de Lubac published an article entitled "Joachim de Flore jugé par saint Bonaventure et saint

---

97. De Lubac, *Medieval Exegesis*, 3:327.
98. Henri de Lubac, *Catholicism: Christ and the Common Destiny of Man,* trans. Lancelot C. Sheppard and Sister Elizabeth Englund, OCD (San Francisco: Ignatius Press, 1988), 118.
99. *Medieval Exegesis* 3:327–419 and *Exégèse médiévale* 4:325–44 contain the most extended treatment of Joachim in this four-volume work.

Thomas" that examined the scholastic response to Joachim's historical thinking.[100] The two volume *La Postérité spirituelle de Joachim de Flore* (1979, 1981) soon followed. *La Postérité spirituelle* is an account of the "spiritual posterity," those who would hope for a third age of the Spirit or of the spirit:

> The first, which was not sustained by any élan of thought, is but a withered branch in the present hour. The second is a dense forest. After the thirteenth century, it has constantly metamorphosed, and not only at the interior or on the margins of the churches, but as far as in the secular thought of modernity. More exactly, the Joachimite idea has not ceased to act like a ferment. In the variety of forms that it has assumed, learned or popular, it has constituted one of the principal channels conducing to secularization, that is to say, to the denaturing of Christian faith, thought and action. It has served also to supplement or substitute mysticism for processes of rationalization that couldn't by themselves arouse the necessary enthusiasm for their achievement. Today it has a surprising renewal of life.[101]

While Joachim's "exegetical posterity" lost its vitality long ago, his "spiritual posterity" remained a significant cultural force.

De Lubac's method of interpretation of Joachim follows the pattern of his other historical works. He was interested less in Joachim himself than in the traditions engendered by his thought.[102] In particular, de Lubac focused his attention on ideas that contributed to ruptures within the intellectual tradition. As Emmanuel Falque notes, de Lubac "track[s] ruptures and transitions: such is the method constantly taken by de Lubac since *Exégèse médiévale*."[103] While de Lubac ascribed to Joachim a significant role in a rupture within

---

100. De Lubac, "Joachim de Flore jugé par saint Bonaventure et saint Thomas."

101. Henri de Lubac, *La Posterité spirituelle de Joachim de Flore: de Joachim à Schelling*, vol. 1 (Paris: Éditions Lethielleux, 1979), 14–15.

102. Emmanuel Falque, "La posterité spirituelle de Joachim de Flore ou le principe d'immunité chez Henri de Lubac," *Revue des sciences religieuses* 77, no. 2 (April 2003): 189.

103. Ibid., 190. I would add only that this interest in rupture and transition was at the heart of de Lubac's historical focus since *Corpus Mysticum*.

Christian eschatological thinking and even saw in him the precursor of dangerous philosophical and political movements, he did not read Joachim in merely a critical light. On the one hand, he paints Joachim as an innovator, whose exegetical methodology broke with a centuries-long tradition.[104] On the other hand, he saw Joachim's thought within a historical evolution of "spiritual interpretation" and also as a response to forms of nascent rationalism within the church. De Lubac treats Joachim sympathetically, as a mystic who envisions the "regeneration in spirit" of the church.[105] "His 'internal dynamism' was consequently not an entirely aberrant force."[106] Joachim was probably not aware of the "disruptive" effects that his theology would have.[107]

Consequently, Joachim's reception within the theological tradition was, perhaps, of greater importance than Joachim himself. The great scholastics, including Bonaventure and Thomas Aquinas, confronted Joachim's exegetical and eschatological thought. Bonaventure purified it and integrated it into his theology of history. Thomas Aquinas refuted it without such integration. However, de Lubac suggests that Thomas himself preserved the historical dimensions of Christianity, but that the subsequent scholastic tradition did not.[108]

104. De Lubac's opinion conflicted with that of Leone Tondelli, Francesco Russo, Antonio Crocco, and Marjorie Reeves, who championed the fundamental orthodoxy of Joachim. They argue that Joachim envisioned a purified church of the future whose institutions would remain intact. In contrast, de Lubac argued that Joachim proposed a radical discontinuity between the present and the past. Indeed, Joachim was quite aware of the novelty of his proposals. De Lubac, *Posterité spirituelle*, 1:22. Bernard McGinn, reviewing this debate, states that the differences between the positions could be partially bridged by avoiding the loaded contrast between heterodoxy and orthodoxy. Bernard McGinn, *Apocalypticism in the Western Tradition* (Brookfield, VT: Ashgate, 1994), 9:34.

105. De Lubac, *Medieval Exegesis*, 3:417. Joachim "struggled against the deadly desiccation that seemed to menace the Church, both in her pastors and in her doctors" and "reacted against an inclination toward psychologism and subtlety." Ibid., 3:418.

106. De Lubac, *Medieval Exegesis*, 3:418.

107. De Lubac, *La Posterité spirituelle*, 1:17.

108. Bernard McGinn mentions that Thomas's refutation of Joachim is interpreted differently by modern historians. Some, including Ernesto Buonaiuti, "have seen in Thomas' opposition to the abbot a sign of the loss of the historical and eschatological dimensions of Christianity in

The condemnations, at the Fourth Lateran Council (1215) and the Synod of Arles (1263), of Joachim and of heresies spread under his name marginalized a growing Joachimite eschatological tradition. However, elements of Joachim's historical-eschatological and spiritual vision were transmitted, but increasingly stripped of their links to Christian theology. Thus, de Lubac writes, "defeated in the most beautiful of his dreams, Joachim of Fiore, in the manner of Nostradamus, triumphs in his hermeneutics. People borrow his prophetic historicism without wanting to retain anything of his hope."[109] It was neither Joachim's particular prophecies of the end of time nor his exegetical method that was passed on into modernity; rather, it was his prophetic expectation of a new age within history.

The novelty of Joachim's theology lies not in the expectation of the end of time or a definitive fulfillment, or even the expectation of an imminent end. As Bernard McGinn states, "All medieval thinkers were eschatological in the sense that they accepted the Christian understanding of history that looked forward to the definitive event of the return of Christ and the end of time."[110] Even Joachim's expectation of an imminent end of time was quite common. Joachim is unique, McGinn states, in that he envisioned the third age as "the age of the fullness of revelation and the triumph of the *viri spirituales*, the 'spiritual men.'"[111] This would be the age of the Holy Spirit, "the perfection of the divine within history." In sum, Joachim's eschatology was "radical" because the third age would be a future *historical* age of fulfillment. De Lubac agreed with McGinn's assessment that Joachim is not unique in seeing his own age as the

Scholasticism. Thomist scholars, on the other hand, like Y. Congar, M. D. Chenu, and M. Secklar, have risen up in defense of the doctor claiming that he saved the true dimensions of *Heilsgeschichte* in Christianity by attacking the false variety spawned by Joachim." McGinn, *Apocalypticism in the Western Tradition*, 9:40.

109. De Lubac, *Exégèse médiévale*, 4:344.
110. McGinn, *Apocalypticism in the Western Tradition*, 9:34.
111. Ibid.

last, or in reading in the Scriptures of the tribulations and triumphs to come. This was already part of a long Christian apocalyptic tradition.

According to de Lubac, two lines of Christian thought converge in Joachim's theology. The first, is the notion of a "slow divine pedagogy in the advance of revelation."[112] Throughout history, God's numerous interventions have been a gradual pedagogy and a growth of the human race in its knowledge of God. The writings of Irenaeus are a premier example, but this historical schema is ubiquitous in the early church. The second is, in part, inherited from monasticism, which presented the monks as realizing a "new age." De Lubac notes that the Dionysian notion of successive hierarchies, in which one stage of contemplation points to a higher one, is similar.[113] Joachim takes the notion of contemplative ascent through numerous ontological and epistemological stages and lays it on its side, interpreting it historically as a succession of historical periods.

Understood against the backdrop of the traditional division of the ages of salvation history, Joachim's division of history is the key to understanding the innovation of his system.

> People distinguished generally, according to Saint Paul, in the history of salvation, three successive "ages," or three "states," or three "reigns," attributed respectively to three persons of the divine Trinity. These were the reign of the Father, which extended through the eight "days" of creation; then the reign of the Son, which was inaugurated by the promise of the redeemer made to Adam the day after his sin; lastly, the reign of the Spirit, covering all the time of the Church and was supposed to last until the end of this world: "a new and eternal testament."[114]

De Lubac noted that there were many variations on this division of history, which would characterize the Old Testament as the age of the prophetic Spirit (Irenaeus), or would contain a fourfold, sixfold,

112. De Lubac, *Medieval Exegesis*, 3:412.
113. Ibid., 3:313–14.
114. De Lubac, *La Posterité spirituelle*, 1:19.

194

or sevenfold division. But these variations did not disrupt "the fundamental division, which carried the essential doctrine."[115] In Joachim, the traditional historical division was radically altered:

> As many before him, on the other hand, Joachim divided the universal history into three parts, according to the sacred number of the Trinity, recommended by the scriptures. Only, he no longer placed the two caesuras, or the two thresholds, in the same place. For him, the age of the Father is extended until the hour of the redemptive incarnation; at that time was begun the age of the Son, which was the one of the present Church; but soon, already "initiated" or announced in figure, a third age (he said more willingly a third state or a third time) was supposed to succeed it, even on this earth, the last, which would be characterized by the reign of the Holy Spirit. This was a radical transformation.[116]

According the traditional schema, the third age, "the age of the Spirit," is the time of the present church. Perhaps motivated by the scriptural account of Pentecost, the tradition has the Christian living in the final age of history under the reign of the Spirit. Because of continuity between the present church and the future heavenly kingdom, eschatological expectation concerns the fulfillment and completion of the present order. In the case of Joachim, we are now anticipating the age of the Spirit and the bringing about of a new order of salvation history.

The rupture between the second and third age, in effect, governed other aspects of Joachim's thought. First, borrowing a title from the book of Revelation, he contrasted the "carnal gospel" with the "eternal gospel." Both Origen and Joachim prominently used this latter term. For both, the "eternal gospel" was a spiritual interpretation of the Gospel given to us in the New Testament. De Lubac states that for Origen, the "eternal gospel" is the future state of the present gospel, not an addendum. For Joachim, the eternal gospel

115. Ibid., 1:20.
116. Ibid., 1:21–22.

will supersede the carnal gospel and will establish a new spiritual society within time.

Second, but closely related to the first point, Joachim's biblical hermeneutics indicated a radical change in the spiritual interpretation of Scripture. Joachim's exegesis was governed by the "concord" between the three ages of history, the first age corresponding to the Old Testament, the second to the New Testament, and the third remaining in the future. Each age has an interior process of development, so that its initial "germination" is followed by a "fructification" and its "passing away."[117] The ages overlap; when one is just beginning, the previous has reached its midway point of development. Joachim's principle of concord assured a correspondence of external characteristic between past and future events, such that one historical figure is likened to another, one war is likened to another, one liturgical practice is like another. De Lubac insisted that concord was fundamentally different from the principle of spiritual interpretation in Origen and much of the tradition. The guiding principle of spiritual interpretation is "interiorization." Christ recapitulates events of the Old Testament by subsuming them to himself. The "interiorization" of the New Testament is the spiritual recapitulation of the New in the life of the church. De Lubac argued that the relationship between the Old Testament to the New is no longer for Joachim a relationship of letter to spirit, but instead is a relationship of "one letter to another letter."[118] Joachim's exegesis mirrors the correspondence between "two external histories."[119] The persons, figures, and events of the Old Testament have concordances

---

117. De Lubac, *Medieval Exegesis*, 3:334.

118. Ibid., 3:336.

119. Ibid. De Lubac notes that traditional principles of spiritual interpretation held apocalypticism, always present in the church, in check. "It is precisely that doctrine [of the *intelligentia spiritualis*, the "spiritual understanding"], that principle of interpretation, sometimes inexactly described as 'idealist,' which turns out to be missing in Joachim." Ibid., 3:407–08.

within the New Testament, and also prophetically prefigure the persons, figures, and events in the third age, which is presently arriving. Joachim's prophesies concerning the third age of the spirit are essentially allegorizations of the New Testament.

Within the normative tradition of spiritual exegesis, however, the New Testament could not be allegorized. He explains in *Exégèse médiévale*:

> If it [the New Testament] is the spirit of the Old Testament, which is its letter, it is clear that we couldn't possibly treat it newly as a letter from which we could then extract the spirit. From here, we would be launched into a *processus in indefinitum*, a fruit of a wanton imagination, destructive of the Christian reality. To admit an explication of the New Testament analogous to this explication of the Old Testament that itself constitutes, would be to remove all the specific content from the word "spirit." It would be to admit that the New Testament is susceptible, as the Old was, of an ulterior transformation or surpassing. It would be to make its very substance a call to something beyond itself. This would be to make the faith in Christ a relative and provisional faith, to see in Christ and in his Gospel the figures of another Savior to come, which would have in its turn the power to transform and surpass its figures "in spiritualem intellectum" [in the spiritual meaning]—without doubt until that third Savior, who would no longer be the supreme and true savior.
> . . .
>
> To believe that the New Testament in its plain and complete meaning no longer contains an allegorical or spiritual meaning is simply to believe in Jesus Christ, of which his testament is "novissimum"—that is to say last, definitive, eternal, new—in an absolute sense. That is to believe that "with Jesus, eschatology has entered into history." After Jesus Christ, we no longer have anything to understand or to receive. Outside Jesus Christ, we no longer have anything to hope for.[120]

---

120. De Lubac, *Exégèse médiévale*, 4:109–10. The phrase *in spiritualem intellectum* is taken from Anselm of Laon, *In Matt.* 7 (PL 162:1318c). "With Jesus, eschatology has entered into history" is taken from *Revue Biblique* 49 (1940), n.p.

To say that there can be no allegorization of the New Testament indicates that Christ transforms the world and that we await no other savior. It claims that Christ is definitive and last. It claims that any future world transformation, including that at the end of history, is a working out of the one already realized in his person.

The rupture that Joachim advances between the second and third age poses a danger to the definitive action of Christ. By locating the third age within history, Joachim dissociated the events of salvation history and its future fulfillment. According to de Lubac, it is because the "time of the Spirit" intervenes between the gospel and eternity that a rupture occurs between the present church and the eternal church, between the work of Christ and that of the Spirit.[121] The age of the Spirit will supplant the present economy of salvation. By placing the age of the Spirit within history, Joachim calls into question the "definitively fulfilling character of the work accomplished by Jesus Christ."[122] As de Lubac indicates, "Joachim has compromised—without intending to, it seems—the full sufficiency of Jesus Christ."[123] Similarly, the caesura between the second and third age affected how Joachim conceived the relationship between present ecclesial institutions and those of the future age. There is some debate about the extent to which Joachim believed that ecclesial institutions, the papacy, and the sacraments must pass away in history. However, he envisioned a disjunction between the institutions of the present age and those that come, between the Christians of this age, and the "spiritual men" of the subsequent age. Where Origen saw continuity between the present and the eternal, Joachim saw a rupture. According to de Lubac, the rupture between present and

121. De Lubac, *Medieval Exegesis*, 3:418.
122. Ibid., 3:387.
123. Ibid., 3:418.

future introduced by Joachim goes so far as to endanger the centrality of Christ and the church in the coming era of salvation.

For de Lubac, Joachim both contributes to and is the witness of a shift in a Christian understanding of eschatological expectation. The awareness that the "kingdom of God is near" is common in Christianity. In the early church, this awareness is an expectation of the imminent end of the world. Joachim expected a new temporal order, a spiritualization of the gospel that is just beginning to take ecclesial and political shape. The spiritual tradition inspired by Joachim transmitted an anticipation of a new era, already germinating, in which humanity would come of age. This expectation carried well beyond the boundaries of biblical interpretation or theology, and well into modernity. In *La Posterité spirituelle*, de Lubac argued that this spiritual tradition would become entirely horizontal, historical, and secular.

Conclusion: The Unity of *Oeconomia* and *Theologia*

Simply put, history matters. In *Catholicism,* de Lubac claims that Christianity, unlike other religions and political ideologies, unites the mystical movement toward the transcendent with a consciousness of historical development. Retaining a balance between the mystical and the eschatological (or vertical and horizontal) elements of the Christian faith were important to de Lubac from his earliest work, *Catholicism.* In *Catholicism,* he argued that Hellenism—as well as Pythagoreanism, Neoplatonism, the Upanishads, and the Bhūmi of Mahayana Buddhism—envision an ascent of the individual soul through various levels of reality, each level being necessary for the attainment of the next. Christianity, he argued, transformed the Hellenistic images of spiritual ascent: "The old image of the ascent of the individual from sphere to sphere soon gives way to that of a collective progress from one age to another."[124]

The achievement of patristic Christianity was to unite collective progress through history with the transcendence beyond it. By holding together eschatological hope and mystical ascent, Origen's eschatology exemplified the essential characteristics of this Christian synthesis. The subsequent dissociation between the *futura* and *invisibilia* within Christian eschatology, particularly during the twelfth century, engendered two principal eschatological impulses. The first was Pseudo-Dionysian in form; the second was Joachimite. The first engendered a mysticism that viewed the historical figures and realities of the Bible as figures for the unthematizable transcendent. This impulse threatened to disregard the historical character of Christianity and see history as a myth. This second was radically historical insofar as it projected a form of eschatological fulfillment into the historical future.

Both the Joachimite and the Pseudo-Dionysian eschatological impulses ruptured the sacramental-historical economy of salvation by dividing *oeconomia* (God's actions in history) from *theologia* (knowledge of God). Dionysian mysticism threatens to ascend *beyond* the salvation enacted by Christ, leaving it behind for its deeper meaning. It threatens to see the historical or sacramental signs as things to be transcended. The Joachimite apocalyptic threatens to progress *beyond* the present economy of salvation by anticipating an age in history that has transcended signs or figures. According to de Lubac, Dionysian mysticism is a *theologia* divorced from *oeconomia* while Joachimite eschatology is *oeconomia* that is fulfilled within history alone.[125] The Dionysian and Joachimite traditions were not so much opposed theological traditions as mirror opposites. The

124. De Lubac, *Catholicism*, 145. Originally published as Henri de Lubac, *Catholicisme: les aspects sociaux du dogme*, Unam Sanctam 3 (Paris: Éditions du Cerf, 1938).

spiritual consequences for the modern world were significant: on the one hand was a theology that was inattentive to the reality of God's grace already working in history; on the other hand was a secular spiritual tradition that refused anything beyond history.

De Lubac's negotiation between Dionysius and Joachim reflected a continued attempt to negotiate a passage between the Scylla of modern realized eschatologies and the Charybdis of pronounced future eschatology (apocalyptic), especially in their secular forms. Both extremes undermine the realism and efficaciousness of the actions of Christ in the economy of salvation. Following a pattern in Dionysius, some realized eschatologies accentuate the manifestation of God in the present moment at the expense of God's presence in history. As de Lubac noted, Rudolf Bultmann's realized eschatology located revelation in the existential time of encounter and decision. For Bultmann, God acts historically. Yet, because of God's transcendence, the historical account of the Gospels can never adequately represent God's historical presence. The Gospels are mythologized accounts created by the cultural prejudices of first-century Palestinians. The concrete events of salvation become a mere vehicle for *expressing* or *representing* the salvation already present that transcends human expression. Because the divine cannot be represented, "salvation history" is reduced to nonhistorical existential moments of encounter with the divine. By dissociating God's action in history from the expression of that action in public form in the

---

125. De Lubac describes a unity of *oeconomia* and *theologia* within premedieval theology. *Oeconomia* referred to God's actions in history from the very beginnings to the redemptive incarnation. *Theologia* denotes the ultimate purpose or intention guiding the economy and, at the same time, God's fulfillment of this plan. *Anagogia* was, at least, allied with *theologia*. At the same time, *theologia* affirmed God's transcendence even with regard to God's actions in history. See Henri de Lubac, "La Révélation divine: Commentaire du préambule et du chaptre I de La Constitution 'Dei Verbum' du Concile Vatican II," in *Révélation divine—Affrontements mystiques—Athéisme et sens de l'homme*, vol. 4, Oeuvres complètes (Paris: Éditions du Cerf, 2006), 83. Originally published as Henri de Lubac, *La Révélation divine: Église Catholique Romaine, Concile Vatican II [1962–1965]* (Lyon: La Bonté, 1966).

Bible, Bultmann repeats a Dionysian pattern.[126] The result of this intensified realized eschatology is the loss of the reality and efficaciousness of the historical events narrated in the Gospels for bringing about our salvation.

The legacy of Joachimite future-oriented eschatologies is the same, only turned on its side. Joachim leaves behind salvation history via a progression through history. For Joachim, salvation truly takes historical form. However, this salvation is future and yet to come. Historical progress is itself identified with salvation, that is, realization or actualization of the universe. Repeating the Joachimite pattern, Hegel and Marx conflate salvation—though it is conceived in differing ways—with the historical process. In each case, the universe has an intraworldly goal. For de Lubac, the legacy of Joachim was theological as well as philosophical. Some contemporary theologians, de Lubac wrote, were incautious in reuniting protology and eschatology, or creation and fulfillment. Conflating "creation" and "covenant," they envisioned the unfolding of history as the goal, rather than a means to a further goal beyond history. In these cases, prioritizing the historical future results in a fundamental insufficiency or incompleteness in the salvific events of Christ's life, death, and resurrection. Jesus becomes a sign and anticipation of the culmination of history, but no longer its focal point that takes history beyond itself.

In contrast to the legacy of Joachim, de Lubac insisted that history's function is to pass into eternity. In "La Révélation divine," de Lubac explains,

> "The history of salvation is not its own end" (L. Malvez). Its purpose is to introduce us to the heart of the divine life. This is what overly-intrusive notions of the history of salvation seem to forget. God *is revealed* to

---

126. See "La Revelation Divine," 83. Similarly, Kierkegaard's existentialism is a form of making oneself contemporaneous with Christ. But what is most important is the decision.

men as their Savior by intervening into their history, he saves them through history, but that does not evidently signify that the final object of salvation and of revelation would be history.[127]

Again, he states, "The end of the messianic mystery is the mystery of participation in the intimate life of God, which is not history, but eternity."[128] De Lubac explains that history itself is not a "mediator" of salvation. The events of secular history are not "a supplement somehow to supernatural revelation, they are always 'ambiguous' and 'in waiting' [en attente], and they must be clarified for us by the light of the Gospel."[129]

De Lubac's rejection of Dionysian and Joachimite eschatological impulses served to recover an understanding of history that can affirm the reality of God's intervention in time and its effective transformation of time into eternity:

For that is the expression of the Christian condition: tension, essential to these "last times" that we are living in the Church, between two characteristics—mystical and eschatological—of our faith. "Spe enim salvi facti sumus" (For in hope we are saved). The eschatological boundary is not purely in the future—nor will it ever become purely in the past. The words of the Lord . . . have "begun to put an end to figures," and of course they have done so still in images, accommodating themselves to the present state of our understanding, but this was already "so that the truth begins." And on the other hand, as they will never pass away, they will always be in the process of being realized. The words of Moses and those of the prophets needed to be fulfilled, and once fulfilled by Christ, they had only to disappear. But the words of Jesus Christ are and always remain full—without that fullness ever becoming something past. Origen adds: "et in actu impletionis sunt semper, et quotidie implentur, et numquam perimplentur" (and they are always in the act of being fulfilled, and they are being fulfilled every day, and they are never totally fulfilled). The Lord himself, who pronounced them, "is

127. Ibid., 85.
128. Ibid., 86.
129. Ibid., 134.

still there, but as someone who never ceases to arrive": Is this not the meaning of παρουσία (parousia), at once presence and future?[130]

The tension maintained by Origen between the mystical and eschatological is the optic through which de Lubac narrates his subsequent tracing of Dionysian and Joachimite thought.[131] Part 3 argues that de Lubac's theology of the church, the sacraments, Christology, and the supernatural is governed by this eschatological tension.

130. De Lubac, *History and Spirit*, 261–62.
131. This narrative enables us to understand de Lubac's criticism of contemporary theologies of hope and his interventions in contemporary debates over communism and the theology of history, which I will treat below in part 3.

The Eschatological Structure of De Lubac's Thought

According to Jürgen Mettepenningen, the *nouvelle théologie* movement of the 1930s to 1950s was primarily concerned with rediscovering the place of history in theology and the "positive" sources of theology, the "Bible, liturgy, and patristics."[1] The first, rediscovering the place of history in theology, was the search for an alternative to the speculative and philosophical form of theology common to neoscholasticism. Yves Congar's "Déficit de la théologie" (1934) called for the development of a theology attentive to the contemporary human condition. Marie-Dominique Chenu's *Une École de théologie: Le Saulchoir* (1937) drafted an outline for a new curriculum for theological formation structured around the study of history. Sources Chrétiennes, a series of translated patristic texts, was founded in 1942 by Jean Daniélou, Henri de Lubac, and Claude Mondésert. The mere collation and translation of patristic texts was,

---

1. Jürgen Mettepenningen, *Nouvelle Théologie—New Theology: Inheritor of Modernism, Precursor to Vatican II* (New York: T & T Clark, 2010), 10–11.

for the neoscholastics, a not-so-veiled challenge to the scientific form of theology characterized by deduction from first principles. Marie-Michel Labourdette's "La théologie et ses sources" (1946) argued that Sources Chrétiennes represented an erosion of the timeless truths contained in St. Thomas Aquinas and built upon by the neoscholastics. The controversy that erupted around the *nouvelle théologie*, including the disciplining of Henri Bouillard, Yves Congar, Marie-Dominique Chenu, and Henri de Lubac, was driven by the anxiety over eternal truth.[2] In sum, the neoscholastics could not imagine that truth could be attained in the changing ephemerality of history and believed that the historical turn of the *nouvelle théologie* was a turn to relativism. Theology could be saved from relativism only by the universally valid building blocks of truth, a unified structure of knowledge built upon the ontological structure of reality.

Although the *nouvelle théologie* movement, including de Lubac, privileged sacred history over metaphysics or ontology, recent interpreters have sought to uncover the "ontology" that governs de Lubac's theology. John Milbank states that de Lubac "implicitly proposed a new sort of ontology—indeed, in a sense a 'non-ontology'—articulated *between* the discourses of philosophy and theology."[3] Milbank is correct insofar as he states that de Lubac did not develop a philosophical foundation or substructure independent of theological discourse. However, he insists that de Lubac proposes a theology of the supernatural and natural—essentially a Neoplatonic reworking of Aquinas—that functions as a "new ontological

---

2. See Bruce W. Holsinger, *The Premodern Condition: Medievalism and the Making of Theory* (Chicago: University of Chicago Press, 2005), 40; Jürgen Mettepenningen, "Truth, Orthodoxy, and The Nouvelle Théologie: Truth as Issue in a 'Second Modernist Crisis' (1946–1950)," in *Orthodoxy, Liberalism, and Adaptation: Essays on Ways of Worldmaking in Times of Change from Biblical, Historical and Systematic Perspectives*, ed. Bob Becking (Leiden: Brill, 2011), 149–84.

3. John Milbank, *The Suspended Middle: Henri de Lubac and the Debate Concerning the Supernatural* (Grand Rapids, MI: Eerdmans, 2005), 5.

discourse." According to Milbank, the ontology found in *Surnaturel* (1946) is essentially the substructure to de Lubac's other writings. Hans Boersma ascribes to de Lubac a "sacramental ontology," a theological view of the sacramental relationship between nature and the supernatural, in part inspired by Neoplatonism.[4]

While there are common patterns and structures to de Lubac's thinking, his writings do not articulate an ontology apart from the historical economy of salvation. Although de Lubac should not be described as an antimetaphysical thinker, the primary categories of his theology are derived primarily from the history of salvation (*kairos*) rather than formal ontology (*ontos*). The *nouvelle théologie* movement's shift of methodology is reflected in de Lubac's historical and systematic writings. His wide-ranging historical investigations in *History and Spirit*, *Exégèse médiévale*, and *La Postérité spirituelle* recovered an understanding of how theology had developed in relationship to history throughout the Christian tradition. These sources aided de Lubac's formulation of a theology based on the pattern of the historical economy of salvation. De Lubac tended to integrate historical and ontological categories because, for him, the "being" of the world or human nature is intelligible only from the perspective of God's plan for the world, unfolded in the historical process and awaiting eschatological consummation. As a result, the very categories of his thinking are drawn from his theology of the economy of salvation.

Part 3 interprets de Lubac's systematic theology as a theology that unites history and ontology. Chapter 6, "Sacraments of the Eschaton," examines de Lubac's theology of revelation, Christology, and ecclesiology in terms of a common eschatological pattern. Chapter 7, "Eschatology in the Theology of the Supernatural,"

---

4. Hans Boersma, *Nouvelle Théologie and Sacramental Ontology: A Return to Mystery* (New York: Oxford University Press, 2009), 86–115.

interprets de Lubac's intervention into the controversy over the supernatural as a reflection of his basic understanding of history and his eschatological commitments.

6

Sacraments of the Eschaton

Henri de Lubac's writings covered a vast range of theological topics over a career of almost seventy years. As a result, the unity of his work is difficult to characterize and its significance is hard to express. Hans Boersma identifies the unity of de Lubac's writings with what he calls a "sacramental mindset" or "sacramental ontology," a vision of the terrestrial world as a participation in the heavenly. *Sacrament* constitutes the core of de Lubac's various theological engagements. However, sacrament should be understood primarily within an historical-eschatological framework rather than primarily an ontological framework. Temporal realities are sacraments of the eternal because God has entered into time, transforming the temporal into an effective sign of the eternal.

Origen's threefold division of history into Old Testament, New Testament, and eternal gospel frames de Lubac's synthesis. For Origen, the Old Testament represents the time of preparation whose realities are wholly symbolic, prefiguring a reality to come. The New Testament fulfills and transfigures the Old Testament because in

Christ, the eternal has entered into time. This is a time of fulfillment that awaits consummation. The time of mere figure has passed because Christ has come and salvation is here. However, the Christian still lives in a time that is symbolic and that prefigures the final eschatological reality. It is a time of patient waiting, a time between possession and anticipation. It is the end time. *Sacrament* describes the experience of the Christian in the end time, in possession proleptically of the fullness of salvation in Christ yet still awaiting the consummation of God's plan. The possession of salvation is real, though it is in sacrament. In this sense, the sacramental pattern of de Lubac's thought permeates his body of writings, organically structuring his theology of revelation, Christology and ecclesiology.

The Temporal Interim and the Terrain of Mystery

The relationship between the temporal activity of Jesus Christ and the eschatological consummation is the key to understanding *sacrament.* For de Lubac, Christ initiates the "end times." Through his words and actions he transforms the temporal, making it an effective sign of the eschaton. The sacraments exist in the "interim" between the first coming and the second coming of Christ, the between times that characterize our own historical existence. Christian experience is marked by living in both the "end time" and the "preparatory" time, a time of expectation of the eschaton.

Twentieth-century biblical studies tended to interpret Jesus' own message in various ways. On the one hand, Johannes Weiss (1863–1914) and Albert Schweitzer (1875–1965) emphasized that Jesus announced the Day of the Lord, a future era in which God's promises would be fulfilled. They interpreted Jesus and the early church through the lens of Jewish apocalypticism. Jesus and the early church expected an imminent end of history, marked by the coming of the Lord. On the other hand, C. H. Dodd emphasized another prominent New Testament theme, the presence of the kingdom of God: "the kingdom of God is among you" (Luke 17:21 NRSV). Dodd tempered the imminent expectation of the end with the notion that the end is already here, realized in the ministry of Christ himself. Oscar Cullman offered a kind of mediating position between an exclusively future or exclusively realized eschatology. His *Christ and Time* argued that early Christian writings mark the tension between present and future rather than between the immanent and transcendent.[1] In Cullmann's understanding, primitive Christians looked backward to the life of Christ as the definitive event in which good triumphs over evil. At the same time, they preach that the kingdom is yet to come.[2]

Agreeing with Cullmann's characterization of Christian temporal experience, de Lubac believed that the Christ event initiated the "end time." De Lubac writes, "Christ has inaugurated the eschatological era. His work fructifies, but not by appeal to another. The 'last times' have arrived; salvation is accomplished in Him, and for each generation 'the Church makes the end of history already present to time.'"[3] Jesus claims to fulfill all previous prophesies and bring an end to the era of waiting for the Messiah. In the context of

1. Oscar Cullmann, *Christ and Time: The Primitive Christian Conception of Time*, rev. ed. (Westminster Press, 1964). Originally published as Oscar Cullmann, *Christus und die Zeit: Die urchristliche Zeit- und Geschichtsauffassung* (Zollikon-Zurich: Evangelischer Verlag, 1948).
2. Ibid., 84.
3. Henri de Lubac, "La Révélation divine: Commentaire du préambule et du chapitre I de La Constitution 'Dei Verbum' du Concile Vatican II," in *Révélation divine—Affrontements mystiques—Athéisme et sens de l'homme*, vol. 4, Oeuvres complètes (Paris: Éditions du Cerf, 2006), 93. Originally published as Henri de Lubac, *La Révélation divine: Église Catholique Romaine, Concile Vatican II [1962–1965]* (Lyon: La Bonté, 1966). The book was translated into English with the title *The Sources of Revelation* (New York: Herder and Herder, 1968). Quoting Jean Mouroux, *Le Mystère du temps: approche théologique,* Theologie 50 (Paris: Aubier, 1962), n.p.

Jewish prophesy, the coming of the Messiah marked the coming of the end. The coming of the Messiah was to bring the prophetic age to a close [OT → Christ-Eschaton]. For the earliest Christians, messianic time meant living now in the last days in expectation of the imminent end and Christ's return. However, the drawing out of the eschaton changed things. The end of history was not imminent. Soon, Christians no longer awaited an imminent end, but rather an immanence of God in the present. The coming of the Messiah opened a temporal hiatus between the fulfillment of the Old Testament and its ultimate consummation [OT → Christ-Eschaton]. Christian life exists in a hiatus or interim between the two comings, where God prepares us for the ultimate consummation of God's plan and where we proleptically experience this consummation.

According to de Lubac, two perspectives are conjoined in a Christian understanding of time. The time narrated in the New Testament—the same time in which we live—is both the end time and a preparatory time. The kingdom of God is already inaugurated and made present through the work of Christ; however, we live in a period of preparation that is still symbolic and anticipatory of its final reality:

> The same ambiguity of evangelical time or the mystery of salvation is envisaged . . . "in the plane of our historical experience. There is a fragment of human time too difficult to characterize exactly: does it appear as a preparatory time or the "end time"?" On the one hand, it is anterior to the "consummation of time" that constitutes the event of the Cross-Resurrection-Ascension (Heb. 9:11–12). But on the other hand, in the incarnate Word, heaven and eternity are already made present on earth and in time; the Kingdom is inaugurated in the person of Jesus (*autobasileia*, following the formula of Origen . . .).[4]

4. De Lubac, "La Révélation divine," 120n5.

The New Testament exists as present fulfillment *and* as a sign of what is to come. De Lubac calls this christic time or evangelical time the "Interim."[5] "Insofar as the great 'Passage' is not crossed, history and allegory are not yet absorbed into each other. They are not yet fully unified in the 'Mystery.'"[6] On the one hand, the eschaton is made present through Jesus. On the other, Jesus begins a temporal process of transcending time, a journey opening up for the church. Even if Christ has already come and already brought fulfillment in himself, this fulfillment awaits an ecclesiological completion of which present realities constitute the sacraments.

The time of the Interim, characterized by a tension between realized and future, already and not yet, end and preparation, marks out the terrain of the sacraments, which is also the terrain of mystery. This "terrain" makes sacramentality possible. In this vein, de Lubac writes that sacramental reality "is essentially related to our present condition, which is not one embodied in the epoch of figures pure and simple [that is the Old Testament], nor yet one which includes the full possession of the 'truth.'"[7] For de Lubac, sacramentality is possible only in our present temporal condition, living after the fulfillment in Christ and in anticipation of the eschatological consummation.

The Structure of Sacramentality in de Lubac

For de Lubac, the Interim—the time between the time of figures and that of complete truth—forms the terrain of sacramentality.[8]

---

5. Henri de Lubac, *Medieval Exegesis: The Four Senses of Scripture*, trans. E. M. Macierowski, vol. 2 (Grand Rapids, MI: Eerdmans, 2000), 183. Originally published as *Exégèse médiévale, 2: Les quatre sense de l'Écriture* (Paris: Éditions Montaigne, 1959).

6. De Lubac, "La Révélation divine," 2006, 120.

7. Henri de Lubac, *The Splendor of the Church*, trans. Michael Mason (San Francisco: Ignatius Press, 1986), 204. Originally published as Henri de Lubac, *Méditation sur l'Église*, Foi vivante 60 (Paris: Aubier-Montaigne, 1953).

The sacrament is a figure of the truth to come, making it temporal and teleological. The truth signified is the purpose or end of the sacramental sign. It is its future state. The sign's inner "intention"—its finality—overflows its bare materiality, making it participate in the mystery signified while, at the same time, not yet bringing the signified to complete presence. The mystery signified exercises a hidden power over the sign that makes the sign what it is. The key terms of de Lubac's sacramental lexicon—*sacrament* and *mystery*—are embedded in the tension between realized and future eschatology, between *making present* and *anticipating* the future. Two of the most elusive and dynamic terms in de Lubac's theological lexicon—sacrament and mystery—are terms he employs frequently and are the most elemental to his theological vision. While these terms possess multivalent meanings, their meanings should nonetheless be understood as pointing to something common. De Lubac's terminology should be read synoptically.

One of the complications is that, as de Lubac notes, *sacrament* and *mystery* were used synonymously in the early church. The word *sacrament* is not found in the New Testament. *Sacramentum* became a Latin translation for the Greek μυστήριον (*mysterion*), which is prominent in the New Testament, especially in Paul's letters. Paul's Epistle to the Colossians refers to the word of God as the "mystery

---

8. While de Lubac did not use the adjective *sacramental* or noun *sacramentality*, he spoke generally of the attributes of sacraments. He did not explicitly examine sacramentality apart from particular sacramental loci, that is, Christ, the church, and the seven sacraments. To speak of a sacramental structure in de Lubac's work is, therefore, an abstraction from particular cases. *Sacramental* or *sacramentality* can describe the underlying intelligibility of the seven sacraments. Paul McPartlan explains that in the early twentieth century, Catholic treatment of sacraments followed, more or less, a polemical anti-Protestant defense of the seven sacraments. The apologetic of the number seven was deficient in showing the underlying intelligibility of the sacraments, or getting "behind the number seven." The theology of de Lubac and Karl Rahner, among others, influenced a shift in Catholic perspective toward grounding the intelligibility of the sacraments in Christ and in the church. Paul McPartlan, "Catholic Perspectives on Sacramentality," *Studia Liturgica* 38, no. 2 (January 2008): 219.

[*mysterion*] that has been hidden throughout the ages and generations but has now been revealed to his saints" (Col. 1:26 NRSV). Similarly, Paul writes, "With all wisdom and insight he has made known to us the mystery [*mysterion*] of his will, according to his good pleasure that he set forth in Christ, as a plan for the fullness of time, to gather up all things in him, things in heaven and things on earth" (Eph. 1:8–10 NRSV).[9] In its translation into Latin, the Greek *mysterion* received a Latin form, *mysterium*. De Lubac notes that *sacrament* and *mystery* are often synonymous in the fathers, both referring to something sacred.

These synonyms began to be distinguished with Augustine, for whom sacrament was a "sign" of the mystery hidden within it.[10] The sacrament is the visible sign of the mysterious secret. "The *sacramentum* would therefore play the role of container, or envelope, with regard to the *mysterium* hidden within it."[11] The two are opposed while united. De Lubac concedes that in the patristic tradition, the meanings of both *sacramentum* and *mysterium* floated between the two poles of *sign* and *secret*, depending on the author. Yet the Augustinian definitions of sacrament and mystery were more or less retained until the twelfth century.[12]

In de Lubac's exposition, *mysterium* has a double meaning. On the one hand, it possesses a substantive, inert meaning as a "secret." It is the mysterious reality or the secret thing signified by the sacramental sign. On the other hand, it possesses a relational and active meaning.

---

9. See ibid., 223.
10. "They always appear—beyond the permanent allusion to something sacred ('*divine and mystical*', '*sacred and mystical*') and all the resonances which such an allusion comprises—with the two fundamental senses, united in variable proportions, of sign and secret—'*arcanum*'—which are still the two senses attached respectively to our two words sacrament and mystery." Henri de Lubac, *Corpus Mysticum: The Eucharist and the Church in the Middle Ages*, trans. Gemma Simmonds, CJ, Faith in Reason (Notre Dame, IN: University of Notre Dame Press, 2007), 47. Originally published as Henri de Lubac, *Corpus mysticum: l'eucharistie et l'Église au Moyen âge. Étude historique*, Théologie 3 (Paris: Aubier, 1944).
11. Ibid.
12. Ibid., 45.

Mystery indicates not the sign or the signified separately, but the relationship between the sign and signified: between *tupos* (figure, type) and *aletheia* (truth).[13] Mystery indicates the *passage* from figure to truth. In this sense, "mystery of salvation" or "sacrament of salvation" conveys a *movement* from figure to truth and their unity at the same time. Therefore, the "Mystery" is not only the "secret thing" revealed, but an action joining the sign and secret signified, the type and truth.[14] In *Corpus Mysticum*, he explains that the mystery is "the *secret power* [*virtus occulta*] by which the thing [is in] the sign and through which the sign participates, here again in widely differing ways, in the higher efficacy of the thing."[15] In its active meaning, the mystery is the active power drawing the visible sacrament into participation with what it signifies. In sum, the mystery can be the whole process by which the sacrament signifies and participates in its sacred goal. According to this Augustinian distinction-in-relation of mystery and sacrament, the sacramental reality is requisite for discovering the mystery. It is through the power of the mystery operating *in* the sacrament that the sacrament possesses its characteristic as a sign. The mystery is present in its visible aspect, the sacrament.

The relationship between sacrament and mystery helps to illumine de Lubac's characterization of sacramental reality in *Splendor of the Church*:

That which is sacramental—"the sensible bond between two worlds"—has a twofold characteristic. Since, on the one hand, it is the

13. Ibid., 53.
14. Ibid., 51–52. De Lubac invokes the "communication of idioms" or exchange of attributes to describe the mutual participation of sign and signified. The "communication of idioms" is especially pertinent when speaking of the humanity of Christ and the divinity, where it literally applies. He notes that depending upon the kind of sacrament about which we are speaking, this *communicatio idiomatum* will be different.
15. Ibid., 52.

sign of something else, it must be passed through, and this not in part but wholly. It is not something intermediate, but something mediatory; it does not isolate, one from another, the two terms which it is meant to link. It does not put a distance between them. It is essentially related to our present condition, which is not one embodied in the epoch of figures pure and simple, nor yet one which includes the full possession of the "truth."[16]

Sacraments possess a twofold characteristic: first, a sacrament is a sign that must be passed through entirely to reach the mystery; second, the sacrament cannot be discarded at will. The sign, the outward visible reality, is not the truth of the sacrament itself. Thus, to stop at the sign is to be arrested by an idol. At the same time, the sacrament is indispensable and necessary to reach the reality of which the sacrament is a sign. De Lubac cryptically explained, "We never come to the end of passing through this translucent medium, which we must, nevertheless, always pass through and that completely. It is always through it that we reach what it signifies; it can never be superseded, and its bounds cannot be broken."[17] The sacrament is the singular way to approach the mystery and its necessity is never compromised. Yet we must envision the sacrament as a passage rather than the end, or rather as an unending passage.

Sacrament : Mystery :: History : Eschatology

For de Lubac, the unity and duality of *sacramentum* and *mysterium* is structurally the same as the unity and duality of history and eschatology. It is unsurprising to find the same structure involving this second pair because sacraments are always visible and historical events, realities, and rituals that signify a mysterious eschatological reality. The important point is that, for de Lubac, the sacrament is the

16. De Lubac, *The Splendor of the Church*, 203–4.
17. Ibid., 204.

visible reality that makes the mystery proleptically present and that mediates the eschatological consummation.

As mentioned above, the term *mysterium* "floats" between sign and secret. It similarly "floats" between historical reality and the eschatological consummation. According to de Lubac, *mystery* suggests God's plan for salvation or God's intention: "The mystery is somehow linked to God's design for man, whether as marking the limit of or the means of realizing this destiny."[18] In other words, it refers to the whole plan of salvation, but its meaning can be focused on either the means by which this design is accomplished or the final reality accomplished. If restricted to the means, the mystery refers to its visible, historical, and tangible form. The mystery, de Lubac states, "concerns us, touches us, acts in us, reveals us to ourselves. To this end, it must have a tangible aspect, the incarnated Word of God, expression of the Inexpressible, the efficacious sign to realize the plan of salvation."[19] Mystery can encompass the "end" or intended reality intended by God, but also the "means" of salvation by emphasizing the inner meaning or reality of that means. Sign or sacrament suggest the "means"—emphasizing its visible aspect—but always in union with the "end."

For de Lubac, the eschatological is not merely the future, but the depth dimension of the present. Mystery is not an inert intention of God, but an active power of eternity reaching into history to bring it into eternity at the end. The mystery is the reality that actively draws the *signum* to be a participation in itself. More precisely, the mystery, as the final reality intended by God, makes its own visible aspect, the sacrament, a means to the final consummation, imbuing

18. Henri de Lubac, *The Church: Paradox and Mystery*, trans. James R. Dunne (Staten Island, NY: Alba House, 1969), 13. Originally published as Henri de Lubac, *Paradoxe et mystère de l'Église* (Paris: Aubier-Montaigne, 1967).
19. *The Church: Paradox and Mystery*, 14.

the sacrament with mystery.[20] In *The Splendor of the Church*, de Lubac draws the precise parallel between mystery and eschatology:

> Like the whole of the Christian reality, of which she is the summing-up, the *Ecclesia Sanctorum* was in [the eyes of early Christians], when taken in the full sense of the words, something essentially eschatological. They were, of course, very far from regarding her as something which was merely "to come." After all, the eschatological is not something simply absent from the present, any more than what is transcendent is exterior to everyday reality; on the contrary, it is the foundation of the present and the term of its movement—it is the marrow of the present, as it were, and exercises over it a hidden power.[21]

De Lubac employs the same language of "exercising a hidden power" here to describe how the eschatological enters into the present as he does to describe the mystery's entering into the sacrament in *Corpus Mysticum*.[22]

If we can summarize the perspective which illumines de Lubac's understanding of sacramentality, it would be in a twofold eschatological perspective:

1. *From visible sign to signified*: The inner "intention" of the sign overflows its bare materiality, allowing it to participate in the higher order of the signified. The visible and historical sacrament

---

20. It is in this sense that de Lubac describes the *sacramenti molitio* from Augustine. Augustine interprets everything in light of a great idea "'of which each is a particular expression.' The remark can be understood for the ensemble of ancient commentators, to refer to the whole of Scripture. The Model to come disposes and orders among them all its past imitations. These are organized in a homogeneous series, which develop throughout history. It is the elaboration of a single great 'sacrament'—'sacramenti molitio'—and by it we have understood at the same time the thing signified and its sign. It is 'the order of prefiguration, begun with Adam.' It is a 'universal prophecy' coextensive with duration until Christ. Prophecy in act, a vast and unique word." Henri de Lubac, *Exégèse médiévale: Les quatre sens de l'écriture*, vol. 4, Théologie 59 (Aubier: Éditions Montaigne, 1964), 81.
21. De Lubac, *The Splendor of the Church*, 117.
22. Elsewhere, de Lubac emphasizes that the eschatological ensures the meaningfulness of history. See de Lubac, "La Révélation divine," 86.

has a finality that makes it tend toward what it anticipates and signifies.

2. *From the signified to the visible sign*: The signified exercises a hidden power over the sign, making it what it is. The eschatological signified is present in the sign, making the sign efficacious as a sign. The sacrament possesses the quality of signifying and bringing about because the eschatological enters into it, exercising a power over it.

De Lubac's theology of revelation, Christology, and ecclesiology follow a structural pattern whereby the visible sacrament possesses a finality for its eschatological term, while the eschatological is present proleptically within the sacrament, its power effecting the finality of the sacrament. Although de Lubac is unsystematic in his presentation, employing various terminology and models in his work, this eschatological structure operates similarly within the particular sacramental loci.

The Eschatological Structure of Revelation and Salvation

Despite his extensive research into the history of biblical interpretation, de Lubac's writings did not contain a general theory of revelation. His writings on revelation derive from his involvement in the Preparatory Theological Commission leading to the Second Vatican Council (1962–1965).[23] A subcommission of the Preparatory

23. In 1960, de Lubac happened to read in a periodical that he had been appointed, along with the Dominican Yves Congar, as a theological consultor to the Preparatory Theological Commission for the Second Vatican Council. Henri de Lubac, *At the Service of the Church: Henri de Lubac Reflects on the Circumstances That Occasioned His Writings* (San Francisco: Communio Books, 1993), 116. Originally published as Henri de Lubac, *Mémoire sur l'occasion de mes écrits*, Chrétiens aujourd'hui 1 (Namur, Belgium: Culture et Vérité, 1989). While on the Commission as a theological expert, he relates, he "in particular gave the impression of being a hostage, sometimes even of being a defendant." *At the Service of the Church*, 117. De Lubac's participation as a consultant to the Preparatory Commission led to his appointment as a *peritus*

Theological Commission, called "De fontibus Revelationis," had produced a preparatory schema entitled *De fontibus Revelationis* (On the sources of revelation). The working schema reflected classical positions taken as a development of the Council of Trent (1545–1563) and in anti-Protestant literature. For Trent, the "source" of revelation is the gospel. However, the subsequent scholastic tradition treated Scripture and tradition as independent supernatural sources of knowledge of God in order to combat the Protestant principle of *sola scriptura*. Tradition, it was claimed, constituted the unwritten revelation handed down from the apostles, which supplemented Scripture, the written revelation. The Vatican I document, *Dei Filius* (1870), spoke of revelation as the supernatural knowledge of God, but did not identify Scripture and tradition as distinct sources. In the preparatory document, *De fontibus Revelationis*, Scripture and tradition are described as distinct "sources."[24] The document sought to "resolve" open debates over the Catholic understanding of revelation, Scripture, and tradition in favor of a neoscholastic and anti-Modernist school. Evidently, de Lubac had very little sway as a theological expert on the Preparatory Commission.

During conciliar debate over *De fontibus Revelationis*, Edward Schillebeeckx and Karl Rahner provided widely distributed and influential criticisms of the schema. *De fontibus Revelationis* became so controversial that it took an act of John XXIII to push the discussion over the document to the side. The final document, ratified in 1965, bears little resemblance to its predecessor and testifies to a radical shift in perspective of thinking about revelation. *Dei Verbum*, Vatican

---

(expert theological adviser) to the Council itself, which allowed him to attend meetings of the Theological Commission.

24. Giuseppe Ruggieri, "The First Doctrinal Clash," in *History of Vatican II: The Formation of the Council's Identity: First Period and Intersession, October 1962—September 1963*, ed. Giuseppe Alberigo and Joseph A. Komonchak, vol. 2 (Maryknoll, NY: Orbis Books, 1997), 135.

II's Dogmatic Constitution on Divine Revelation, prioritized the historicity of revelation and Christ as the center of revelation. It placed an emphasis on revelation as a personal encounter with God, not simply knowledge about God. Moreover, revelation is fully present in Christ, not in the biblical text.

It is unclear what role de Lubac himself played in resisting the draft schema. While he certainly influenced the formation of a new document, called the 1964 Schema, he never revealed the precise nature of his role in the formation of the document. De Lubac's 1966 commentary on *Dei Verbum*, "La Révélation divine," is not only a commentary from a participant at Vatican II. It is also an attempt at influencing the reception of the document in the church. His commentary produces a radically historical understanding of revelation as the sensible or visible sacrament through which salvation occurs. According to de Lubac, salvation is already taking place through the revelation of the incarnate Word, but it is nonetheless only complete in a future consummation.

De Lubac's understanding of revelation can be summarized by the following phrase: *Dando revelat, et revelando dat* (In giving God reveals, and in revealing God gives). Revelation is intimately bound to the gift of salvation. De Lubac explained that the Council's intent is not to explicate the "doctrine on revelation," but rather the "proclamation of salvation itself," that is "revelation itself that is transmitted to us."[25] The intimate union between the proclamation, that is revelation, and the salvation that it proclaims is made particularly clear in the prologue of *Dei Verbum*, which quotes 1 John 1:2–3: "We proclaim to you the eternal life which was with the Father and was made manifest to us—that which we have seen and heard we proclaim also to you, so that you may have fellowship

---

25. De Lubac, "La Révélation divine," 58.

with us; and our fellowship is with the Father and with his Son Jesus Christ." In 1 John, the proclamation is of the "eternal life" who was with the Father and made manifest. The proclamation effects ecclesial fellowship and the fellowship with the Father and the Son, which constitute "eternal life."

Following John, the entire first chapter of *Dei Verbum* attests to the "indissoluble union of revelation and salvation."[26] De Lubac speaks of this union between revelation and salvation in two ways: first, revelation "contains" salvation; second, salvation is the object or end of revelation. First, revelation communicates the very reality of salvation: "The announcement of salvation contains the salvation announced. The object revealed does not consist in notions, by themselves without vital efficacy, which would just barely have as their goal to make explicit a Christianity existing already in an 'implicit' state, or to name finally a reality until then 'anonymous.'"[27] De Lubac's mention of an "anonymous salvation" sounds like a criticism of Karl Rahner's notion of "anonymous Christianity."[28] However, it is more likely that de Lubac was criticizing an "intellectualist" notion of revelation as the communication of a series of abstract truths. Catholic intellectualist theories of revelation tended to oppose "supernatural revelation"—those truths beyond the capacity

---

26. Ibid., 59.
27. Ibid.
28. It is possible that he had Rahner in mind, since Rahner had promulgated his thesis on "anonymous Christianity" prior to de Lubac's "La Révélation divine." The idea of anonymous Christianity appeared in "Grundzüge einer katholisch-dogmatischen Interpretation der nichtchristlichen Religionen" in *Pluralismus, Toleranz und Christenheit,* Veröffentlichungen der Abendländischen Akademie (Nürnberg, 1961), 55–74. This essay was published as "Das Christentum und die nichtchristlichen Religionen" in *Schriften zur Theologie 5: Neuere Schriften,* (Einsiedeln: Benziger, 1962), 136–58. The same essay was translated into English and published as "Christianity and the Non-Christian Religions" in *Theological Investigations,* vol. 5: *Later Writings* (London: Darton, Longman and Todd, 1966), 115–34. Although de Lubac did not read German and Rahner's *Schriften zur Theologie* was not published in French, de Lubac may have had access to the English translation or have otherwise been exposed to Rahner's terminology. However, it is not clear that Rahner is the target of de Lubac's criticism.

of the mind to attain by its own power— to "natural knowledge" or "natural revelation"—those truths about God that can be known by human reason alone. As a matter of course, intellectualist theories deemphasized the historical nature of revelation because history could not easily be categorized into "natural" or "supernatural." If revelation consists primarily of "concepts," those concepts have no power to save. Their only function would be to bring us to explicit consciousness of the salvation already available implicitly or anonymously. De Lubac, therefore, implies that the intellectualist view of revelation espoused by some neoscholastics supports a view of salvation attributed to the Modernists and condemned by the neoscholastics themselves.[29]

In contrast, de Lubac's theology of revelation is radically historical. His "La Révélation divine" emphasizes that revelation consists in *events* that can be seen, heard, and touched, namely the deeds and words of God. Because they are God's actions in history, these deeds and words "contain" the salvation that they announce. The second paragraph of *Dei Verbum* reads,

> It pleased God, in his goodness and wisdom, to reveal himself and to make known the mystery of his will [*Seipsum revelare et notum facere sacramentum voluntatis suae*] (cf. Eph. 1:9). His will was that men should have access to the Father, through Christ, the Word made flesh, in the Holy Spirit, and thus become sharers in the divine nature (cf. Eph. 2:18; 2 Pet. 1:4). By this revelation, then, the invisible God (cf. Col. 1:15; 1 Tim. 1:17), from the fullness of his love, addresses men as his friends (cf. Ex. 33:11; Jn. 15:14–15), and moves among them (cf. Bar 3:38), in order to invite and receive them into his own company. This economy of Revelation is realized by deeds and words [*gestis verbisque*], which are intrinsically bound up with each other. As a result, the works performed by God in the history of salvation, show forth and bear out the doctrine and realities [*doctrinam et res*] signified by the words; the words, for their part, proclaim the works, and bring to light the mystery they contain.

29. I am indebted to Rev. Joseph Mueller, SJ, for this observation.

The most intimate truth which this revelation gives us about God and the salvation of man shines forth in Christ, who is himself both the mediator and the sum total of Revelation.[30]

Instead of speaking of Scripture and tradition as "two sources" of revelation, *Dei Verbum* speaks of the "economy" of revelation manifested through the words and deeds of God. Moreover, this manifestation is centered in Christ.

De Lubac emphasizes the "sacramental" relationship between the external actions and words within the historical economy and the salvation that they bring about. *Dei Verbum* overtly employs the language of the sacraments to confirm the efficacious character of God's interventions in history. The revelation communicated in "deeds and words" (*gestis verbisque*) unveil the "teaching and things the words signify" (*doctrinam et res*). According to de Lubac, *res* was intended to evoke the *res sacramenti*, that which the sacrament signifies and brings about.[31] The *res* is not the external action or utterance but the profound reality united to the external action or utterance:

> The "*res*" of which it [*Dei Verbum*] speaks overflows the "*opera*" or "*gesta*" taken in their sole visibility . . . because the "*res verbis significatae*" that it mentions designates a reality more complex and more profound than the "*gesta*": they [things that the words signify] comprehend at the same time the "*consilium Dei*" [the plan of God] and, in their interior efficacy, the "*facta salutaria*."[32]

According to de Lubac, the *res verbis significatae* of *Dei Verbum* comprehend both God's saving actions in history (*facta salutaria*) and the plan or purpose of God (*consilium Dei*). The historical, visible

---

30. "Dei Verbum," in *Vatican Council II: The Conciliar and Postconciliar Documents*, ed. Austin Flannery, OP, rev. ed. vol. 1 (Northport, NY: Costello, 1996), 750.
31. De Lubac, "La Révélation divine," 70n5.
32. Ibid., 70–71.

events of salvation (*facta salutaria*) are no mere exterior or phenomenal gesture but are sacramentally united to their salvific purpose and goal (*consilium Dei*).

De Lubac understands the saving deeds (*facta salutaria*) and the plan of God (*consilium Dei*) in sacramental terms:

Sacramentum	Res Tantum
Deeds (*facta salutaria*)	Plan of God (*consilium Dei*)
Revelation (God's self-manifestation)	Salvation (God's self-gift)

In the language of the sacraments, through the visible sacramental sign (*sacramentum*), God effects the reality signified by the sign (*res tantum*). In de Lubac's commentary, the exterior or visible events of salvation are efficacious in bringing about the salvific plan of God. This structure is at the heart of a Christian sacramentalism: external rites and realities are both signs of and mediations of a reality that surpasses them.

De Lubac's interpretation of *Dei Verbum* not only stresses the historicity of revelation but also the eschatological nature of salvation. The object or end of divine revelation is "eternal life," that is, salvation. Eternal life is, de Lubac explains, "the last end of revelation" (*la finalité dernière*), that is, the participation in the communion with the Father and the Son.[33] The historical manifestation of God and participation in communion with God can be distinguished without being dissociated. De Lubac explains, "It is impossible to dissociate, even in thought . . . the self-manifestation of God and the self-gift of God; in other words, revelation and its end."[34] For de Lubac, the

---

33. Since God calls a whole people, "communion with God and communion among the faithful are then the two aspects of the same reality: the participation in eternal life." Ibid., 56.
34. Ibid., 57.

historical revelatory manifestation is united to the salvific gift of God, yet the two are distinguished teleologically, as means and end. In sum, in de Lubac's understanding of revelation, revelation is always visible, sensible, and historical. Salvation, which de Lubac expresses as the "the last end" (*la finalité dernière*), is the eschatological goal of history, united to that history, and brought about by it.

Christ, the Sacrament of Salvation

Catholicism, de Lubac's earliest book, vibrantly portrays the sacramental dimensions of temporality in a Christian perspective:

> Of necessity we must establish a foothold in time if we are to rise to eternity; we must use time. The Word of God submitted himself to this essential law: he came to deliver us from time, but by means of time—*propter te factus est temporalis, ut tu fias aeternus* [he was made subject to time on account of you, in order that you might be made eternal]. That is the law of the incarnation, and it must undergo no docetist mitigation.[35]

The rise to eternity is a transition from time. However, this transition from time to eternity takes place only by means of time, the sacrament of eternity. The key to de Lubac's sacramental understanding of temporality is Christ, who stands at the center of the sacramental economy. Because of the unity of humanity and divinity in Christ, his *human actions* manifest the fullness of revelation and bring about the fullness of salvation.[36] In de Lubac's christocentric theology of revelation, the eternal is made temporal in the historical self-emptying (*kenosis*) of the incarnate Word. Through

---

35. Henri de Lubac, *Catholicism: Christ and the Common Destiny of Man*, trans. Lancelot C. Sheppard and Sister Elizabeth Englund, OCD (San Francisco: Ignatius Press, 1988), 144. Quoting Augustine, *In I Joan.*, tr. 2, n. 10.

36. *Dei Verbum*, he argues, expresses the "concrete unity. . . of revelation and salvation, and, at the same time, the personal unity of the twofold object of revelation: the end to which it tends and the means willed to realize this end." De Lubac, "La Révélation divine,", 63.

this self-emptying, the Word becomes the means by which humanity joins in this self-emptying.

For de Lubac, the humanity of Christ is the sacrament of the divine presence. De Lubac emphasizes that Jesus is revelation in person: the incarnate Word is the "absolute Presence of God among us;"[37] revelation is identical to the "God-man."[38] But, it is precisely through the humanity of Jesus that we are placed in the presence of God:

> The presence of Jesus Christ, illuminating and salvific at the same time, is the presence of the eternal Logos (Word), the only Word of God, the only Son of the Father. But it is at the same time a human presence, of a true man, a "man sent to humanity" in order to say from a human mouth "the words of God": *et habitu inventus ut homo.*[39]

In the mystery of the incarnation, God speaks to human beings and is present to them through a human presence. The visible *humanity* of Jesus does not merely extrinsically signal the divine presence but mediates it: "The one who sees Jesus sees the Father—but one sees him through the humanity of Jesus."[40] De Lubac refuses a monophysite theology of revelation that minimizes the humanity of the Son as the precise site of the revelatory and salvific action of God. The "hypostatic union" between the human and divine natures is not merely a static ontological reality. Instead, it is Christ's concrete actions as both human and divine.[41] The humanity of Jesus functions

37. Ibid., 116. Quoting Karl Rahner, "Considérations generales sur la christologie," in *Probléms actuels de christologie* (Paris: Desclée de Brouwer, 1965), 30.
38. "God speaks . . . to reveal himself and make us know the mystery of his will, 'hidden since the beginning,'" and who is "Christ among us, hope of the glory." De Lubac, "La Révélation divine," 61, quoting from Eph. 1:9 and Col. 1:26.
39. De Lubac, "La Révélation divine," 115.
40. Ibid., 116.
41. "Any representation of the Incarnation that sees in the humanity of Jesus only the vestment that God uses in order to signal his speaking presence, is a heresy. And it is properly *this heresy*, rejected by the Church in its fight against Docetism, Apollinarianism, Monophysitism and Monothelitism, that is today considered as mythic, and refused as mythology, but not the authentic orthodox Christology." Ibid.

as a sign of his divinity and a means of bringing about the divine presence.

Moreover, de Lubac suggests that the humanity of Jesus is a sacrament because it is the site of the self-emptying (*kenosis*) of God in the world:

> "Already the divine Kenosis was announced in the Word of the ancient Law. In Jesus Christ, the temporality of the human experience and the eternal truth are joined together." It is in "emptying himself" and in taking "the form of a slave" that he is made present to us in history to reveal to us "what the eye has not seen, nor the ear heard, what is come to the heart of man, all that God has prepared for those who love him."[42]

Divine revelation radiates through Jesus because in him human experience and eternal truth are united together. For de Lubac, the divine self-emptying unites the eternal truth and human experience. In many Christian accounts of salvation, the self-emptying of the Son is associated primarily with the passion and death rather than with the incarnation. De Lubac's view is closer to the account in Philippians, in which the self-emptying of the Son is accomplished first by taking on human form (Phil. 2:6–11). For de Lubac, the self-emptying act of the Son is the act by which the Son becomes historically and visibly present. The self-emptying of the Son occurs in his entire historical activity. The Word is articulated in history through an act of self-emptying. As a result, de Lubac implies that revelation as such is the self-emptying of God's self. The Word must empty himself in order to speak to us, not just to save us.

By identifying the kenosis of the Son with revelation, de Lubac also implies that this kenosis makes salvation present to time and

---

42. Ibid., 117. Quoting Hans Urs von Balthasar, "Dieu a parlé un langage d'homme" in *Parole et Liturgie*, Lex Orandi 25 (Paris: Éditions du Cerf, 1958), 71–103, Phil 2:7, and 1 Cor. 2:0. De Lubac indicates that the quotation from 1 Corinthians, "What the eye has not seen . . . ", is found in Origen's *In Matt.* and *In Jerem.* "La Révélation divine," 117n3.

history. Christ's kenotic self-revelation is indeed the same kenosis that constitutes the divine life. The Triune God *is* the kenotic *perichoresis*, the eternal and infinite exchange that constitutes the divine life. When the incarnate Word empties himself, the divine and eternal self-emptying reveals itself in a human and historical form. The historical revelation of the Son is *pro nobis* in the most intimate sense. It makes the intimate communion between the Father and the Son present to us.

Christ's historical self-emptying is an invitation to humanity to unite in his self-emptying. The self-emptying of Christ in his humanity becomes both the temporal site of revelation and the efficacious sacrament of salvation that makes us sharers in the divine self-emptying. De Lubac interchangeably referred to Christ as the "sacrament of salvation," "sacrament of God," "universal sacrament," and "mystery."[43] Christ is a sacrament of God because he is both a sign and a means: "The mystery of Christ . . . in the unity of his person, is for us the 'sacrament' of God." He notes that "sacramentum = at the same time sign and means."[44] Calling Christ the sacrament suggests two interrelated characteristics. First, Christ mediates God's presence to us through the sign of his humanity. This is the symbolic or revelatory function of the sacrament. Second, as means, Christ is the way to salvation who draws us to the Father. This is the salvific function of the sacrament. The sacrament is not merely a window onto a transcendent reality, but it is the means by which we ascend to that reality.

In this perspective, Christ is the sacrament of God because his saving action is figurative in nature. He is the universal sacrament because he signifies or prefigures a future salvation of humanity. This

---

43. De Lubac, *Catholicism*, 76; de Lubac, "La Révélation divine," 125; de Lubac, *The Church: Paradox and Mystery*, 14.

44. De Lubac, "La Révélation divine," 63.

salvation is envisaged as the *totus Christus*, the whole Christ, that is, Christ the head and members united to the head, who is united to God the Father. If, as mentioned above, salvation is both communion between the Father and the Son, and communion among the entire church, then salvation must be embodied socially. The saving actions of Christ, according to de Lubac, are what bring about this social salvation of humanity united in and through Christ. The same action by which he reveals God to us is the action by which he constitutes the church as the social locus of salvation. The church hopes for its future completion as the *totus Christus* at the end of time.

The language referring to Christ as the "sacrament of God" or the "universal sacrament" could conceivably raise objections on the ground that Christ is envisaged as the sacramental means to an ecclesial end. De Lubac's often-employed binary language—*type* and *antitype, figure* and *truth, sign* and *signified*—describes the sacramental mediation from visible symbol to reality signified. Sacraments are *means* to a future end, that is, something that we pass through to reach that end. The problem is that "Christ as sacrament" could suggest that he falls on the side of figure or sign but not on the side of the truth signified. Under this lens, Christ's historical action is a means to something else, something to leave behind once we reach the end of the journey. In other words, echoing the interpretation of history in Joachim of Fiore, the work of Christ is not the definitive act of God but only a preparation for that act.

De Lubac's account of spiritual interpretation corrects this misinterpretation. In the normative tradition of spiritual exegesis, the New Testament is the allegorization of the Old Testament, but the New Testament itself cannot be allegorized. The New Testament is definitive and complete because Christ's action is definitive and complete. At the same time, Christ, the allegory of the Old Testament, is the figure for the tropological and anagogical meanings. Christ is the figure for the church and for the heavenly Jerusalem. In this case, tropology and anagogy follow allegory and are developed *within* it. While the historical actions of Christ signify a future, eschatological fulfillment, that fulfillment is essentially *in* Christ.

Christ is indeed a sacrament and sign of a future eschatological consummation. However, there is a priority of the signover the signified. The Old Testament was a figure of the New Testament, where the New Testament was the greater reality that fulfilled the Old. However, when we speak of the allegory as a figure of tropology and anagogy, the figure is the dominant reality.[45] The figure of Christ assimilates to himself (*concorporatio*) what he signifies.[46] Tropology and anagogy develop "within" allegory as the further explication and deepening of the meaning of Christ in the life of the church.[47] The movement of spiritual meaning is, in fact, incomplete without tropology and anagogy. The New Testament allegory must engender further meanings:

> It is really a sign, an efficacious sign. It is not any longer only mystery; it is the whole mystery in its principle. Tropology will describe only the fruit, anagogy will evoke only the consummation. It would not be grasped in its depth, it would even be truly mutilated, if it were not contemplated in this double prolongation. But this word itself of prolongation is inadequate, because in reality the investigation of the two last senses contributes nothing to the Mystery of Christ; it does not carry us outside of or beyond it; it only manifests its fecundity.[48]

45. De Lubac, *Exégèse médiévale*, 4:112.
46. Ibid., 4:112–13.
47. "At the same time it is the allegory of the Old Testament, its 'truth', its 'mystery', this great Fact constitutes up to a certain point the equivalent of what was, in the Old Testament, the *historia*. For it is really a real fact, happened in a certain place, in a certain time; it has then completely an exterior face, and, as the *historia*, it is really the foundation of all that there remains to inventory within the New Testament, that is to say, inside itself, by *tropologia* and *anagogē*. It is truly really the sign, or the figure of all that the establishment of the two last senses must expose." Ibid., 4:111.
48. Ibid.

In *Exégèse médiévale*, de Lubac affirms the continuity of the "mystery of Christ," from his earthly life to the eschatological consummation: "Everything is being produced right now, everything is living on and buckled up inside one and the same mystery: *Christ is substantially always the same; Christ signifies himself.*"[49] Although Christ is a sacrament, he is also the mystery signified.

Yet de Lubac carefully balances the completeness of Christ's work with an eschatological reserve. In practice, the New Testament *was* interpreted as a "letter." The Christ event is a sign pointing to the future salvation of the church, a salvation embodied in the tropological and anagogical meanings of Scripture. Although the Christ event was definitive, tropology and anagogy were something truly "to come." In this way, without moving *beyond* Christ, the tropological and anagogical meanings are something more than allegory. De Lubac addresses this issue in *Exégèse médiévale*, where he asks whether the literal or spiritual sense is more important. If one is thinking of the Old Testament, he says, then clearly the New Testament, its spiritual sense, is more important: "The Mystery of Christ is superior to all its prefigurations." However, de Lubac explains,

> if one considers the New Testament, the response appears less simple. Here the literal sense is itself spiritual, as the Mystery of Christ, even under its first aspect of historical fact, is the "truth," that is to say, "the spirit" of the Old Testament. On the other hand, as this Mystery contains in itself, in the manner just explained, the two last senses which arise from its "letter," this letter itself must be called the most dignified. The assimilating figure prevails clearly over the assimilated reality. The personal Act of Christ dominates the constitution of his "mystical body," the Head is superior to the members. Nevertheless, this Act has for its end only the constitution of this "body." The Head is desired for the members, the Word of God is incarnate only "*propter nos*

49. De Lubac, *Medieval Exegesis*, 2:202.

et propter nostram salutem," [for us and for our salvation] and the Church is the "pleroma" or the plenitude of Christ. More than the letter of the Old Testament, the intention of the Spirit is only that one remains at the letter of the New, and since the spirit of this letter, that is to say tropology and anagogy of which it is the sign and the foundation, does not surpass it really but finds in it all its substance, it is here not improper to say that it is the Mystery taken in its totality, the final reality wished by God, that constitutes the sense otherwise the most "dignified," at least the most complete and, in the end, the most important.[50]

God's ultimate intention, the mystery of Christ taken in its final state, takes priority. The actions of Christ recounted in the New Testament are truly anticipatory, prefiguring the eschatological consummation. When de Lubac speaks of Christ as the sacrament of salvation or the sacrament of God, he means that the historical actions of Christ are truly efficacious in bringing about a new situation between God and humanity. Yet this salvation remains yet to come. The incarnation and his historical action remain the foundation and the sign of the accomplishment of salvation, which, though accomplished in his humanity, still awaits its full extension to the rest of humanity at the end of the world.

Eschatology as Ecclesiology

Henri de Lubac's ecclesiology organically unfolds from Christology, just as, in spiritual exegesis, the allegory gives rise to tropology or anagogy. He writes, "The Church is a mystery; that is to say that she is also a sacrament. She is 'the total locus of the Christian sacraments,' and she is herself the great sacrament which contains and vitalizes all the others. In this world she is the sacrament of

---

50. De Lubac, *Exégèse médiévale*, 4:113–14. De Lubac addresses a highly debated question in the history of Christianity, namely whether the incarnation was necessary due to sin and whether the Son would have become human had humanity not sinned. De Lubac sides with Robert Grosseteste and Duns Scotus against Thomas Aquinas (*ST* III, qu. 1, art. 3). I am grateful to Rev. Joseph Mueller, SJ, for alerting me to this broader debate.

Christ, as Christ Himself, in His humanity, is for us the sacrament of God."[51] De Lubac's dominant ecclesiological metaphor is the church as sacrament. The visible communion of the church is the sign and means to union with God. While a definitive account of de Lubac's sacramental ecclesiology is impossible here, this section merely shows that de Lubac's metaphor of the church as sacrament closely corresponds with his eschatological vision.[52] Henri de Lubac's eschatology takes the form of an ecclesiology because the church at the end of time, the "whole Christ," is the goal of all of God's salvific action. The visible actions of the church in time constitue the sacramental anticipations of the church of eternity.

Before correlating de Lubac's ecclesiology and eschatology, it is necessary to address a dubious reading of de Lubac's ecclesiology, namely that de Lubac fails to distinguish between the practices of the visible church and salvation itself.[53] Under this reading, there is no partition between God's actions and the church's actions, God's

---

51. De Lubac, *The Splendor of the Church*, 203.

52. The literature on de Lubac's ecclesiology is vast. For key readings of de Lubac's sacramental ecclesiology, see Hans Boersma, "The Eucharist Makes the Church," *Crux* 44, no. 4 (Winter 2008): 2–11; Francesca Murphy, "De Lubac, Ratzinger and von Balthasar: A Communal Adventure in Ecclesiology," in *Ecumenism Today: The Universal Church in the 21st Century* (Burlington, VT: Ashgate Publishing, 2008), 45–81; Lisa Wang, "Sacramentum unitatis ecclesiasticae: The Eucharistic Ecclesiology of Henri de Lubac," *Anglican Theological Review* 85, no. 1 (December 1, 2003): 143–58; Robert Franklin Gotcher, "Henri de Lubac and Communio: The Significance of His Theology of the Supernatural for an Interpretation of Gaudium et Spes" (PhD diss., Marquette University, 2002); Dennis M. Doyle, *Communion Ecclesiology: Vision and Versions* (Maryknoll, NY: Orbis Books, 2000), chap. 4; Susan K. Wood, *Spiritual Exegesis and the Church in the Theology of Henri de Lubac* (Grand Rapids, MI: Eerdmans, 1998); Paul McPartlan, "The Eucharist, the Church, and Evangelization: The Influence of Henri de Lubac," *Communio* 23, no. 4 (1996): 776–85; Elie Koma, "Le mystère de l'Eucharistie et ses dimensions ecclesiales dans l'oeuvre d'Henri de Lubac" (ThD diss., Pontificia Universita Gregoriana, 1990); Marc Pelchat, *L'Église mystère de communion: l'ecclésiologie dans l'œuvre d'Henri de Lubac*, Collection Brèches théologiques 2 (Montréal: Éditions Paulines, 1988); Hubert Schnackers, *Kirche als Sakrament und Mutter: Zur Ekklesiologie von Henri de Lubac*, vol. 22, Regensburger Studien zur Theologie (Frankfurt am Main: Peter Lang, 1979).

53. Some contemporary critics of de Lubac accuse him of doing the opposite, of undermining the necessity of the church in salvation. Because this misreading is drawn as a necessary consequence of his theology of grace and not of his ecclesiology, I will respond to this objection in chapter 7, below.

saving activity and the liturgical practices of the church, or God's transformation in grace and the efforts by the church to establish social justice. De Lubac's sacramental ecclesiology collapses the saving activity of God into the liturgical and social practices of the visible church.

For instance, John Webster is critical of de Lubac's ecclesiology in particular and communion ecclesiologies in general for the lack of partition between the agency of the visible church and the agency of God. According to Webster, communion ecclesiologies propose that salvation is embodied within a particular ecclesial communion, as "essentially visible as a form of common life and part of the world's historical and material economy."[54] While Webster recognizes the need to overcome an overly individualistic notion of salvation, he believes that most communion ecclesiologies fail to safeguard the "unparticipable perfection of God's triune life."[55] When the very life of God is seen as being embodied within a particular church's social, sacramental, or liturgical practice, God's "utter difference" in relation to creatures is lost. As a result, communion ecclesiology risks undermining God's freedom and grace with regard to the church: "The very density of the resultant ecclesiology can sometimes become problematic. Ecclesiology can so fill the horizon that it obscures the miracle of grace which is fundamental to the church's life and activity."[56] While Webster takes particular exception to John Milbank's theology, he believes that Milbank, Robert Jenson, and de Lubac fall within a spectrum of the same teaching. De Lubac's ecclesiology, which he says depends upon a "metaphysical substructure" found within *Surnaturel,* is a principal example of a confusion of the divine and human within communion

54. John Webster, *Confessing God: Essays in Christian Dogmatics II* (New York: T & T Clark, 2005), 161.
55. Ibid., 163.
56. Ibid., 155.

ecclesiologies. As a result of this confusion, de Lubac's ecclesiology emphasizes the visible and social life church as the site of salvation itself.

While Webster opposes de Lubac's ecclesiology on the grounds that it confuses divine and human agency, John Milbank suggests that de Lubac's ecclesiology is valuable because it proposes ecclesial practice as the unique site of participation in the divine. In this interpretation, the liturgical and social practice of the visible church is the "site" of God's salvation. For Milbank, de Lubac's understanding of the supernatural grounds all other aspects of his theology. De Lubac defended the thesis that humanity possesses a single, supernatural finality, resulting in an unquenchable desire for God at the depth of human nature.[57] According to Milbank, de Lubac's defense of supernatural finality implies that there is no "purely natural" domain existing as a space closed to the divine or defined apart from the supernatural. Indeed, the distinction between nature and the supernatural, or nature and grace, is false.[58] As a result of this ontology, there is no distinction between social practice and grace, between ecclesial performance and supernatural life, or *praxis* and *theoria*. Indeed, Milbank's collapse of God's saving activity into the social, sacramental, and liturgical action of the church is really why he depends upon de Lubac's theology.[59] For Milbank, de Lubac's

---

57. See Henri de Lubac, *Surnaturel: Études historiques*, Théologie 8 (Paris: Aubier-Montaigne, 1946). Originally published in 1944. See also Henri de Lubac, *Le mystère du surnaturel*, Théologie (Paris: Aubier, 1965); Henri de Lubac, *Petite catéchèse sur nature et grâce*, Communio (Paris: Fayard, 1980).

58. For the pivotal texts on Milbank's interpretation of de Lubac, see John Milbank, *The Suspended Middle: Henri de Lubac and the Debate Concerning the Supernatural* (Grand Rapids, MI: Eerdmans, 2005); John Milbank, "Henri de Lubac," in *The Modern Theologians: An Introduction to Modern Theology since 1918*, ed. David F. Ford (Malden, MA: Blackwell, 2005); John Milbank, *Theology and Social Theory: Beyond Secular Reason*, 2nd ed. (Malden, MA: Blackwell, 2006), 220–25.

59. To be fair, Milbank often speaks of the incompleteness of the church, the church as the initiation of God's plan, or the proleptic anticipation of God's peace. He writes, "In the Incarnation, God as God was perfectly able to fulfil the worship of God which is nevertheless, as worship, only possible for the creature. This descent is repeated and perpetuated in the

ontology helps to establish that the church itself is an alternative social space in which the ecclesial community participates visibly in God's salvation through concrete practice.

De Lubac's 1939 book *Corpus Mysticum* is critical to Milbank's interpretation. *Corpus Mysticum* traced the evolution of the meaning of the "mystical body" from the patristic to medieval periods. Before the twelfth century, the "real" body of Christ referred to the church, while the "mystical" body referred to the Eucharist. De Lubac showed that the modern meanings of the terms *mystical body* and *real body* came about through an inversion of meanings that took place primarily during the twelfth century. In modernity the "real" body of Christ was understood as the Eucharist and the "mystical" body of Christ was the church. This shift in meanings led to the overemphasis on the Eucharist as the "real presence" of Christ—what Laurence Paul Hemming calls the "fetishization" of the Eucharist—and the neglect of the social dimension of salvation. De Lubac sought to recover a theology in which the Eucharist was the sign and sacramental means of the church, the "real body." The dominant reading of *Corpus Mysticum* from Michel de Certeau and Radical Orthodoxy interprets de Lubac's recovery of the eucharistic meaning of *corpus mysticum* as a response to the individualistic spirituality that arose in modernity. The key point is that by recovering the idea of the Eucharist as the "mystical body," de Lubac shifted our attention to the assembled body of believers and their ecclesial practices as the

Eucharist which gives rise to the *ecclesia*, that always 'other-governed' rather than autonomous human community, which is yet the beginning of universal community as such, since it is nothing other than the lived project of universal reconciliation. Not reducible to its institutional failures and yet not to be seen as a utopia either, since the reality of the reconciliation, of restored unity-in-diversity, must presuppose itself if it is to be realizable (always in some very small degree) in time and so must be always already begun." *Theology and Social Theory*, xxxi. Rather than failing to distinguish between the *ecclesia* and Christ, or between the visible community and grace, here Milbank describes the church as the already-begun "universal reconciliation." Here, Milbank's ecclesiology is far from triumphalistic and emphasizes the incomplete nature of the church's identity as the reconciliation of humanity.

object signified by the Eucharist.[60] The visible ecclesial community is the "real body" of Christ that gathers to constitute the "mystical body," the Eucharist, a sign and performative manifestation of the "real body." The church is the salvation of Christ realized socially in the practice of the community.

However, this reading of de Lubac tends to distort de Lubac's ecclesiological vision by delimiting the scope of the "real body" to the present, visible communion.[61] Laurence Paul Hemming suggests that de Lubac does not objectify the social practice of the visible church because the visible church anticipates its eschatological completion:

> Only at the end of time is the Church in its entirety to be understood as fully present, and so only then is the identity of the Church with the Body of Christ visible and complete. At this point, sacraments, and above all the sacrament of the altar, cease to be, no longer needed as the mediation of the incompleteness of the *Corpus mysticum* (the end of time and the glorification of Christ's mystical Body, and the point at which the Body ceases to be mysterious, or a matter of significations, and is completed). Von Balthasar himself emphasizes the importance of this eschatological aspect in de Lubac's work, and notes: "the Origenistic thought, which finds so strong an echo through history. . . that Christ and the blessed attain their ultimate beatitude only if the whole 'Body of Christ,' the redeemed creation, is gathered together in the transfiguration, is honoured in its lasting spiritual meaning." This occurs, von Balthasar tells us, only in "the heavenly Jerusalem." There is

---

60. Catherine Pickstock, *After Writing: On the Liturgical Consummation of Philosophy* (Oxford: Wiley-Blackwell, 1998), 158–66; John Milbank, *The Word Made Strange: Theology, Language, Culture* (Oxford: Wiley-Blackwell, 1997), 163; Michel de Certeau, *The Mystic Fable: The Sixteenth and Seventeenth Centuries*, vol. 1, trans. Michael B. Smith, Religion and Postmodernism (Chicago: University of Chicago Press, 1995), 75–85.

61. Hemming contends that under de Certeau's and Milbank's reading, de Lubac presents the church, the visible assembled community, as the locus of God's saving power: "The result—caricature indeed—has been the fetishisation, not of the sacred species, the eucharistic host, but of the community itself, the one that has assembled for the Eucharist, and so the *Anwendung* of the interpretation has been a turning-in on ourselves, to intensify the objectification of the subjects for whom the host has become mere object." Laurence Paul Hemming, "Henri de Lubac: Reading Corpus Mysticum," *New Blackfriars* 90, no. 1029 (September 2009), 528.

a hermeneutical key proposed in the text that most commentators have, as far as I can see, overlooked.[62]

For Hemming, the key to de Lubac's ecclesiology is his eschatology. The sacramental, liturgical, and social practices of the visible church are incomplete anticipations of the eschatological church. For de Lubac, the present, visible church must await its transfiguration in glory. As long as de Lubac's ecclesiology is understood as an eschatology, there is no objectification of the visible church, confusion of human and divine action, or "fetishization" of the assembly.

Instead, de Lubac's primary ecclesiological metaphor, the "church as sacrament," is thoroughly eschatological.[63] The sacramental metaphor for the church functions to bring together two sides of the church's paradoxical nature. In his post–Vatican II work, *The Church: Paradox and Mystery*, de Lubac examines the church in terms of paradox, opposing truths that must be somehow reconciled or joined together. To neglect either pole of the paradox would be to

62. Ibid., 530. Quoting from the German, Hans Urs von Balthasar, *Henri de Lubac: Sein organisches Lebenswerk* (Einsiedeln: Johannes, 1976), 32. Although Hemming argues that the hermeneutical key of *Corpus Mysticum* is eschatological, he overlooks Susan K. Wood's *Spiritual Exegesis and the Church*, in which she correlates de Lubac's understanding of Scripture, the church, and the sacraments. Wood notes that de Lubac did not explicitly capitalize on the eschatological orientation of spiritual exegesis in his work on the sacramentality of the church. Ibid., 127. I am indebted to Wood's analysis for my understanding of eschatology as key to de Lubac's ecclesiology.

63. We should note that de Lubac's ecclesiology weaves together the central biblical and patristic metaphors for the church: body of Christ, spouse, mother, mystery. Each metaphor is incomplete in itself and must be supplemented by the others. As Susan Wood notes, the church as sacrament supplements the "body of Christ" metaphor. Ibid. A too literal application of the "body of Christ" to the church could suggest that the incarnation of the Word in Jesus extends literally in the through the church in an "ongoing incarnation." De Lubac himself said that the divine and human are united in the church: "The Church is really Christ perpetuated among us, Christ 'spread abroad and passed on,'" and the "'permanent incarnation of the Son of God.'" De Lubac, *The Splendor of the Church*, 48. Quoting Jacques-Bénigne Boussuet, "Allucution aux Nouvelles Catholiques," in *Oeuvres Oratoires* IV (Paris: Librairie Hachette, 1922), 508. Wood claims that the metaphor of sacrament functions to temper the body of Christ or incarnation metaphor.

deform its reality. Paradox is characteristic of our present state, where we lack the intellectual perspicacity to rationally resolve both poles. The paradox is "resolved" only by recognizing the mystery, in which the parallel lines meet only at the horizon, the limit of history. "The mystery always transcends our definitions."[64] Referring to the church, de Lubac elaborates on three paradoxical pairs: the church is of God and of humanity; the church is visible and invisible; and the church is of time and of eternity.

First, de Lubac states the "Church is of God (*de Trinitate*) and she is of men (*ex hominibus*)."[65] On the one hand, de Lubac describes the church with the highest ecclesiological descriptors: she is "a mysterious extension in time of the Trinity," "the incarnation continued," the "presence of Christ on earth," "the spouse of Christ and his body."[66] On the other hand, he warns that these descriptions are inadequate because the church is also very human, faulty, and sinful. De Lubac warns us to avoid an "ecclesiological 'monophysitism'" that recognizes the divine source of the church without seeing its human nature. But the parallel between Christ and the church is limited. Unlike Christ, the church has a "borrowed splendour," just as the moon borrows its light from the sun.[67] Nevertheless, this borrowed splendor can only be seen by penetrating her shabby humanity. He writes, "The Church disguises her borrowed splendour in a shabby garment: the contradiction is, therefore, part and parcel of her nature and only the penetrating regard will know how to discover the beauty of her face."[68] One must penetrate the human side of the church to reach the divine. The idea

---

64. De Lubac, *The Church: Paradox and Mystery*, 18.
65. Ibid., 23.
66. Ibid., 24.
67. On the lunar symbolism for the church, see ibid., 16.
68. Ibid., 25.

of "sacrament" remains in the background of this exposition, which are filled out by two additional paradoxes.

Second, de Lubac describes the church as visible and invisible at the same time. Here the sacramental nature of the church becomes clearer: "The mystery, the efficacious sign, is not separated from that which it signifies and, on the other hand, what is signified can only be grasped through the mediation of the sign."[69] The visible, hierarchical, ministerial, and historical reality of the church is a sign pointing to its invisible reality. In the church, a "reciprocal interiority" pertains between the visible and the transcendent. We must keep in mind that the relation between visible and invisible is, for de Lubac, the relation between the "visible ecclesial communion" and the "invisible communion with the Trinity":

> Communion is the objective—an objective which, from the first instant, does not cease to be realized in the invisible; the institution is the means for it—a means which even now does not cease to ensure a visible communion. But their reciprocal interiority could not be understood ... if we did not believe that the Christian life is received from above, a life to which we are begotten and in which we are nourished by a ministry coming from Jesus himself and which realizes historically a communion victorious over all history.[70]

Here the church generates a visible ecclesial communion while at the same time acting as a means to the invisible. It is a means, but the invisible is already present, already acting within the visible communion. What is critical is that the visible communion is an historical "means" to an invisible, eternal "end."

---

69. Ibid., 26.
70. Henri de Lubac, *The Motherhood of the Church: Followed by Particular Churches in the Universal Church and an Interview Conducted by Gwendoline Jarczyk* (San Francisco: Ignatius Press, 1982), 35. Originally published as Henri de Lubac, *Les églises particulières dans l'Église universelle; suivi de La maternité de l'église, et d'une interview recueillie, par G. Jarczyk*, Intelligence de la foi (Paris: Aubier-Montaigne, 1971).

This leads us to the third paradoxical pair: the church is of time and of eternity. It is historical and eschatological. In *Motherhood of the Church*, de Lubac describes the church as the "eschatological anticipation, within the temporal order itself, of that Kingdom of God proclaimed by the Gospel."[71] In *The Church: Paradox and Mystery*, he states, "The reign of God is yet to come: but 'without waiting for history to run its course, it has already, in a mysterious anticipation, made its appearance in the inner marrow of history.' Since the fact of Christ and his resurrection, "time-after" is already present in the interior of time.'"[72] The church is a visible and historical communion that anticipates the eschatological communion and is the site for the eschatological acting within the temporal. There remains an identity as well as distinction between the present and eschatological church. The present church is the *sacrament* that signifies and brings about the eschatological *mystery*.

De Lubac's criticism of the Vatican II constitution on the church, *Lumen gentium*, is helpful for understanding the relationship between the church in time and the eschatological church. De Lubac approved of *Lumen gentium*'s recovery of a virtually lost ecclesiological theme, the "people of God journeying towards a common destiny."[73] This theme recovered the historical dimensions of ecclesial existence as a communal pilgrimage on the way to a goal that transcends history. However, de Lubac took issue with the document for reintroducing a modern dualism between the "pilgrim church" and the "heavenly church." De Lubac explains that *Lumen gentium* articulated an important eschatological perspective of the church, a perspective arising in recent centuries. Although *Lumen gentium* melds together

---

71. *Motherhood of the Church*, 126.
72. De Lubac, *The Church: Paradox and Mystery*, 52. Quoting Christopher Butler, *The Idea of the Church* (Baltimore: Helicon, 1962), 213.
73. *The Church: Paradox and Mystery*, 47.

corporate and individual eschatologies, he says, it vertically juxtaposes the pilgrim church and the heavenly church in a spatial framework. This vertical juxtaposition—originating from a modern focus on individual eschatology against corporate eschatology—obscures the sacramental dimensions of the church, namely that the terrestrial is already making the heavenly present. As a result, *Lumen gentium* is not sufficiently eschatological and represents a "narrowing of the patristic horizons."[74] For the fathers, the church is both terrestrial and heavenly, existing as a terrestrial anticipation of the eschatological kingdom constituted by the whole Christ.[75]

De Lubac's sacramental ecclesiology communicates the identity and gulf between the present church and the eschatological church. He states that the church is the "church on pilgrimage" and the "church as already filled with Christ and the Spirit."[76] The church militant is not other than the church triumphant: in de Lubac's perspective, they are different states of the same reality.

> The Church which gave them life in the waters of baptism, this Church—visible and terrestrial herself—was therefore for them at the same time "the heavenly Church," "the heavenly Jerusalem, our mother." . . . In this all-embracing view of the mystery the Church is identified with Christ, her spouse, who is himself the kingdom: "autobasileia," as Origen admirably puts it. Now this view corresponds to the deepest logic of Christian eschatology and to depart from it could lead to many abuses of both thought and action.[77]

At the same time, there is a gulf between the present church and the eschatological church, a gulf that the "church as sacrament" describes. As Susan Wood explains, "The Church as a sacrament of Christ is Christ, yet it is different, and the difference can, at least in part,

---

74. Ibid., 51.
75. Ibid., 52.
76. Ibid.
77. Ibid.

be expressed as the difference between sacramental mediation of that which is complete eschatologically and its full eschatological manifestation."[78] To put it differently, the visible communion exists in anticipation of a more perfect communion.

The church is a sacrament of the eschaton in two complementary ways: the church makes the eschaton, the whole Christ, present in time; and the church is the means to the eschaton. First, to speak of the church as a sacrament is to say that the church makes Christ present. But this making present is equally a making the end of time present to us, since Christ has entered into that fullness in his own person. The temporal church, therefore, makes present the eschatological church, that is, the end of history constituted by the unity of all humanity through Christ. Second, the temporal church is a means to its own eschatological realization: "The Church is the ark that saves us from death. But we are not mere passengers on this ark: we *are* the ark, we are the Church."[79] The church constitutes the sacramental means to the eschatological end. As means, she is a present, visible, organic, and incomplete unity that is the sacrament of her eschatological culmination in the whole Christ, the heavenly unity of all humanity. The eschatological élan of de Lubac's communion ecclesiology moderates a triumphalist fusion of church and kingdom that would presume an identity between the Roman Catholic Church with the kingdom. It balances the "already-present" with a "not-yet."[80]

---

78. Wood, *Spiritual Exegesis and the Church*, 127.

79. De Lubac, *The Church: Paradox and Mystery*, 21.

80. Similarly, in his "Le Fondement théologique des missions," de Lubac describes the catholicity of the church as what the church is called to be. Catholicity is not a description of the geographical extent of the Roman Catholic Church. Rather, it is an essential aspect: "It is an idea and a force. It is an ambition and exigence. Its catholicity is its vocation, which is melded with its being." Henri de Lubac, "Le Fondement théologique des missions," in *Résistance chrétienne au nazisme*, vol. 34, Oeuvres complètes (Paris: Éditions du Cerf, 2006), 47. This essential mark of the church is its calling.

De Lubac's undoubtably high ecclesiology and sacramental realism presents a typically Roman Catholic theology, historically an obstacle for Protestants. The emphasis on the church as the visible *communio sanctorum* could conceivably detract from the centrality and efficacy of Christ and lead to a form of triumphalistic ecclesiology. However, de Lubac's high ecclesiology is balanced by an eschatological reserve. The concrete, visible practices of the church participate sacramentally in the eschaton, but the church remains "in waiting" (*en attente*), sustained by hope. De Lubac's ecclesiology makes it clear that the church does not supplant Christ's historical presence. Because de Lubac grounds ecclesiology in the economy of salvation, the church should not be seen as a competitor to Christ but the very participation in his mystery. At the same time, de Lubac's ecclesiology preserves a strong sense that the church constitutes a concrete visible participation in the life of Christ. Its life is lived between the two comings of Christ, but never apart from him. The "mystery" has entered into time and transformed it. The "mystery" continues historically as the ongoing development of God's plan in time that draws us to the consummation. Without denying the centrality of Christ in the economy of salvation, de Lubac's ecclesiology presents an account of the church as the concrete and social participation in the Trinitarian life. This balance between the church's visible, terrestrial dimensions and an eschatological reserve make de Lubac an important theological interlocutor with Protestant ecclesiology and sacramental theology.

Liberation Theology, Temporal Progress, and the Kingdom

If the Christian church is a visible unity that anticipates and mediates the kingdom, and if that unity is social, concrete, and historical, it would follow that this concrete, social unity of the church anticipates and mediates the kingdom. De Lubac's earliest writings suggested that God's salvation is social and that social salvation is experienced within time and history, raising the prospect of a close relationship between social conditions and salvation. His ecclesiology implied that if salvation is being anticipated proleptically in the concrete, historical reality of the church, then this anticipation of salvation assumes particular relationships, political dimensions, and social structures.[81] For de Lubac, grace, embodied in the church, takes social and historical form and functions as a sacrament of the eschatological fullness of grace. As an implication, one would think that social and political conditions, as an extension of the visible church communion, would participate in this sacramental relationship.[82] However, de Lubac's work reveals his deep conflict on the relationship between social conditions and the kingdom of God.

Although he admitted that there is some relationship between temporal social conditions and the kingdom, he also insisted that "progress" and "liberation" cannot lead to the kingdom. In his *Petite*

81. De Lubac's theology of grace appears to concur with Gustavo Gutiérrez's *A Theology of Liberation*, which challenged a distinction of two planes, the religious and the secular, and proposed a close relationship between lived historical experience and salvation. Gutiérrez, *A Theology of Liberation: History, Politics, Salvation* (Maryknoll, NY: Orbis Books, 1973). Originally published as *Teología de la liberación, Perspectivas* (Lima: CEP, 1971). Recently, Robert M. Doran, SJ, outlined the concept of "social grace," the notion that elevation of the consciousness to participation in divine life occurs through a shared life. "The state of grace . . . is a social, interpersonal situation." Robert M. Doran, "Social Grace," in *Essays in Systematic Theology: An E-Book*, 14, http://www.loneranresource.com/pdf/books/1/35 - Social Grace.pdf

82. This implication in de Lubac's work is developed by a number of authors, including Bryan C. Hollon, *Everything Is Sacred: Spiritual Exegesis in the Political Theology of Henri de Lubac* (Eugene, OR: Cascade Books, 2009); Hans Boersma, "Sacramental Ontology: Nature and the Supernatural in the Ecclesiology of Henri de Lubac," *New Blackfriars* 88, no. 1015 (2007): 242–73; Jean-Yves Calvez, *Chrétiens, penseurs du social*, Histoire de la morale (Paris: Éditions du Cerf, 2008); Milbank, *Theology and Social Theory*; Wood, *Spiritual Exegesis and the Church*; David L. Schindler, *Heart of the World, Center of the Church: Communio Ecclesiology, Liberalism, and Liberation* (Grand Rapids, MI: Eerdmans, 1996); Susan K. Wood, "The Church as the Social Embodiment of Grace in the Ecclesiology of Henri de Lubac" (PhD diss., Marquette University, 1986).

catéchèse sur Nature et Grâce (1980), he admitted of a "reciprocal relation" between social conditions and the kingdom, or in the words of Pope Paul VI, between "evangelization and human progress, development and liberation."[83] He recognized a distinction, but not a separation, between "the progress of the modern world and the coming of the Kingdom."[84] There are, he claimed, close ties between our historical experience and the eschaton, and between progress within our world and the kingdom. However, in the same book, de Lubac rejected the notion of a causal relationship between the two, insisting on the nonidentity of temporal progress and the kingdom of God. He argued human liberation is fundamentally ambiguous in its relationship to salvation:

> "Liberation of man," understood as a social emancipation, is a human undertaking which, even when inspired by faith, brings about . . . by human means certain changes in the organization of temporal society, and which becomes part of human history, with all the hazards . . . of going from bad to worse, which will always remain possible in this groping and sinful world. "Salvation in Jesus Christ," on the contrary, is essentially a divine undertaking which comes about in the depths of hearts and is inscribed in eternity. This makes clear the proper role of the Church; she is the messenger and bearer of this salvation and hence she cannot be assimilated, either in her structure or in her aims, to any of our human societies.[85]

De Lubac maintained the absolute transcendence of the grace of salvation with respect to the structures of political society. He distinguished between liberation as a social program and liberation as the freedom from sin. The first is fundamentally ambiguous in relationship to the latter. Furthermore, he suggested that this strong

---

83. Henri de Lubac, *A Brief Catechesis on Nature and Grace*, trans. Brother Richard Arnandez, F.S.C. (San Francisco: Ignatius Press, 1984), 102. Originally published as *Petite catéchèse sur Nature et Grâce* (Paris: Librairie Arthème Fayard, 1980). Quoting Paul VI, *Evangelii nuntiandi*, no. 31.

84. *Brief Catechesis*, 102

85. Ibid., 159–60.

distinction between liberation in the social sphere and spiritual liberation preserves the independence of the church from any external social program.[86]

De Lubac's considerations on the relationship between salvation and human progress are illuminated by his response to Edward Schillebeeckx. De Lubac reacted to Schillebeeckx's characterization of the church as the *sacramentum mundi*, the "sacrament of the world." The question de Lubac posed concerned the ultimate reference of the church as sacrament: is the church the sacrament of the world or the sacrament of Christ?[87] Schillebeeckx's interpretation of Vatican II's *Gaudium et Spes* suggests that the church makes Christ explicit to the world where God's salvation is already mysteriously active.[88] "The church is the sign that effects, by experiencing and helping others experience what will be given concrete and full shape in the whole human fellowship when the salvation is fully realized."[89] The entire world is in an historical process towards an eschatological salvation. God's universal will to save humanity is manifested in the struggle for a better world, even though this manifestation does not explicitly thematize salvation. For Schillebeeckx, the salvation of the world through God's grace, coinciding with the unity of humanity, is made explicit within the church.[90]

---

86. The context of *Petite catéchèse* can help explain its tone. It was written during the Cold War and at a time when Marxist thought was influencing Christian theological reflection on the coming of God's kingdom and the role of temporal progress and development. It was also written a year after the first volume of de Lubac's *La Postérité spirituelle* was published, which traced Hegelian, Marxist, and other future-oriented philosophical eschatologies back to Joachim. When he writes about human progress, he is thinking of a tradition of secular humanists that include Hegel and Marx. See de Lubac, *Brief Catechesis*, 162. Moreover, it was written at a time during which liberation theology was emerging as a new perspective.

87. Wood, *Spiritual Exegesis and the Church*, 109–17.

88. See Edward Schillebeeckx, *The Mission of the Church*, trans. N. D. Smith (New York: Herder and Herder, 1973); Edward Schillebeeckx, *The Real Achievement of Vatican II* (New York: Herder and Herder, 1967).

89. Anthony Lee, "From Sacrament of Salvation to Sign that Interrupts: The Evolution in Edward Schillebeeckx's Theology of the Relationship between the Church and the World" (PhD diss., Notre Dame, 2011), 92.

De Lubac argued that Schillebeeckx's description of the church as *sacramentum mundi* presented the church as the expression of a salvation already available in the secular world. As a result, the church explicitly thematizes a salvation implicit within sociopolitical projects. Schillebeeckx fails to articulate the fact that salvation transcends all the features of our historical world. Concerning Schillebeeckx's position, he asks, "Does the 'eschatological kingdom' not appear, in all this, as the culmination of our 'earthly expectations,' as their supreme fulfillment and consummation? . . . So, in practice, human history and salvation history would be one and the same."[91] The problem, as de Lubac saw it, was that the eschatological kingdom for Schillebeeckx is merely the endpoint of secular progress and not the transfiguration of the world that takes the world beyond itself. Schillebeeckx ultimately confuses the supernatural and nature and it collapses "creation and divinization."[92]

De Lubac's desire to maintain infinite difference between nature and the supernatural leads him to reject the notion that the natural unfolding of history results in the radical transformation of this world:

> Since the world as a whole is going to its death, "it cannot be considered an immanent reflection or an anticipation of the Kingdom of God." Hence it cannot be, as such, the goal of our hopes. We must, then, take care not to confuse the "progress of this world" (itself a very ambivalent term) with the "new creation." We must avoid slipping from conversion of heart, by which the "new man" is born in Christ, to the unfolding of history (dialectic or not) that bears "as in its womb" the societies of the future.[93]

90. See Hans Boersma, *Nouvelle Théologie and Sacramental Ontology: A Return to Mystery* (Oxford and New York: Oxford University Press, 2009), 260.
91. De Lubac, *Brief Catechesis*, 225.
92. Ibid., 226.
93. Ibid., 101. Quoting Teilhard de Chardin, Letters to Fr. Auguste Valensin, December 8 and 12, 1919.

Neither human progress nor world history should be considered an anticipation of the promised kingdom:

> In its social meaning liberation of every kind belongs to time; salvation is for eternity, and for that reason anticipates time. We should not even say, strictly speaking, that the more or less perfect accomplishment (it always remains imperfect) of the first of these two goals is at least the indispensable preparation for the second; for this would amount to saying that the Christian hope is necessarily situated in the prolongation of the objective results obtained by human efforts.[94]

Human liberation cannot be confused with the spiritual renewal that occurs in the human heart and that transcends history and progress.

There are two fundamental theological insights at play throughout de Lubac's writings that never achieve a perfect reconciliation. On the one hand, de Lubac refused to separate nature and grace into two (spatial) planes of existence. His theology of the supernatural avoided severing all relationship between the visible, temporal order and the supernatural. De Lubac's engagement with early modern theories of pure nature in *Surnaturel* emphasized that nature and grace are unified within a single historical experience. On the other hand, de Lubac preserved the distinction between nature and grace. He wished to avoid the identification of temporal and secular progress with the coming eschatological kingdom. Salvation is infinitely different than the immanent world process, including human liberation and political progress. The infinite difference between creation and redemption is preserved in the difference of orders between human progress and the kingdom of God. De Lubac's engagement with Joachim and Joachim's posterity reflects his insistence that the kingdom of God cannot be reduced to temporal progress. Although de Lubac attempted to balance the historicity of salvation with the

94. Ibid., 107.

distinction between the natural and supernatural orders, his work emphasizes one or the other in different contexts.

De Lubac's sacramental ecclesiology reflects his insight into the unity between nature and grace within a single historical experience. For de Lubac, the church itself is the temporal reality—a visible communion and sacramental anticipation—that makes the kingdom present. The church is the sacrament of the eschaton. As in all sacramental reality, the visible sacrament cannot be an end in itself. It achieves its identity as sacrament when it is a means to the final end, a means that we must pass through, but will never do so completely. The church embodies a certain way of life that takes on social, liturgical, and political dimensions, which constitute her visibility. Salvation proleptically enters into these dimensions. Yet this social and political space is always an anticipation and, as such, is incomplete. In de Lubac's view, it would be false to absolutize a certain set of practices—including sacramental practices like baptism—as definitively embodying salvation. His communion ecclesiology cautions against it. We enter into communion with God through the ecclesial communion. It would be a mistake, however, to confuse the exterior dimensions of the ecclesial communion, conceived of as exterior practices and structures, with communion with God. The rearrangement of institutions, structures, and practices is no guarantee of salvation; and salvation is not reducible to these institutions, structures, or practices.

In *Brief Catechesis on Nature and Grace*, de Lubac primarily attended to the distinction between the supernatural and natural orders. His manner of speaking of temporal progress and human liberation is telling, for he defined "human liberation" as the restructuring of temporal society by *only* human means. Human liberation is the rearrangement of the deck chairs on the sinking ship of history. It is a social or political rearrangement considered independently from the revolution of God's grace, the conversion of heart. Conceived as only a human effort to reorganize the bureaucracy of social existence, the pursuit of social justice appears enclosed within its own very human order. Unfortunately, de Lubac did not apply the notion of sacramentality to human liberation or the ecclesial practices that proleptically embody salvation. He did not extend his understanding of the church to the matrix of social existence that constitutes the church. This neglect is caused by de Lubac's tendency to think of social progress in terms of the ontological "nature-supernatural" distinction. Created "nature" is of an entirely different order than grace, or the supernatural. Nature cannot, by its own power and without the gift of grace, rise to the supernatural. However, the "history-eschatology" distinction is not entirely the same as the "nature-supernatural" distinction. History is not entirely natural because history allows for the encounter with God in time, in Jesus, in the church, and through the sacraments. We could say that both nature and the supernatural are to be found in a single historical frame. However, by thinking of human progress as merely human efforts, de Lubac failed in this instance to apply or realize the broad scope of his sacramental vision. Unlike Johann Baptist Metz or Gustavo Gutiérrez, de Lubac did not elaborate how social and political practices, the struggle for justice, or the social aspects of ecclesial communion could be anticipatory of the consummation of God's plan.

Conceivably, de Lubac's understanding of the church as sacrament—of God and of humanity, bearing both the invisible and visible, uniting the eschaton with history—could be reclaimed for interpreting the church's sociopolitical dimensions. Keeping in mind that these social dimensions of the church remain ambiguous, they might appear as sacraments of the eschaton. Communion with God and others must be embodied visibly. In this sense, practices that embody communion, namely all of those human actions in the world in pursuit of communion, should be considered *within* the sacramental economy of salvation as anticipatory of the eschatological kingdom.

Conclusion

A sacramental perspective governs de Lubac's writings on revelation, Christ, and the church. Sacraments possess a twofold characteristic. First, the sacramental sign's "intention" overflows its bare materiality, enabling it to participate in the mystery signified. Second, the mystery signified exercises a power over the sign, making it what it is, making it efficacious as a sign. As a consequence, the sacraments (as visible, concrete, historical realities) are loci of the eschaton entering into history. The sacramental sign is an anticipation of the eschaton but also a making present of its transcendent reality. The sacred is discovered within our concrete, historical experience, yet is not reducible to that experience.

The exemplar of sacramentality is the historical actions of Jesus. In Jesus, the Word becomes human without reserve. Jesus's kenotic life, death, and resurrection make the eschaton visible historically. He is eternity in history. Yet his historical existence is also a sacrament because it is the sign and means of the eschatological unity of the human race at the eschaton. Christ inaugurates the beginning of the end. Thereafter, the Christian lives in the wake of Christ's action, seeking a unity that cannot entirely be achieved in history. The visible, social dimensions of the church become a sacrament of the eschatological consummation in the *totus Christus*, the union of all humanity in Christ. De Lubac preserves the sacredness of the concrete and historical while not conflating it with the eschatological.

In dialogue with post–Vatican II theologies of history, de Lubac opposed the identification between temporal progress and the kingdom of God. His opposition to Joachimite thought influenced his position in *A Brief Catechesis on Nature and Grace* that, just as the natural is not a seed of the eternal, temporal progress cannot in any sense "anticipate" the coming kingdom. Although his position is consistent with his refusal to collaborate with political regimes or to allow theology to underwrite political ideologies, on this point it is not entirely consistent with his understanding of the sacramentality of the temporal order, especially when we are speaking of ecclesial practices that embody communion in the world. The next chapter shows that de Lubac's theology of nature and the supernatural was built upon his basic eschatological insights and sought to preserve the sacred in temporal existence.

7

Eschatology in the Theology of the Supernatural

Although almost seven decades have passed since the publication of Henri de Lubac's *Surnaturel* (1946), his theology of supernatural remains at the center of an unsettled debate.[1] De Lubac's most vehement critics claim that his insistence that human beings have

1. See C. C. Pecknold and Jacob Wood, "Augustine and Henri de Lubac," in *T & T Clark Companion to Augustine and Modern Theology* (New York: Bloomsbury T & T Clark, 2013), 197–222; Sean Larsen, "The Politics of Desire: Two Readings of Henri de Lubac on Nature and Grace," *Modern Theology* 29, no. 3 (2013): 279–310; Christopher J. Malloy, "De Lubac on Natural Desire: Difficulties and Antitheses," *Nova et Vetera*, English Edition, 9, no. 3 (2011): 567–624; Matthew Bernard Mulcahy, OP, *Aquinas's Notion of Pure Nature and the Christian Integralism of Henri de Lubac: Not Everything Is Grace*, American University Studies (New York: Peter Lang, 2011); Lawrence Feingold, *The Natural Desire to See God according to St. Thomas and His Interpreters* (Washington, DC: Sapientia Press, 2010), 2010; David Braine, "The Debate between Henri de Lubac and his Critics," *Nova et Vetera*, English Edition, 6, no. 3 (2008): 543–90; Nicholas J. Healy, "Henri de Lubac on Nature and Grace: A Note on Some Recent Contributions to the Debate," *Communio* 35, no. 4 (2008): 535–64; Raymond Moloney, "De Lubac and Lonergan on the Supernatural," *Theological Studies* 69, no. 3 (Spring 2008): 509–27; Noel O'Sullivan, "Henri de Lubac's Surnaturel: An Emerging Christology," *Irish Theological Quarterly* 72, no. 1 (2007): 3–31; Reinhard Hütter, *"Desiderium Naturale Visionis Dei—Est Autem Duplex Hominis Beatitudo Sive Felicitas*: Some Observations about Lawrence Feingold's and John Milbank's Recent Interventions in the Debate over the Natural Desire to See God,"

a single "supernatural finality" compromises the gratuity of grace, endangers the intelligibility of the natural order, and construes grace as universally available through the natural. If God made humanity with a single supernatural end, and if humanity required grace to reach this end, then would not God then be under obligation to supply that needed grace? Moreover, if God *must* give grace to everyone, are not the church and sacraments superfluous? The consequence—though not intended result—of de Lubac's theology is the irrelevance of Christ, the church, and the sacraments as means to our supernatural end. De Lubac's defenders insist that his position on human finality is crucial for rejecting a view of the natural world autonomous from God's grace. If human beings have a purely natural end that can be reached by their own power and if they can be fully happy by attaining this end, does not God's offer of supernatural grace become something extra or superfluous? The consequence—though not the intended result—is the irrelevance of Christ, the church, and the sacraments as means to our supernatural end. The stakes of the debate remain high.

The current debate over the supernatural reflects profound divisions surrounding post–Vatican II Catholicism. The Second Vatican Council prompted a fundamental shift from antagonism to engagement in the Catholic Church's stance toward the modern world. The Council's tone was irenic and dialogical rather than combative. It also opened the door to theological methods that were attentive to the human experience of God and the reality of God's universal presence. Catholic theologians such as Karl Rahner, Edward Schillebeeckx, and Hans Kung became representatives of the theological, liturgical, and cultural revolution in the Catholic Church surrounding the Council. De Lubac's theology of the supernatural is

Nova et Vetera, English Edition, 5, no. 1 (2007): 81–132; Milbank, *The Suspended Middle: Henri de Lubac and the Debate Concerning the Supernatural* (Grand Rapids, MI: Eerdmans, 2005).

also symbolic of these changes. Guy Mansini claims that *Surnaturel* is *the* most pivotal book of twentieth-century Catholic theology because it demarcates a before and an after—that is, before and after scholasticism.[2] Furthermore, de Lubac's *Surnaturel* anticipated the shift in emphasis following the Council toward the attentiveness to the universal presence of God and the universal availability of grace. Today, the legacy of the Second Vatican Council is contested. The Catholic Church in Europe and the United States has experienced effects of secularization in the form of empty churches, lessened social prestige, and loss of political power. The Council's openness to the world interpreted through the postconciliar theological climate, some argue, downplayed the necessity of Christ, the Catholic Church, and the sacraments. Given this context, the recent criticism of de Lubac's theology of the supernatural is also a referendum on post–Vatican II Catholic theology.

Although de Lubac employed the theological categories of modern scholasticism, he intentionally reenvisioned the categories under which the modern controversy over the supernatural had been fought. Because he had to defend his work in terms of a neoscholastic methodology employed nearly universally in Catholic institutions, his writings on the supernatural reflected the Aristotelian ontological and anthropological categories of neoscholasticism. Yet his theology of the supernatural also reflects his historical and eschatological thinking. Despite the deep connections between ontology and history in de Lubac work, his writings on the supernatural have often been considered in isolation from the rest of his theological production, often exclusively within a framework of metaphysics,

---

2. Mansini, "The Abiding Theological Significance of Henri de Lubac's Surnaturel," *The Thomist* 73, no. 4 (2009): 593–619. However, Mansini says that Marie-Dominique Chenu's *Le Saulchoir, une école de théologie* is a close rival for the most pivotal Catholic theological text of the twentieth century.

ontology, and anthropology. These thematic or disciplinary partitions, however, are unnatural to his thinking. As de Lubac states, to attain a vision of the whole one must "unite in order to distinguish."[3] De Lubac's writings on the supernatural finality of human nature united without entirely reconciling ontology and history. An accurate assessment of his theology of the supernatural requires one to interpret it in light of his theology of history and eschatology. The earlier debate over nature and supernatural in the nineteenth and twentieth centuries transitioned into a debate over history and eschatology by the middle of the twentieth century. De Lubac's most controversial writings straddle this transition.

Apologetics and the Supernatural

De Lubac's most controversial work, on the theology of the supernatural, was congruous with his proposed transformation of apologetics. Most of modern apologists sought to prove the existence of God and the Christian truth with a barrage of philosophical and pseudoscientific arguments. This apologetic method tended to obscure rather than reveal the truth of Christianity. De Lubac argued that Christianity becomes credible only when God is revealed to the depths of the human heart, that is, in the recognition of God's gift of grace as a fulfillment of one's existence. The apologetic task is no longer to convince using extrinsic argumentation, but to present the totality of dogma as a whole. The implication of de Lubac's apologetics is that humanity has a "natural desire for the supernatural" by which we can recognize in God's offer of salvation the fulfillment of human desire. His theology of the supernatural followed his shifts in apologetic and theological methods.

---

3. De Lubac, *Catholicism: Christ and the Common Destiny of* Man, trans. Lancelot C. Sheppard and Sister Elizabeth Englund, OCD (San Francisco: Ignatius Press, 1988), 330.

De Lubac delivered his opening lecture for his course in fundamental theology at *Université Catholique de Lyon*, entitled "Apologetics and Theology," in 1929. It treated the problem of the separation of apologetics and theology in twentieth-century Catholicism. Apologetics, he argued, had "engulfed theology" in the modern period. The object of faith, the self-revelation of God to humanity, known through the liturgy and Scriptures, took a secondary role in the intellectual efforts of the church. Apologetic arguments attempted to prove the existence of God, the revelation of God in Christ, and the validity of that revelation without describing what that revelation is. De Lubac proposed a close interrelation between apologetics and theology: reason is fulfilled by faith in revelation because the human being has an inner orientation to union with God. The "natural desire for the supernatural" is the rationale for his apologetic method.

The overarching concern of the neoscholastics was to trace a path between the Charybdis of fideism and Scylla of rationalism. The fideism that they attributed to Protestants failed to secure the rationality of the act of faith and denied human reason the capacity to arrive at truth. Rationalism, attributed to the post-Kantian theological tradition, made faith an act of human reason apart from grace. The concern to avoid fideism and rationalism drove the neoscholastics to maintain the distinction between the *preambula fidei* and the "act of faith," that is, between those things that human reason could know securely independent of grace and the supernatural act of faith itself.[4] Vatican I's *Dei Filius* appeared side with the neoscholastics. Against rationalism, *Dei Filius* stated that "authority of God revealing" (*auctoritatem Dei Revelantis*) through the gift of supernatural faith

---

4. Gabriel Daly, *Transcendence and Immanence: A Study in Catholic Modernism and Integralism* (Oxford: Clarendon Press, 1980), 8–9.

is the only motive to believe. Against fideism, the Council fathers claimed that the act of faith is itself reasonable.

The discipline of apologetics, therefore, establishes the reasonableness of faith based on natural reason prior to the act of faith. The problem that always troubled this approach to apologetics was how the mind can assent to the truth of faith prior to supernatural virtue. How can natural reason know with certainty there is a moral obligation to assent to a proposition of faith without knowing the proposition is true? The neoscholastics maintained a clear distinction between the natural assent of the mind to arguments—a "natural faith"—and the supernatural assent to the authority of God by faith. Louis Billot, SJ (1846–1931), at the Gregorian University in Rome from 1888 to 1911, argued that the reasonableness of the act of faith is established by the *preamubla fidei* that established God's authority through '*argumenta seu signa*' (arguments or signs) that resulted in the removal of doubt. In the act of faith, the mind adheres to the truth to be believed because God revealed it. Gabriel Daly points out the schizophrenia involved: "*A priori* agnosticism about the nature and content of revelation and an *a posteriori* fideism in its appeal to *signs* (miracles and fulfilled prophesies) . . . give extrinsic guarantee of credibility."[5] Establishing the credibility of revelation was extrinsic to and prior to the act of faith. The act of faith is merely a response to God's authority, previously made reasonable by philosophical argumentation and external signs and miracles.

According to de Lubac, the apologetic project became a barrage of "scientific" arguments, providing historical and metaphysical "demonstrations" to lead the nonbeliever to an act of "natural faith." The rationalistic apologetics of the nineteenth to twentieth centuries became an abuse of science on the one hand, and distanced this

5. Ibid., 17.

rationalistic apologetics from the heart of the Christian mystery on the other. This apologetics poorly interprets the meaning of Vatican I, for which only God's revelation makes God credible. According to de Lubac, this division between apologetics and theology could only be resolved by following another precept of Vatican I: "Has the First Vatican Council not summoned us to search for the links between the two [grace and nature] when it teaches that the theological method consists of studying the relationships that exist not only among the various dogmas but also between the totality of dogma and its ultimate end?"[6] God is the ultimate author of both nature and grace and nature *in anticipation of* grace. Therefore, de Lubac argued, the relationship between creation and redemption forms the pivot on which both apologetics and theology turn.

De Lubac's apologetic was based on two key premises: the natural world as a whole has a finality in God's divine plan, and dogma as a whole is essentially related to the ultimate end of humanity. The "the supernatural brilliance of doctrine," he writes, "is a brilliance by which the doctrine becomes its own sign, a brilliance by which God bears witness to himself in the deepest part of the human heart."[7] De Lubac denied that one could prove the mysteries of faith by a chain of extrinsic rational arguments. His apologetics is not a method of resorting to signs external to revelation itself. Instead, doctrine sheds light on the whole of human reality and experience because it sheds light on the purpose of human life. Because the human being is made in the image of God and called to union with God, human life is only illuminated by its divine destiny. De Lubac illustrated the intrinsic connection between human life and its destiny with the fulfillment of Judaism in Christ. Put simply, authentic doctrine presents an

---

6. Henri de Lubac, "Apologetics and Theology," in *Theological Fragments*, trans. Rebecca Howell Balinski (San Francisco: Ignatius Press, 1989), 95.
7. Ibid., 101.

integrated vision of human reality that explains the antinomies of human existence and, therefore, is convincing. By beginning from the rich conception of reality communicated by Christian doctrine, the apologist is freed from unconvincing assertions of signs and miracles as proofs for Christianity.

De Lubac's 1929 lecture became programmatic for his work as a whole. Rather than searching for external signs and miracles that make doctrine credible, de Lubac argued that doctrine becomes its own sign because it represents a fulfillment of human existence. Faith is credible to reason because reason is fulfilled in faith. This key idea indicates a trajectory, not usually expounded with systematic consistency, but nonetheless foundational for de Lubac's subsequent writings. He developed it in a christological direction, where natural mysticism anticipates its fulfillment in the mystery. It is developed in his ecclesiology, in which the Israel is an anticipation of the church, and the church anticipates the whole Christ. It is developed within his sacramental theology, in which the sign points towards and anticipates the reality signified.

De Lubac's style of apologetics closely correlates with his theology of natural desire for the supernatural. His core argument suggests that the human being is made in the image of God and that the image is, in itself, incomplete until it attains to the likeness of God. Human reason desires knowledge of ultimate causes and faith is reasonable because it constitutes knowledge of the divine source, its ultimate cause. In sum, de Lubac's apologetics requires that humanity possesses a supernatural finality, a natural orientation to the divine. Thus, all of de Lubac's writings on the supernatural defend the idea quoted in *Le Mystère du surnaturel* from Augustine's *Confessions*: *Fecisti nos ad te, Deus* (You have made us for yourself, O God).[8] The incomplete

---

8. Henri de Lubac, *The Mystery of the Supernatural*, trans. Rosemary Sheed (New York: Crossroad, 1998), xxxvii. Quotation from Augustine, *Confessions*, book 1, chapter 1.

quotation prompts the reader to recall the second half of the quoted line, *Et inquietum est cor nostrum donec requiescat in te* (and our heart is unquiet until it rests in you).

Three Theses on the Supernatural

De Lubac's early writings on the supernatural—*Surnaturel: Études historiques* (1946) and an article, "Le Mystère du surnaturel" (1949)[9]—contained a provocative set of theses:

1. *Historical thesis*: Contemporary neoscholastics depended upon a modern tradition of interpretation that distorted the teachings of St. Thomas Aquinas concerning human nature by erecting a system of "pure nature" beginning in the sixteenth century.
2. *Theological thesis*: Contemporary neoscholastic anthropology implied a human nature without the desire or élan for the supernatural and, therefore, conceivably fulfilled without it. Instead, according de Lubac, human beings have a "natural desire for the supernatural."
3. *Practical thesis*: Contemporary neoscholastic theology assumed an ontological dualism between the supernatural and natural orders not dissimilar to the anthropology assumed by atheist humanist philosophers of the nineteenth and twentieth centuries.

The theological thesis accused modern scholastic theologians of creating a theological anthropology that mischaracterized the human desire for the supernatural by minimizing it or by making it not constitutive of what it means to be human. The historical thesis

---

9. De Lubac, *Surnaturel: Études historiques*, Théologie 8 (Paris: Aubier-Montaigne, 1946). References are to the original 1946 version of *Surnaturel*. Henri de Lubac, "Le Mystère Du Surnaturel," *Recherches de Science Religieuse* 36 (1949): 80–121.

accused them of infidelity to their own theological master. The practical thesis accused them of being unwittingly complicit with the atheist intellectual enemies of the faith. Understood correctly, *Surnaturel* incited a theological revolution in Roman Catholic theology.

The historical thesis has proven the most explosive because it attacked the very legitimacy and relevance of the neoscholastic schools. The neoscholastic movement claimed to be a recovery of medieval scholasticism along with its perennial philosophical and theological principles. If neoscholasticism had distorted medieval scholasticism on something so critical as the supernatural order, then its methods were suspect. Much of the recent scholarship touching de Lubac's thesis concerns the interpretation of Thomas Aquinas: the accuracy of de Lubac's interpretation of Aquinas; whether the Baroque scholasticism of the commentary tradition, including that of Denis the Carthusian, Cajetan, Báñez, and Suárez accurately interpreted Thomas Aquinas; and whether, in turn, contemporary iterations of scholasticism are the legitimate heirs to Thomas Aquinas.[10] Because de Lubac presented *Surnaturel* as a series of historical studies, many responses to de Lubac's work have been historical studies on Thomas Aquinas and the scholastic commentary tradition.

The theological thesis of *Surnaturel* is that human beings have a single, supernatural finality. Human beings are made for a transcendent end that is beyond their power to attain and failure to attain this end is frustration of their purpose.[11] The only end of

10. Serge-Thomas Bonino, *Surnaturel: A Controversy at the Heart of Twentieth-Century Thomistic Thought* (Ave Maria, FL: Sapientia Press of Ave Maria University, 2009); Feingold, *The Natural Desire to See God*, 2010; Mulcahy, *Aquinas's Notion of Pure Nature*; Malloy, "De Lubac on Natural Desire."

11. On the issue of natural desire, de Lubac sided with the Augustinian or Aegidian school of interpreting Thomas Aquinas that was inspired by Giles of Rome (1246–1318) and revived

humanity that can make humanity happy is union with God, also described as the beatific vision. The scriptures, the fathers, and the medieval theologians testify to this fact. Human beings possess an innate desire for God, what de Lubac calls the "natural desire for the supernatural." The natural desire for the supernatural is, in de Lubac's view, the volitional and noetic expression of supernatural finality. Human beings desire God as their only end.

De Lubac rejected the modern scholastic position that desire for the supernatural is merely conditional. Some neoscholastics invoked the principle that finality is delimited by form, that is, the immanent powers and properties of nature. In other words, the immanent constitution of human nature is the principle that determines the end toward which nature moves. The finality of a human being is limited to ends proportionate to its nature: natural virtue, natural knowledge, and so on. To desire something above one's nature, one must be moved by a principle proportionate to that end. The desire for the supernatural depends upon receiving grace, which generates the desire for the supernatural. In other words, desire for the supernatural is conditioned by the reception of grace. De Lubac agreed that our natural desire for God was powerless to achieve its end without grace, though he believed making desire for the supernatural conditional made it also unnecessary. *Surnaturel* affirmed in the strongest terms that natural desire was essential to what it meant to be human: "L'esprit est donc désir de Dieu" ("The spirit is, then, the desire of God").[12] Natural desire, he states, is absolute, "the most absolute of all the desires."[13] The theological difficulty that emerged for de Lubac is how to maintain God's freedom against the

---

by Guy de Broglie, S J (1889–1983), in the twentieth century. See Pecknold and Wood, "Augustine and Henri de Lubac," 200–3.

12. De Lubac, *Surnaturel*, 483.

13. Ibid., 484.

absolute requirement of the creature: If grace is what we require, then how can God be free to *not* grant it?

De Lubac's rejection of "pure nature" is implied in his affirmation of a single, supernatural finality. The earliest medieval construct *pura naturalia* was used to consider whether God could have made humanity without grace yet without the fault of sin.[14] It was a philosophical construct of nature apart from any state, that is, independent from the original human nature before the fall of Adam and Eve and independent from fallen human nature. According to de Lubac, these earlier medieval speculations were employed for a new purpose by Thomas Cajetan (1469–1534), who laid the foundation for a system of pure nature by restricting the end and purpose of a being—its finality—to what can be achieved by its own powers and constitution. Francisco Suárez (1548–1617) hypothesized a third state apart from *natura integra* (integral nature) and *natura lapsa* (fallen nature), which is "supposed to lay the foundation for the historic states."[15] Apart from the state of integral nature, in which human beings existed in grace and harmony with God before the fall, and apart from the state of fallen nature, there exists a third state underlying both, *natura pura*. Following Suarez, neoscholastic theologians depended upon the construction of pure nature as the extant anthropological reality upon which grace can operate. Pure nature is, therefore, a conception of the human who is destined only for a terrestrial goal, who can be fulfilled by its attainment, and seeks nothing more. Pure nature is, in principle, opposed to de Lubac's conception of the human being fundamentally unfulfilled without grace.

14. Pierre-François Moreau, "De la pure nature," *Revue Philosophique de la France et de l'etranger* 103, no. 3 (1978): 347.
15. Ibid., 348

De Lubac's practical thesis, which he expanded in *Le Mystère du surnaturel* (1965), is that the "theory of pure nature" assumed an ontological univocity between nature and supernatural. Originally the theory of pure nature functioned as a *hypothetical* construct used for preserving the gratuity of grace. It asked the question, "What would the created order look like had God not given it a supernatural end, sent the prophets, and sent the Son?" Although pure nature was originally thought of as a hypothetical or counterfactual scenario, it morphed into a whole system of thinking about nature (*as it really is*) as something entirely independent of a supernatural end. The theory of pure nature became the basis for understanding the existing order of creation. In turn, the existing natural order became an oppositional concept: *supernatural = not natural*. The theory of pure nature encouraged one to see "nature and supernature as in some sense juxtaposed, and in spite of every intention to the contrary, as contained in the same genus, of which they form as it were two species."[16] Nature and the supernatural were conceived of two univocal "things" competing for space on the same ontological plane.

The result was a dualistic theology in which nature and the supernatural were thought of as occupying two orders of reality, complete in themselves, with little interaction. In practice, the supernatural was thought as being in the same genus as nature, losing its fundamental ontological difference and distinctiveness. Modern scholastic theology tended to contrast natural virtue and supernatural virtue, natural knowledge and supernatural knowledge, natural grace and supernatural grace. "In the complete system, the two series—pure nature and supernaturalized nature, or nature called to the supernatural—flowed along parallel channels in complete harmony."[17] The supernatural would be conceived as a supersized

16. De Lubac, *The Mystery of the Supernatural*, 37.
17. Ibid., 41.

version of the natural. The otherness and transcendence of the supernatural was almost entirely lost.

Modern Catholic theology colluded with a post-Englightenment understanding of the natural order that became dominant, namely a self-enclosed and self-sustaining sphere of forces, natures, and powers. Under this view of nature, humanity loses nothing by denying the relevance of the supernatural order altogether. The rejection of the supernatural in modern philosophers—like Comte, Feuerbach, Proudhon and Nietzsche—had its roots in a conception of the supernatural that placed it on the same plane as the natural and thereby made it a redundant version of the natural. As a result, God is seen as a coercive force intervening from the outside and from which one must escape to ensure freedom and dignity. This was the concern in de Lubac's 1944 *Le Drame de l'humanisme athée. Surnaturel* was written with the movement of atheist humanism in mind.

The Problem of Finality

De Lubac's systematic thesis that human beings have a single supernatural end has been controversial from the beginning. In a 1948 review of the brewing dispute over the supernatural, Philip Donnelly identified the critical issue concerning finality: "Herein lies the central point of the entire controversy. P. de Lubac not only maintains that the beatific vision is the normal and only possible goal of a spiritual being, but is also convinced that this thesis expresses the constant thought of St. Thomas, and even constitutes an essential doctrine of Christian philosophy."[18] To identify the vision of God as the sole finality of the spiritual being implied that God would be compelled to supply the grace to achieve the beatific vision. Here, Donnelly points to a fundamental tension in de Lubac's account of

18. Phillip J. Donnelly, "Disussions on the Supernatural Order," *Theological Studies* 9, no. 2 (1948): 226.

natural desire: on the one hand, de Lubac speaks of our desire to see God as "inefficacious," powerless on its own; on the other hand, de Lubac characterized this desire as "absolute," that is, in Donnelly's words, "infrustratable." An "absolute" desire suggested a desire that must be attained as a requirement of the nature of the person. The problem that has followed de Lubac ever since is how to maintain God's freedom to give grace (or not to) in the face of an "absolute" need for grace on the part of the human being for grace.

Initially, the debate that followed *Surnaturel*'s publication in 1946 was vibrant but civil. The initial critical responses were largely from Jesuit scholars, mostly Suarezian and Thomistic scholastics, including Leo Malevez, Jacques de Blic, SJ, Charles Boyer, SJ, Guy de Broglie, SJ, and Philip Donnelly, SJ. The Jesuits critical of de Lubac generally treated the controversy as an academic dispute rather than a heretic trial (as Donnelly stated, "The Church does not forbid under pain of heresy the habit of philosophizing irrationally.")[19] However, *Surnatural* soon became implicated in the controversy over the *nouvelle théologie*, which became a public fight between the Dominicans at the the Pontifical University of St. Thomas (The Angelicum) in Rome and the Jesuits of the scholasticate at Fourvière in Lyon.[20] Reginald Garrigou-Lagrange, OP, and Marie-Michel Labourdette, OP, linked de Lubac's theology with the ideas of the Modernists condemned earlier in the century by the Catholic magisterium. Now, the argument against "natural desire for the supernatural" became essentially an extension of argument against rationalism. Just as human beings cannot achieve supernatural knowledge of God by the natural power of their intellect, so also,

19. Phillip J. Donnelly, "Current Theology: A Recent Critique of P. de Lubac's *Surnaturel*," *Theological Studies* 9, no. 4 (1948): 557.
20. For an overview of the controversy, see Aidan Nichols, OP, "Thomism and the Nouvelle Théologie," *The Thomist* 64 (2000): 1–19.

they cannot desire God with the natural power of their will. De Lubac's book was associated with a resurgent Modernism for its denial of traditional doctrine and theological methodology.

In 1950 Pope Pius XII promulgated the encyclical *Humani generis*. For de Lubac, it was a conversation ender. One line of the text was critical: "Others destroy the gratuity of the supernatural order, since God, they say, cannot create intellectual beings without ordering and calling them to the beatific vision."[21] The text was seen as targeting de Lubac's *Surnaturel*. His Jesuit superiors soon removed him from the teaching faculty at Fourvière, exiling him to Paris. De Lubac stated that he did not believe that *Humani generis* targeted his writings. He was not rehabilitated as a Catholic theologian until just before the Second Vatican Council. His subsequent writings on the supernatural constituted a defense of his original thesis, expanded to meet the doctrinal concerns raised by *Humani generis*. *Le Mystère du surnaturel* (1965) and *Augustinianisme et théologie moderne* (1965) appeared together as an expansion of *Surnaturel* and the 1949 article "Le Mystère du surnaturel." *Petite catéchese sur nature et grace* (1980) expands on some of the ideas in *Le Mystère du surnaturel*.

The theological tension in de Lubac's argument pointed out by Donnelly remains at the heart of the current debate. Christopher J. Malloy's sympathetic critique of de Lubac identifies the theological inconsistency between two of de Lubac's affirmations concerning natural desire. On the one hand, de Lubac insists that desire for God is innate, unconditional, and absolute: "It is so absolute that its eternal non-fulfillment would cause the pain of damnation."[22] In this way, de Lubac underscores that union with God is absolutely necessary to human happiness and denies the sufficiency of terrestrial happiness.

---

21. *Humani generis*, 26.
22. Malloy, "De Lubac on Natural Desire," 575.

On the other hand, de Lubac stated that this desire is "inefficacious . . . 'no kind of divine seed' of glory."[23] It is unable to reach its goal by its own power. In the first affirmation, de Lubac characterized natural desire as essential to human nature. In the second, he characterized human nature as unable to attain its goal without grace. Malloy says that these two assertions are really on a collision course. He asks whether God could "without injustice or failure in wisdom never meet this desire."[24] If God *could not* withhold grace, it would appear that God is obligated to human beings. Grace would then be due to humanity. If God *could* withhold grace, never fulfilling this desire, it would seem that God has created an absurd world in which God creates a being for an unattainable destiny. Thus, in the attempt to preserve the absoluteness of natural desire for the supernatural, de Lubac's theology results in the arbitrary nature of divine liberty. At the same time, de Lubac's anthropology suggests that human nature, in itself (without grace), lacks any orientation toward the good and is "wretched" to the core.[25]

Lawrence Feingold finds a similar tension in de Lubac's understanding of human finality. On the one hand, de Lubac conceives finality as an *intrinsic ordering* of the human being to the supernatural. On the other hand, de Lubac states that this intrinsic ordering is completely natural, not due to grace.

> It is *ultimately contradictory to suppose that our nature or being itself—without the addition of a supernatural principle—could be intrinsically determined by a supernatural finality*, or have a supernatural finality inscribed upon it, or have an "essential finality" that is supernatural. If this were the case, our nature itself would be supernatural or divine, for every nature is defined by its end. *A nature with a divine end can only be the divine nature.*[26]

23. Ibid., 576. Quoting de Lubac, *The Mystery of the Supernatural*, 84.
24. Ibid., 584.
25. Ibid., 120.

According to Feingold, de Lubac's assertion that supernatural finality is "essential" to what it means to be human implies either (a) that nature requires grace, thereby placing requirement on God to give grace or (b) that it is already somehow contains in itself a supernatural principle that orders it to a supernatural end. In contrast to de Lubac, for Thomas Aquinas, there exists a natural, essential end and another supernatural, gratuitous end. Feingold argues that we are ordered to our supernatural end by the reception of grace and the supernatural virtues and not *essentially* ordered to a supernatural end. Grace is gratuitous in relation to the essential order of the concrete person: a "supernatural end is gratuitous because it is not required by the principles of the nature itself, as it concretely exists."[27] Since grace is not *essentially* required by nature, "it cannot be maintained that a supernatural finality—generating an innate absolute desire to see God—is imprinted on our nature prior to our reception of sanctifying grace."[28]

The ambiguity in de Lubac's account of finality has been exploited by John Milbank. Milbank suggests that de Lubac can claim supernatural finality belongs essentially to human nature because he dismantled the ontological partition between the natural and supernatural. Like contemporary Thomists, Milbank recognizes a tension in de Lubac's account of finality insofar as de Lubac claims that the human being possesses a finality to the supernatural ontologically prior (not historically) to grace. But Milbank dissolves the tension altogether by denying that de Lubac distinguished between supernatural and natural orders. According to Milbank, de Lubac's rejection of the theory of pure nature implied the rejection of

26. Feingold, *The Natural Desire to See God*, 321–22. Emphasis in the original.
27. Lawrence Feingold, *The Natural Desire to See God according to St. Thomas Aquinas and His Interpreters*, Dissertationes Series Theologica 3 (Rome: Apollinare studi, 2001), 622.
28. Ibid., 624.

any aspect of human nature formally distinct from the supernatural. To analytically separate the natural from the supernatural within human nature would be to set aside that part of human nature that is conceptually distinguishable, a "pure nature."[29] De Lubac embraced a patristic ontology ambivalent to the distinction between supernatural and natural and that implied a rejection of nature that is not already *constituted* by grace. By insisting that human beings have a single supernatural telos, de Lubac dismantled any formal distinction between the natural and the supernatural altogether. Milbank's reading leads to the suspicion that de Lubac cannot account for a "nature" presupposed by grace. In other words, everything is grace. While Milbank's interpretation achieves a kind of philosophical consistency, it has fundamental problems on an exegetical level because it ignores or rationalizes away all of the places in which de Lubac insists on the difference between the natural and supernatural orders.[30]

Although one might attempt to interpret de Lubac on the supernatural by "bracketing" the ontological problems, one cannot entirely escape ontology. For instance, one contemporary method approaches de Lubac's intervention into the controversy over the supernatural in light of its political implications and not exclusively as a metaphysics. Sean Larsen suggests that the conflict of interpretations of de Lubac is premised "on the idea that de Lubac is answering a metaphysical question, and there is good reason to think that he is not in fact trying to do that."[31] Larsen claims that de Lubac should be read in terms of how his theology "shows something

29. According to Milbank, Cajetan employs a doctrine of pure nature because he "explicitly states that human nature in actuality is fully definable in merely natural terms." Milbank, *The Suspended Middle*, 17.
30. See, for instance de Lubac, *Surnaturel*, 488; de Lubac, *The Mystery of the Supernatural*, 23, 28, 31, 34–35; de Lubac, *A Brief Catechesis on Nature and Grace*, trans. Brother Richard Arnandez, F.S.C. (San Francisco: Ignatius Press, 1984), 32, 65.
31. Larsen, "The Politics of Desire," 309–10.

about how we are constituted relationally, both individually and communally," that is, the implications de Lubac's theology has for communal, social, and political life.[32] It is true, as Larsen observes, that de Lubac is not entirely consistent as a metaphysician. However, to claim that de Lubac is a nonmetaphysical theologian or that his account of the supernatural is not "ontological" would be a misrepresentation. The preface to *The Mystery of the Supernatural* reads, "Starting from the classic question of the relationship between nature and the supernatural, he [the author, de Lubac, speaking of himself in the third person] has restricted his theological reflections to the sphere of formal ontology where they are normally carried out, without any attempt to make them more concrete."[33] Not only did de Lubac intend to communicate something true about human nature, but he restricted himself methodologically in *The Mystery of the Supernatural* to "formal ontology." One might question whether formal ontology was a good starting place or whether de Lubac was consistent in his methodology. However, de Lubac would probably object if we characterized his theology of the supernatural as a strategy or rhetorical practice as opposed to an account of what is true.

Although de Lubac was certainly making an "ontological" claim, his lack of systematic coherence remains an obstacle.[34] David Braine

---

32. Ibid., 310.

33. De Lubac, *The Mystery of the Supernatural*, xxxiii.

34. De Lubac invited the suspicion of intellectual inconsistency by appealing to the paradox of human nature. *Surnaturel* reads, "Paradox of the human spirit: created, finite, it is not only a kind of dual nature; it is itself nature." De Lubac, *Surnaturel*, 483. In *The Mystery of the Supernatural* he again appealed to paradox, even in the titles of chapters: "6. The Christian Paradox of Man"; "7. The Paradox Unknown to the Gentiles"; "8. A Paradox Rejected by Common Sense"; "9. The Paradox Overcome in Faith." However, in his theological lexicon, *paradox* does not refer to an irrational contradiction: "Paradox is the search or wait for synthesis. It is the provisional expression of a view which remains incomplete, but whose orientation is toward fullness." Henri de Lubac, *Paradoxes of Faith*, trans. Paule Simon and Sadie Kreilkamp (San Francisco: Ignatius Press, 1987), 9. Not only do our minds lack the power to construct a complete synthesis, resulting in a tension between truths, but the realities themselves are

argues that de Lubac's inconsistent exposition of nature and finality led to a "disaster."[35] According to Braine, finality exists not as something inhering within a *nature*, but within a *substance* or *person*. Finality consists in a *relation* of human nature, connected to the whole plan of God's salvation, rather than something inhering *in* the nature itself. De Lubac confuses the issue because he speaks of an "essential," "absolute" finality inhering in the nature of the human being. Some of de Lubac's critics are also mistaken, he says: "This supernatural finality consists not in a 'form' as something 'real' *in the nature of human beings* (contrary to Feingold's presumption), but is a finality belonging to them *as persons* arising in virtue of a relation."[36] The supernatural finality of humanity cannot be found within the structure of human nature as such, but instead in its relation to God's providential plan of salvation. Braine affirms de Lubac's basic intuition that human beings possess a supernatural finality by virtue of God's plan of salvation but denies that this finality inheres in human nature. Braine suggests that if de Lubac wanted to follow Thomas he should have affirmed that finality is a relation of a nature and doesn't belong to nature itself.

Braine presents a plausible and coherent rapprochement between scholastics and de Lubac on supernatural finality, and a reasonable criticism of de Lubac's use of the term *nature*. However, to describe finality as a "relation of nature" cannot be easily reconciled with de Lubac's fundamental intuition that supernatural finality belongs to the deepest human reality. De Lubac avoided speaking of finality

also paradoxical: "Paradoxes: the word specifies, above all, then, the things themselves and not the way of speaking of them." Ibid., 10. Paradox, for de Lubac, *is* ontological. Paradox is, in a sense, the noetic consequence of supernatural finality by which the human intellect has an "orientation . . . toward fullness" but lacks the power itself to attain that fullness.

35. Braine, "The Debate between Henri de Lubac and his Critics," 567.
36. Ibid., 552. Braine's solution is not very far from Karl Rahner's "supernatural existential." See David Coffey, "The Whole Rahner on the Supernatural Existential," *Theological Studies* 65, no. 1 (March 2004): 95–118.

as a *relation* because in Thomistic terms relation is an accidental property of a thing (like its color or mass). The accidental property does not enter into the definition of what a thing is, such that it could exist with that property or without it. But de Lubac insisted that supernatural finality is more than an accidental property. A set of affirmations found throughout de Lubac's work echo the claim that finality affects the deepest reality of humanity: the human spirit itself *is* the longing for God; it is possible to imagine that God, in a different order, could create intellectual creatures not destined for the beatific vision, but these creatures would be very different from what we are; it is God's call to humanity that establishes our supernatural finality and makes us what we are. At the same time, de Lubac affirmed that finality exists in relation to God's intention for humanity. Even if we cannot call finality something inhering in the nature as its principle or power, *nature* is constituted by a *relation*, namely the order that God has established in the economy of salvation. What humanity is is constituted by the order of salvation established by God's calling to discipleship and imitation of Christ.[37] In other words, de Lubac's understanding of finality stretches the scholastic categories of *relation* and *nature* for it contains elements of both.

In what follows, I propose that the tension in de Lubac's understanding of finality is shaped by his combining ontological–anthropological categories with historical–eschatological categories. De Lubac's understanding of human finality is shaped by his perspective of the finality of all of history for its eschatological end.

---

37. As Nicholas J. Healy suggests, "The real bone of contention, then between Lubacians and Neo-Thomists is not whether or not there is a relative integrity to nature, but whether or not (at least in the present economy) nature itself is best understood in light of Mary's immaculate divine motherhood and the filial existence of the Son." Healy, "Henri de Lubac on Nature and Grace," 563.

As a result, human finality is intimately tied to the historical economy of salvation.

The *Mystery* of the Supernatural

Although de Lubac often spoke the ontological language of the neothomists, his idea of finality is derived from God's historical plan of salvation. Certainly, his use of scholastic terminology appears imprecise. *The Mystery of the Supernatural*, in particular, engages ancient thought forms using the language of neoscholasticism, resulting in inconsistent terminology. De Lubac suggested that Baroque scholasticism, consumed by the *supernatural*, often forgot other ways of thinking about the relationship between God and humanity common to the patristic and medieval period. The very categories of the Bible and the early church—*grace, image of God, desire for God, creation, redemption,* or *economy*—do not easily correlate with *substance, accident, supernatural,* or *natural.* Modern scholasticism had difficulty appropriating the singular, the particular, or the historical. Moreover, it had difficulty recognizing that God's revelation ruptures all of our philosophical categories.[38] The tensions in de Lubac's account of finality can be traced to the fact that he was operating with a historical-eschatological framework that did not readily map onto scholastic categories. Instead, he was revising those categories in light of a broader theological tradition.

The very title, *The Mystery of the Supernatural,* invokes the purpose of de Lubac's writings on the supernatural: the historical-sacramental language preferred during the patristic period (*mysterion*) is placed side by side with the language of the medieval and modern period (*supernaturalis*). De Lubac did not intend to cleanse theology of the modern dyad, *natural* and *supernatural*: he explained that "the realities

38. De Lubac, *The Mystery of the Supernatural*, 88, 224.

expressed by these terms are and remain fundamental."[39] Instead, he proposed a corrective to a modern theological tradition that produced a dualistic view of the world by reinscribing *natural* and *supernatural* into the biblical and patristic tradition.

The third part of *Surnaturel*, entitled "Aux Origines du mot 'Surnaturel'" (At the origins of the word *supernatural*) indicates de Lubac's interest in correcting or reorienting a modern understanding of the supernatural. It consists of a study on the historical genesis, development, and application of the concept of the supernatural from the Bible to the modern period.[40] Although this part of the book has generated the least controversy and, therefore, the least research, it is perhaps the most critical section.[41] Although, de Lubac explained, the concept of the supernatural is "as essential to Christianity as perhaps, for example, the idea of revelation, or incarnation, or sacrament," its entrance into theological usage comes much later.[42] He explained that it does not appear in Scripture, though its concept might be close to a combination of the biblical terms *mysterion* (mystery) or *charis* (grace). *Supernaturalis* emerges in Christian theology through the translations of pseudo-Dionysius (sixth century) into Latin by John Scotus Eriugena (815–877) and Hilduin (775–840). De Lubac argues that it did not initially catch on. It was not until Thomas Aquinas began to use this term that its commerce spread.

Supernatural does not enter ecclesiastical-doctrinal milieu until the Council of Trent in the sixteenth century, after which it becomes an obligatory theological theme and is expounded everywhere. After

---

39. De Lubac, *Brief Catechesis*, 8.
40. This section was previously published as Henri de Lubac, "Remarques sur l'histoire du mot 'Surnaturel,'" *Nouvelle Revue théologique* 61 (1934): 225–49; 350–70.
41. For the only book-length study on the supernatural in Henri de Lubac, see Raúl Berzosa Martinez, *La teología del sobrenatural en los escritos de Henri de Lubac: estudio historico-teológico (1931–1980)*, Publicaciones de la Facultad de Teología del Norte de España, Sede de Burgos 57 (Burgos, Spain: Ediciones Aldecoa, 1991).
42. De Lubac, *Surnaturel*, 325.

Trent, *supernatural* invades "dogmatic exposition" and forms the foundation for the emergence of a "new vast and technical direction" to theology.[43] The *supernatural*, de Lubac argued, took on a very different role in modern theology: "According to this new meaning, it is no longer a matter, at least directly, of a sensible fact or of a metaphysical object, or of an effect or of a substance. One currently speaks of a supernatural plane of the world, of a supernatural order, of an economy, of a supernatural destiny."[44] The systematization of the natural-supernatural dyad effected a new dualistic image of the world: "If 'the natural order is a complete order,' if the supernatural order appears simply superimposed on a nature that already is sufficient itself, one does not see how the passage to this new order would be made obligatory."[45] Catholic theology then colludes with a naturalistic view of the world in which the supernatural is an unnecessary superimposition.

John Milbank argues that de Lubac was attempting to utterly dismantle the distinction between created nature and grace, something originally foreign to Christianity. Milbank writes, "The essential contrast [in Christian theology], up until the High Middle Ages, remained one between *natural* and *moral* and not *natural* and *supernatural*."[46] He quotes de Lubac's *Surnaturel*:

> Here de Lubac shows that he thinks the older Augustinian natural/moral (in contrast to the natural/supernatural) distinction remains valid: "'Ordre de la nature' et ordre de la 'moralité,' ces deux ordres contiennent tous les conditions—les unes essentielles et nécessaires, les autres personnelles et libres [The order of 'nature' and the order of 'morality,' these two orders contain all the conditions—the former essential and necessary, the latter personal and free]."[47]

43. Ibid., 421.
44. Ibid.
45. Ibid., 427.
46. Milbank, *The Suspended Middle*, 17.
47. Ibid., 19n3. Quoting de Lubac, *Surnaturel*, 487.

Milbank chooses to not quote the rest of the sentence:

—propres à nous faire attendre notre fin surnaturel, et tous deux sont contenus à l'intérieur d'un même monde, d'un monde unique, qu'on peut appeler pour cela même, quoiqu'il contienne des éléments tout naturels, monde surnaturel [—to cause us to await our supernatural end, and both are contained at the interior of the same world, the only world, that one can call for that reason, though it contains some completely natural elements, the supernatural world].[48]

The second half of the quotation, including the words "completely natural elements," might complicate Milbank's interpretation. De Lubac was not attempting to dismantle the ontological distinction between nature and the supernatural or trying to rehabilitate a Neoplatonic ontology. Indeed he explicitly rejected Neoplatonist ontological metaphors for the relationship between creation and Creator, metaphors that fail to preserve the difference.[49] The word *supernatural*, though imperfect, protects the Christian patristic notion of participation while maintaining a distinction between the created and uncreated orders. The problem was that the nature/supernature dyad became a dualism that resulted in the loss of the existential unity and interrelationship between the two.

Instead, de Lubac responded by reinscribing a dualism of principles (nature/supernatural) within a single historical-eschatological order. As stated in *Surnaturel*, "The only world . . . [is] the supernatural world." The dualistic consideration of nature and the supernatural is possible only by considering the two apart from God's plan for salvation, a consideration that was only possible in modern theology.

---

48. De Lubac, *Surnaturel*, 487.
49. De Lubac, *The Mystery of the Supernatural*, 234. While it is true that *supernatural* is a rather late terminological development, it would be inaccurate to attribute a consistent Plotinian hierarchy of being to the Christian patristic and medieval traditions. The fundamental difference between Neoplatonic metaphysics and the Christian patristic metaphysics influenced by Neoplatonism consists precisely in the difference between uncreated and created being, a reworking of a Neoplatonic hierarchy of being.

In *The Mystery of the Supernatural*, de Lubac addresses this concern directly: "In the Fathers, and especially in Augustine, we do not find this clear-cut opposition between the abstract 'essential' order, a *de iure* order, and a concrete 'historical' order which is merely *de facto*, an opposition which fills a large part of certain modern treatises. For them the created essence is itself 'historical' and history in that sense is essential."[50] Even the medieval scholastics, including Thomas Aquinas, consider human nature in the context of the historical order.[51] What characterizes modern scholasticism is the "radical separation between abstract essence and the existing world."[52] The *natural* became associated with the essential, necessary order of essences, but the *supernatural* became associated with the unessential, historical order of God's actions in history. In other words, modern scholasticism separated ontology—the unchanging, essential, and necessary—from history—the changing, unessential, and contingent. Such a division between necessary essences and contingent history would make no sense for Origen, Gregory of Nyssa, or Augustine, for whom God's actions in history reveal the very life of God, the only thing strictly necessary.

Although he claimed in *The Mystery of the Supernatural* to restrict himself methodologically to "formal ontology," de Lubac employs a range of theological idioms—creation and consummation, image and likeness, covenant and mystery—that better preserve a dynamic understanding of nature in its historical-eschatological dimensions. De Lubac explains that "the dogma of creation has profoundly and permanently transformed the idea philosophers must have, whether of individual natures or of the totality of the universe."[53] The nature/

50. Ibid., 64.
51. Ibid., 66.
52. Ibid., 67.
53. Ibid., 19.

supernatural dyad as it has emerged in modernity is incapable of expressing both the finality of human beings for union with God and the freedom with which God gives grace. However, the *image/likeness* and *creation/consummation* dyads preserve their relatedness. De Lubac explains that when the church fathers spoke of "'the image' which is in us is made in the 'likeness' of God, and that therefore we have to pass from the 'dignity of the image' received at the 'first creation' to the 'perfection of the likeness which is 'reserved for the consummation of all things,' they were in no sense intending to affirm by this that this 'likeness' was of the same nature as the 'image.'"[54] De Lubac remarks that "creation as it exists, with the unique final end which it has, that creation as effected by God precisely with the object of giving himself to it; that creation as finally illuminated for us by the good news announced to mankind one night in Bethlehem." [55] Humanity in its concrete existence cannot be understood apart from its dynamic relatedness to God as a creature and the destiny to which God has called it, a destiny revealed in the life of Jesus Christ.

Just as de Lubac places nature within a historical–eschatological framework, he understands the supernatural in terms of *mystery*, the goal of the historical-eschatological order. The supernatural, he says, "is something belonging to a different order."[56] The supernatural should not be thought of as a "supernature" juxtaposed with nature, as an entity.[57] It is "created grace," becoming a "sharer in the divine nature." The supernatural reflects the union with God and humanity as well as the difference: "It is a relationship of reciprocity in unity," the "admirable exchange."[58] It is that which elevates humanity and

---

54. Ibid., 31. Quoting from Origen, *Periarchon*, book 3, c. 6, n. 1.
55. Humanity knows itself only in reference to this mystery, such that "by revealing himself to us . . . God 'has revealed us to ourselves.'" *The Mystery of the Supernatural*, 214.
56. De Lubac, *Brief Catechesis*, 28.
57. Ibid., 34–35.

that humanity cannot achieve on its own. Most importantly, he characterizes the supernatural as *mystery*: "This mystery of the supernatural, which is the mystery of our divine destiny, appears rather like the framework within which all other mysteries of revelation have their place."[59] Mystery does not suggest merely the unknown as much as it concerns the destiny of humanity, its "last end," its "vocation," which de Lubac calls "supernatural."[60] It is the "fullness" of the mystery to which the human mystery is oriented.[61] Thus, the Mystery is the supernatural the goal of creation and God's final intention for humanity known through historical revelation.

As a whole, de Lubac's writings on the supernatural reintegrate the nature-supernatural dyad into a holistic understanding of the economy of salvation. *Surnaturel*'s key idea was the inherent limitation of the nature-supernatural distinction for describing the Christian mystery. *The Mystery of the Supernatural* proposed a personal and covenantal understanding of the supernatural. His *A Brief Catechesis on Nature and Grace* defended the relevance of the nature-supernatural dyad, though he used biblical and patristic sources to defend it. In *Athéisme et sens de l'homme*, his commentary on the Second Vatican Council's *Gaudium et Spes*, he explained that the Council had returned to a more unified, organic conception of the relationship between God and the world. Quoting Jean Mouroux, de Lubac noted that the dualistic notion of two "orders"—natural and supernatural—had been replaced by a conception of a single order of "the Covenant" that unites the creation, the Christ event, and the consummation.[62] The covenant

58. Ibid., 42–44.
59. De Lubac, *The Mystery of the Supernatural*, 217.
60. De Lubac, *Brief Catechesis*, 65.
61. De Lubac, *The Mystery of the Supernatural*, 209.
62. Henri de Lubac, "The Total Meaning of Man and the World," *Communio* 35, no. 4 (2008): 620. Originally published as Henri de Lubac, *Athéisme et sens de l'homme: une double requête de*

provides a more adequate framework than nature and the supernatural for understanding the relationship between the world and God. Quoting Edward Schillebeeckx, de Lubac explains, "The problem as it was expressed classically in the still too abstract terms of nature and grace, now becomes for us 'a problem set out for us in terms of the relations that unite earthly expectation (or earthly activity) and eschatological kingdom.'"[63] Although de Lubac did not entirely depart from the ontological categories of natural and supernatural, he stretched them in such a way that they include the economy of salvation and its orientation to an eschatological consummation. As a result, the very categories in which de Lubac describes supernatural finality reflect his historical–eschatological framework.

The Nature of Finality

One of the principal points of contention is whether finality belongs "essentially" to the constitution of humanity or whether it is accidental, elicited by God's offer of grace. On the one hand, de Lubac describes finality as "essential," belonging to human nature or the constitution of human beings as such. De Lubac explains that supernatural finality is "inscribed in the depths of my nature" and "inscribed on my very being as it has been put into this universe by God. . . . My destiny is something ontological, and not something I can change as anything else changes its destination."[64] On the other hand, he describes finality as arising from the fact that God has destined human beings to the supernatural. We possess a supernatural

---

Gaudium et Spes, Oeuvres Completes, vol. 4 (Paris: Éditions du Cerf, 2006), 471–500. Quoting Jean Mouroux, "Sur la dignité de la personne humaine," in *L'Église dans le monde de ce temps*, "Vatican II," no. 65 b (Paris: Éditions du Cerf, 1967), 232.

63. De Lubac, "Total Meaning of Man and the World," 629–30. Quoting Edward Schillebeeckx, "Foi chrétienne et attente terrestre," in *L'Église dans le monde d'aujourd'hui* (Mame, 1967), 150.
64. De Lubac, *The Mystery of the Supernatural*, 55, 62.

destiny because of God's "calling." Although finality belongs to the nature of the human being, *nature* does not describe a discrete center of capacities and inclinations abstracted from its destiny. This account of finality appears inconsistent. The key to unraveling this tension is to recognize that de Lubac's theology does not create a dichotomy between an essential, ontological order inhabited by abstract natures and a contingent, historical order that is the order of salvation. Finality, for de Lubac, belongs "by nature" to human beings because their ontological constitution is determined by and affected by God's actions in history and final intention for humanity.

De Lubac's corporate understanding of human nature is key to his conception of finality. Finality results from "belonging to humanity, as it is, that humanity which is, as we say, 'called.' God's call is constitutive" of what a thing is and humanity as a whole is "called."[65] By human nature, he means the whole of humanity as a corporate body: "Human nature is, in its way, a reality. But the fact that we all share in it is precisely, at least in part, because we all have the same essential finality."[66] In *Catholicism* de Lubac specifies that "our fundamental nature" consists of a "common destiny" and forms the anthropological foundation for salvation.[67] The natural unity of the human race, consisting in sharing the same image of God, is the precondition for the supernatural unity of the mystical body of Christ. Our common human nature is not properly an *individual* substance, since it is constituted by all humanity, living and dead. If our destiny is a union with Christ and all of humanity, then our fundamental corporate nature as its natural foundation is ontologically relational. Made as one being, humanity will be truly

65. Ibid., 55.
66. Ibid., 63.
67. De Lubac, *Catholicism*, 222.

united only in the body of Christ, a unity that finds its completion at the end of time.

In *The Mystery of the Supernatural*, human nature is a unitary ontological fact, and its unity consists in the "assignation of a single destiny."[68] Finality is constitutive of human nature. *What* the human being is can only be described relationally: horizontally, as a union of all humanity, and vertically, as an anticipation of its ultimate eschatological union in Christ. De Lubac stretched the meaning of *nature* beyond a scholastic or Thomistic framework. Properly speaking, human nature is a corporate reality and we share in the same corporate reality because we have the same supernatural goal. Supernatural finality is not *in* humanity as its actuality or its form. But neither is it something accidental or unessential to being human.

As a result, de Lubac rejects the scholastic notion of a supernatural finality that is superadded to a completely natural finality. The idea of pure nature, he wrote, arose within "an intellectual context of a watered-down idea of what finality is."[69] Under the hypothesis of pure nature, supernatural finality is not "inscribed in a man's very nature" but rather is a "destination given him from outside when he was already in existence."[70] For Cajetan, Suarez, and their followers, the fact of revelation changes the finality of the human being or adds another finality without changing its structure as a whole or the essences that inhabit that structure: "The ultimate destination of the universe has been changed in the course of time, without this fact making any change to the structure of that universe or the essence of the beings who constitute it."[71] De Lubac perceives a subtle nominalism at work in the theory of pure nature insofar as God

---

68. De Lubac, *The Mystery of the Supernatural*, 63.
69. Ibid., 68.
70. Ibid., 68–69.
71. Ibid., 71.

could reassign the finality of a thing by decree. Indeed, he believes that the hypothesis of pure nature supposes a "radical extrinsicism which must destroy either the idea of nature or that of finality, or possibly both."[72] The natural world, including humanity, would be ontologically indifferent to revelation in the sense that humanity remains the same whether or not there is a revelation of God and whether or not humanity is called to union with God.

For de Lubac, the eschatological goal of humanity and the universe as a whole is not something extrinsic to what it means to be human. Instead, the concrete constitution of humanity is affected by the final destination of the universe. In *The Mystery of the Supernatural*, the order in which a thing exists impacts the existence of any single thing in it, such that *nature* is closely associated with *order*.[73] Appealing to St. Thomas Aquinas, he writes, "We know too what reality he attached to what he called the 'order of the universe' [*ordo universi*] or 'order of the parts of the universe in relation to each other'—so much so that for him a single change in the natures making up the universe would be enough to mean that one was really dealing with a different universe."[74] There is an intrinsic relationship between the nature and the order. But also, nature is affected by the finality of that order as a whole. Finality does not just belong "individual natures" but also of the "totality of the universe" and the structure of the universe as a whole.[75] Although a change in the finality of the universe as a whole may not affect the laws of physics, it certainly would effect a

---

72. Ibid., 68. De Lubac, however, does not accurately assess the neoscholastic position, since the neoscholastic idea of "elicited" desire that corresponded to an elicited finality does not envision the natural end being eradicated, but subsumed under the supernatural end.

73. See *The Mystery of the Supernatural*, 19 on the Augustinian understanding of the order of nature, 28 on the supernatural as another order, 34 on the normal development of nature in its own order. His entire discussion of the "inadequate hypothesis" provided by neoscholasticism appeals to the relationship among the orders.

74. Ibid., 71.

75. Ibid., 18, 71.

change in the "intellectual and moral" constitution of humanity.[76] For mere material, physical cogs in deterministic machine, final destiny wouldn't affect the reality of their constitution. In contrast, the intellectual and moral constitution of humanity would be radically changed by a modification in the finality of the universe because this constitution is intimately bound the destination of the universe.[77]

De Lubac's understanding of the concrete, historical finality of human beings resonates with his understanding the senses of Scripture. The "letter" of Scripture describes the history of God's saving actions in the Old Testament. The comprehensive meaning of those actions is its "spiritual meaning." In *Exégèse médiévale*, he explains that the explication of historical facts already presumes the application of "a principle of discernment which can itself be inserted within the facts, but which, as such, pertains to a different sphere and overflows into the observation of the facts."[78] Only by reference to the final causes of realities can we offer a complete understanding of them: "This is why, if any not merely partial and relative but total, comprehensive, and absolutely valid explication of history is truly possible, this explication can be only theological. Only faith anticipates the future with security. Only an explication founded upon faith can invoke a definitive principle and appeal to ultimate causes."[79] God intervened into history only in view of a later

---

76. Ibid., 72.
77. David Grumett argues that de Lubac did not sufficiently escape from the idea of pure nature because he failed to apply his understanding of supernatural finality to material nature. Admittedly, material nature in the order of the world is not something that de Lubac explicitly thematized, as it is in Teilhard de Chardin, but it does not follow that "the concept of pure nature . . . remains intact in his understanding of material nature." See Grumett, "Eucharist, Matter and the Supernatural: Why de Lubac Needs Teilhard," *International Journal of Systematic Theology* 10, no. 2 (2008): 167. De Lubac's description of the ordering of the universe as a whole has parallels in Lonergan's theology of grace that incorporates "horizontal and vertical finality." Raymond Moloney, SJ, points to surprising congruence between the two thinkers. See Moloney, "De Lubac and Lonergan on the Supernatural."
78. De Lubac, *Medieval Exegesis: The Four Senses of Scripture*, trans. E. M. Macierowski, vol. 2 (Grand Rapids, MI: Eerdmans, 2000) 71.

fulfillment in Christ, the "spiritual meaning of Scripture." Just as the letter of Scripture cannot be understood apart from its spiritual sense, so nature cannot be comprehended apart from its final goal.

For de Lubac, history is oriented toward an eschatological goal, which profoundly shapes his exposition of teleology. The ultimate or final cause is classically the telos, that for which a thing exists. Echoing a principle of Aristotle adopted by Thomas Aquinas—"everything is ordered to its end in virtue of its form"—the neoscholastics envisioned the final cause as the goal that within one's power to attain, entailing delimitation of finality to form.[80] The ultimate purpose (e.g., hammering nails) of a thing (e.g., a hammer) is entailed in its natural capacities (its shape and structure.) This delimitation has the advantage of narrowing the boundaries of a science in order to provide a thorough account of causes within a circumscribed sphere of investigation. The advantage is lost when it comes to the discipline of history and Scripture, which deal with dynamic events rather than static things. For de Lubac, any explication of an *event* requires a principle beyond the brute facts of history, namely its telos. For the Christian, the historical events narrated in the Old Testament require a principle beyond themselves to provide an ultimate explanation, which principle is Christ. The manna is fulfilled in the Eucharist; the parting of the Red Sea is fulfilled in baptism; Israel is fulfilled in the church. According to de Lubac, like historical revelation, creation itself requires a principle of explanation beyond itself—its purpose, meaning, and goal. The Christian principle of discernment is "the Mystery of Christ, the absolutely ultimate final cause," which retroactively illumines the depth of the historical event.[81] And for de Lubac, the "Mystery of

---

79. Ibid.
80. Feingold, *The Natural Desire to See God* (2001), 528.
81. De Lubac, *Medieval Exegesis*, 2:72.

Christ" is the telos, the end point of God's historical plan that is already present and active in history.

De Lubac's understanding of ultimate causality in the history of salvation has profound resonances with his understanding of the finality in human beings. The meaning of the human person at the "depths of being" cannot be understood entirely apart from the ultimate intention for the person, the ultimate cause, namely God's call. This calling is not reducible to the human "form," just like the spiritual sense is not reducible to the letter. Human nature takes its ultimate meaning from a principle of a different order than itself, a supernatural principle, namely the whole Christ. Similarly, historical realities take their meaning from a principle of a different order from those realities themselves, namely the Christ event.

Gratuity and Ontological Difference

The perennial accusation leveled against de Lubac is he fails to preserve the gratuity of grace; that is, he fails to preserve God's freedom either to give grace that saves us or not to. Because de Lubac insisted that human beings have a single supernatural finality, he undermined God's freedom of refusal. Although de Lubac insisted otherwise, Pope Pius XII's encyclical *Humani generis* appeared to condemn the implications of his theology of the supernatural. Yet de Lubac persisted in his claim that humanity has a single supernatural end and that the freedom and graciousness of God is not compromised by that end. He appealed to the relationship between Old Testament and the New Testament as a model for understanding how nature can be fulfilled only in the supernatural, with the supernatural remaining gratuitously given.

Contemporary critics of de Lubac argue that de Lubac's theology of the supernatural fails to adequately guarantee the gratuity of grace.[82] If the human being requires God's grace by its very nature, as de Lubac appears to say, then once God creates a human being it would be a human being that demands something from God. God would be placed under obligation to a creature.[83] An intensified version of this argument is made by Lawrence Feingold, who argues that de Lubac compromises the fundamental difference between the natural and supernatural. Feingold states that to have a supernatural finality by nature is to already be supernatural. The neothomist solution that de Lubac rejected was to maintain a double finality: a purely natural end proportionate to nature, and a supernatural end that God offers by grace. Double finality is the only way to preserve the ontological difference between nature and the supernatural and the gratuity of grace.

Ironically, de Lubac claimed that a theory of double finality (in the form of "pure nature") is a symptom of thinking univocally about nature and the supernatural. In the conclusion of *Surnaturel*, de Lubac argued that we have a "spontaneous" tendency to think of God's being and our participated being in the same univocal category.[84] Although we remain dependent upon God for our ongoing existence in each moment, we imagine ourselves as entirely independent beings: "Forgetting, or at least not 'realizing' at its depth our situation as creatures, we reason more or less that if creation is only a fact, a pure extrinsic condition of our position in being, as if it affected only

82. For example, Mulcahy, *Aquinas's Notion of Pure Nature*, 167. John Milbank writes, "The defenders of de Lubac who deny that he was implicated in the statement by Pius XII are surely wrong, and the critics who insist that he was are surely correct." *The Suspended Middle*, x. For a concise overview of the controversy surrounding *Humani generis* as it affected de Lubac, see Noel O'Sullivan, *Christ and Creation: Christology as the Key to Interpreting the Theology of Creation in the Works of Henri de Lubac*, Religions and Discourse 40 (New York: Peter Lang, 2009), 244–47. See also Susan K. Wood, *Spiritual Exegesis and the Church in the Theology of Henri de Lubac* (Grand Rapids, MI: Eerdmans, 1998), 15–16.

83. Malloy suggests that the only alternative would be to argue that God has the freedom to refuse grace. The result, however, would be a world in which the human being needs grace as a requirement of its nature and in which that grace is withheld. This would be an absurd world that violates God's goodness. Malloy, "De Lubac on Natural Desire," 568.

84. De Lubac, *Surnaturel*, 485.

our origin, and not our essence."[85] Since we fail to see creation as an ongoing condition that affects what we are, we wrongly imagine a relationship between two independent beings. As a result, we begin to think of God and humanity as two beings existing in the same category. According to de Lubac, the "infinite qualitative difference" between God's grace and our nature is already compromised. The problem of gratuity is an "illusion" that responds to this already-compromised sense of transcendence. Because the neoscholastics already placed nature and the supernatural in the same ontological category—some even referred to supernature, a "supersized" version of nature—they need to establish their ontological difference. Scholastics attempted to establish the difference between natural and the supernatural ends by speaking of the former as necessary and the other as superadded. The theory of a purely natural human destiny was not only a solution to a false problem. It was a symptom of the pathological thinking about human being as univocal with God's being.

De Lubac insisted on the absolute difference between the natural and the supernatural from the very beginning in *Surnaturel* in order to correct a pathological theology, and not because of the supposed condemnation by *Humani generis*. Each of his books on the supernatural make this point, though *The Mystery of the Supernatural*, written after *Humani generis*, is naturally more explicit: there is a formal difference between the two, "a difference in kind;"[86] a difference between the *donum perfectum* (grace) and the *datum optimum* (nature);[87] the "infinite qualitative difference."[88] The fact of supernatural finality does not imply an ability to achieve its end: "The

---

85. Ibid.
86. De Lubac, *The Mystery of the Supernatural*, 23.
87. Ibid., 91.
88. Ibid., 35.

fact that the nature of the spiritual being, as it actually exists, is not conceived as an order destined to close in finally upon itself, but in a sense open to an inevitably supernatural end, does not mean that it already has in itself, or as part of its basis, the smallest positively supernatural element."[89] In an emphatic reference to the absolute ontological difference, he explains, "Between nature as it exists and the supernatural for which God destines it, the distance is great, the difference is as radical, as that between non-being and being: for to pass from on to another is not merely to pass into 'more being,' but to pass to a different type of being."[90] In other words, de Lubac did not believe that the neoscholastic nature–supernature "layer cake" sufficiently guaranteed the ontological difference between nature and the supernatural. This ontological difference would be necessary to guarantee that nature and the supernatural were not competitors over the same ontological territory. Moreover, this difference is necessary to make something like "supernatural finality" meaningful.

De Lubac's emphatic assertion of the difference between nature and supernatural also points to the limits of the nature-supernatural dyad itself. If viewed as merely a contrast between two *things* or *substances*, the dyad fails to preserve the infinite difference of categories. The categorical difference is lost as well as the intimate relationship between them. This failure occurred in modern Catholic theology. This is why de Lubac describes the passage to supernatural life as a form of "transforming union," a "passive purification," "the 'perfection of the likeness' that is 'reserved for the consummation of all things,'" an entrance into the "fullness."[91] In this way, de Lubac's writings on the supernatural violate his self-imposed methodological restriction to "formal ontology." De Lubac finds that he can only

89. Ibid., 31.
90. Ibid., 83.
91. Ibid., 28, 31, 209.

preserve the ontological difference between natural and supernatural by broadening the theological framework.

The gratuity of the supernatural, he admits, cannot be established if one thinks of it on the analogy of gift that one person makes to another. Instead, he turns to the relationship between creation and the new creation: "There is . . . a genuine parallelism between the first gift of creation and the second, wholly distinct, wholly super-eminent gift—the ontological call to deification which will make of man, if he responds to it, a 'new creature.'" It is a difference between my "natural being" and "my divine sonship."[92] The supernatural is not a substance added to nature, but instead is a participation in charity that requires a self-renunciation and death of selfishness: "The passage to the supernatural order, even for an innocent and healthy nature, could never take place without some kind of death."[93] The passage to the supernatural is not a mere completion of the tendencies inherent in nature because it requires a *kenosis*, a renunciation of the self. Moreover, the supernatural, as the telos of the natural, must be described as a transformative union with God.

De Lubac appealed to the relationship between the Old Testament and its fulfillment in the New as a model for recognizing how nature can be incomplete without grace, yet remain of an entirely different order. The Old Testament anticipation of the Messiah was not already a possession of Christ even if it suggests an incompleteness without Christ.

> If it is true that the whole history of Israel ultimately only receives its meaning from the coming of Christ for which it was a preparation and to which it was directed, should we see this as a reason to deny that, even in relation to Israel, that coming was something totally new and gratuitous? But further, just as the coming of Christ, through fulfilling the history of Israel and giving it meaning, marks the passing into a

92. Ibid., 76.
93. Ibid., 28.

new order, which wholly transcended the order that preceded it—"He brought all that is new" [*omnem novitatem attulit*]—so it is with our supernatural finality.[94]

The relationship of promise and fulfillment in salvation history becomes a model for the supernatural finality of human nature. Israel receives its final meaning from the coming of Christ, yet Christ brings something entirely new. Similarly, supernatural finality does not necessarily imply an inner capacity for the supernatural or the innate possession of it. Finality and infinite difference can be seen as complementary aspects of a single reality. From this perspective, *the finality of the natural for the supernatural precisely depends upon an infinite distinction between the orders.* Otherwise, the passage from one to the other would be either a continuation of the same thing or a destruction of the natural. Just as Christ does not come to "abolish the law" (Matt 5:17) but instead to fulfill it, grace does not abolish nature, but fulfills it on an entirely new level.

"L'esprit est donc désir de Dieu. Tout le problème de la vie spirituelle sera de libérer ce désir, puis de le transformer: conversion radicale, *metanoia* sans laquelle il n'est point d'entrée dans le Royaume"[95] ("The spirit is then desire for God. The whole problem of the spiritual life will be to liberate this desire, then to transform it: radical conversion, *metanoia* without which there is no entry into the Kingdom"). The language of *Surnaturel* is paradoxical and poetic. Its unsystematic and perhaps inexact presentation elicited an entire genre of misinterpretation. It is not entirely surprising that de Lubac has been interpreted as a closet Neoplatonist for whom supernatural finality springs from an ontological parity between the natural and supernatural. However, a close reading of his work will recognize a

94. Ibid., 82–83.
95. De Lubac, *Surnaturel*, 483.

consistent pattern in *Catholicism, Surnaturel,* and *The Mystery of the Supernatural*: de Lubac cannot describe supernatural finality or natural desire without reference to the economy of salvation, the Mystery of Christ, or the fulfillment of the Old Testament in the New.

Conclusion

While the strong parallels in de Lubac between his theology of history and theology of the supernatural do not resolve the ongoing conflict over his work, they indicate that his writings on the supernatural must be read in terms of a broader eschatological engagement that runs throughout his writings. De Lubac writes, "Our divine destiny . . . appears rather like the framework within which all other mysteries of revelation have their place."[96] Human *destiny* is really the primary subject of de Lubac's writings on Scripture and his writings on the supernatural. The rise of the nature-supernatural dyad to such prominence in the modern period helped to displace the theological images more natural to Christianity, like creation and consummation, image and likeness, sacrament and mystery. Despite its indisputable utility, the dualistic theology of nature and the supernatural occluded the absolute dependence of humanity on God for existence and also for its fulfillment. De Lubac's response was to reinscribe the debate over the supernatural into an understanding of the historical economy and its eschatological fulfillment.

Whereas within de Lubac's *Surnaturel* and *The Mystery of the Supernatural* he explicates finality *ontologically*, in that the supernatural is the only end of the natural, in *Medieval Exegesis* he explicates finality *historically*, in that the Old Testament event has its inner completion in the Christ event. The relationship of the Old

---

96. De Lubac, *The Mystery of the Supernatural*, 167.

Testament to the New Testament (alternatively, the historical sense of Scripture to its spiritual sense, or prophecy to fulfillment) is a relationship of a historical event to its spiritual end, meaning, and purpose. Although he never develops a satisfactory systematic correlation between *ontos* and *historikos*, de Lubac opened a space for relating the economy of salvation more closely to the theology of the supernatural and for a negotiation between philosophical and scriptural accounts of human nature. It is clear, however, that de Lubac's writings over the supernatural straddle ontological categories and historical categories without systematic correlation. On the one hand, de Lubac's work might be seen as transitional insofar as he paves the way for more robust systematic correlations between history and systematics. His writings were part of a movement opening Catholic theology to the historical economy as the basis for constructive theology, which bears fruit in the work of very different theologians such as Edward Schillebeeckx, Gustavo Gutiérrez, and Elizabeth Johnson. Furthermore, he helped to transform the debate over the supernatural into a debate over history and eschatology. On the other hand, de Lubac's integration of history and ontology may be seen as a significant in its own right. His writings relate a diversity of theological images in order to preserve the paradox of truth that any single category fails to convey.

It should not be surprising that there are deep resonances between de Lubac's recovery of patristic symbolism in the interpretation of Scripture, his theological anthropology based on the human being as the image of God, and his recovery of a premodern sacramental symbolism. Modern rationalism has a highly circumscribed imagination in which a Christian view of the world and human destiny fails to fit comfortably. In de Lubac's interpretation, rationalistic methods of biblical interpretation ascended to prominence at the same time as the nature–supernatural dyad became dominant. De Lubac's *ressourcement* of premodern exegesis is related to his project of reclaiming a premodern understanding of human nature and a sacramental-symbolic imagination.

Conclusion: Eternity in Time

Henri de Lubac's theological contribution must be read against the backdrop of the crisis of temporality in modern Europe and the rediscovery of history as a theological category among Catholic theologians. The rediscovery of the eternal in time was at the heart of his theological project. He believed that secularization in modernity had resulted from the loss of the sacred and the loss of the spiritual imagination that enables us to recognize it. De Lubac responded to this loss by claiming the church fathers as a source for renewing our spiritual vision. His multiple volumes and articles on the "spiritual interpretation" of Scripture elaborated not so much an exegetical procedure applicable for modern people as a way of reading the world in light of the economy of salvation. The spiritual interpretation of Scripture is a way of relating our experience to the mystery of Christ unfolding in time and of recognizing the eternal in time. According to de Lubac, our time is the time between the two comings of Christ. The transcendent fulfillment of human existence, the mystery of Christ, has already entered history in the incarnation and is already present at the heart of temporal experience. However, the mystery of Christ is still unfolding and incomplete, and will be complete only at his second coming. We live at the ending of time, shaped by the proleptic experience of the eschatological goal and the incompleteness of this experience. Despite the idiosyncracies and the occasional nature of de Lubac's writings, his theology addressed the pivotal discourses of twentieth-century Catholicism, namely the meaning of human historical experience and the mystical experience of God in the temporal.

The Crisis of the Temporal

De Lubac and the *nouvelle théologie* are a critical part of the story of modern Catholicism's struggle to come to terms with historicity. As previously indicated, despite their theological opposition, the *nouveaux théologiens* and the neoscholastics shared a common experience of secularization and a common anxiety. Rapid technological, political, and social changes in Europe resulted in a widespread distress over losing the eternal, which had a range of social manifestations and was elemental to Modernist culture.[1] Catholic theology was hamstrung by a dichotomy between the natural and the supernatural, which effectively became a dichotomy between the unchanging truth (present in perennial church doctrine) and the ever-changing world (history). This struggle over time and eternity has been a pivotal discourse in Catholic theology from the late nineteenth-century to today.

The *nouvelle théologie* was not exempt from the anxiety over the eternal, though its authors strongly affirmed history as part of the eternal plan of God. The *nouvelle théologie* is often characterized by its historical consciousness and its turn to Scripture, the church fathers, and medievals as sources for theology.[2] There are certainly

1. See Stephen Schloesser, "Vivo Ergo Cogito: Modernism as Temporalization and Its Discontents: A Propaedeutic to This Collection," in *The Reception of Pragmatism in France and the Rise of Roman Catholic Modernism, 1890–1914* (Washington, DC: Catholic University of America Press, 2009), 21–58.
2. See Jürgen Mettepenningen, *Nouvelle Théologie—New Theology: Inheritor of Modernism, Precursor to Vatican II* (New York: T & T Clark, 2010), 9–13.

profound differences over the theology of history expressed by the authors connected to the *nouvelle théologie*, though they each were articulating new models of the relationship between the temporal and the eternal. De Lubac rejected the spatial partition between the natural human realm and the realm of God, affirming that history has sacramental depths. We live in a "supernatural world," he said. History is the medium of encounter with God. Human historical experience is the stuff that will be transfigured in eternity. De Lubac and the *nouvelle théologie*'s turn to Scripture and the economy of salvation addresses a widespread concern to affirm the encounter with God through time and the value of historical existence.

The discovery of the eternal in time was thematized in the *nouvelle théologie* and broadly in Catholic philosophical circles, especially following World War II. The socialist philosopher Jean Lacroix's *Marxisme, existentialisme, personnalisme. Présence de l'éternité dans le temps* (1949) addressed the problem in relationship to the dominant trajectories of the French philosophical milieu. The philosopher Jacques Maritain addressed the problem from a Thomistic perspective in a series of lectures entitled "On the Philosophy of History," delivered at Notre Dame in 1955. Gaston Fessard wrote *De l'actualité historique* (1960), an investigation into the theological meaning of the present time.[3] The diocesan priest Jean Mouroux wrote *Le Mystère du temps. Approche théologique* (1962). Catholic philosophers and theologians sought to affirm the role of human beings as historical actors and also to affirm a positive relationship between eternity and historical existence.

Time and eternity constitutes one of the key discourses in the period leading up to the Second Vatican Council (1962-1965) and

---

3. See Mary Alice Muir, "Gaston Fessard, S.J.: His Work Towards a Theology of History" (MA thesis, Marquette University, 1970), 4.

appears as a theme in the documents of the Council. The Dogmatic Constitution on Divine Revelation, *Dei Verbum* (1965), treats God's revelation as primarily personal and historical, rather than propositional. Revelation is God's word in history and is constituted of both words and deeds. Salvation is made present to time and history through revelation. The Pastoral Constitution on the Church in the Modern World, *Gaudium et Spes* (1965), concerns the role of the church in the world and its solidarity with human beings. Its first line reads, "The joy and hope, the grief and anguish of the men of our time, especially those who are poor or afflicted in any way, are the joy and hope, the grief and anguish of the followers of Christ as well."[4] *Gaudium et Spes* presents the church as the mission to the world that seeks "solidarity with the human race and its history."[5] As a result, the social concerns of human beings constitute a properly religious object.

In the period following the Second Vatican Council, the relationship between the church and the world remained a live debate, prompted especially by the interpretation of *Gaudium et Spes*, from which one of the Council's most contentious lines came: "At all times the Church carries the responsibility of reading the signs of the time and of interpreting them in the light of the Gospel, if it is to carry out its task."[6] The Council suggested the church, for its mission of proclaiming the gospel to be successful, must be attentive to the concrete needs and desires of human beings. The short phrase *signs of the times* has caused no end of trouble for the interpretation of a range of social, economic, political, and family and marriage issues. It expresses a confidence that the desires expressed by modern

---

4. "Gaudium et Spes," in *Vatican Council II: The Conciliar and Postconciliar Documents*, ed. Austin Flannery, OP, rev. ed. (Northport, NY: Costello, 1996), 903.
5. Ibid., 903–4.
6. Ibid., 905.

humanity arise from an authentic religious desire rather than from sin. Joseph Ratzinger and Henri de Lubac were critical of a too-optimistic understanding of the modern world expressed in *Gaudium et Spes* and postconciliar discourses. For de Lubac and Ratzinger, to rightly understand the relationship between the world and the church one needed to understand the relationship between history and the kingdom of God.

Given the importance of the Second Vatican Council in Catholic self-interpretation, it is important to recognize that the Church's turn to history and its concern with the church and the world are grounded in the discourses over time and eternity that reach back to the late 1800s. De Lubac's theology of history and eschatology also sought to interpret the "signs of the times." He did not wish to rid Christianity altogether of its apocalyptic impulses—its desire for a new age, the desire for social harmony, and the recognition of the dignity of the temporal order—but instead to integrate these elements into a longing for eternity. We are, according to de Lubac, living in the end of time. But this means that we experience historical existence as a sacrament, lived in proleptic anticipation of eternity. The Christian is to embrace the temporal order as an anticipation of eternity without making her home there.

Mysticism and Modernity

The problem of time and eternity is closely connected to mysticism, a recurring topic in de Lubac's writings. If discovering the "eternal in time" was a religious crisis of modern Europe, much of de Lubac's work is directed toward formulating a response. His book *Sur les chemins de Dieu* (translated as *The Discovery of God*) developed a fragmentary religious epistemology that argued that human beings possess an implicit or preconceptual knowledge of God. *Sur les chemins de Dieu* presents our experience of the finite world as a pathway to God.[7] His 1939 book *Corpus Mysticum* traced the loss of the "symbolic imagination" of the church fathers through which the temporal world was understood as a sign of the eternal. In an essay entitled "Internal Causes of the Weakening and Disappearance of the Sense of the Sacred" (1942), de Lubac lamented our inability to recognize the sacred in the world. *Exégèse médiévale* traces the evolution of mysticism from something central to Christian experience to a specialization of monks. All of these writings concern the discovery of God in the temporal order or the discovery of the temporal order as a symbol of God. De Lubac's *ressourcement* of the spiritual sense of Scripture was a recovery of mysticism, a way of recognizing the mystery operating in the historical, temporal order.

It is surprising, then, that de Lubac never attempted an intensive study on mysticism from a systematic or an historical perspective. In 1956, he claimed that his unwritten book on mysticism inspired much of his thinking.[8] Beyond his powers to begin, this book sits at the center of his theology. While de Lubac failed to articulate the systematic core of his thinking, his failure is congruent with his mysticism itself, in which the very ideas and concepts that we vitally need to reach God, in the end, must be transcended. It is no wonder that de Lubac's theological reflections on mysticism are fragmentary

7. Interpretation of this work is made difficult by the fact it reads more like Pascal's *Pensees* than a treatise on religious knowledge: it gathers together fragmentary thoughts, quotations, and prayers of praise under a single title. Instead of presenting a demonstration for theistic belief, it leads the reader to move beyond the constructions of our limited intellects and recognize in those constructions the traces of God.

8. Henri de Lubac, *At the Service of the Church: Henri de Lubac Reflects on the Circumstances That Occasioned His Writings* (San Francisco: Communio Books, 1993), 113. Originally published as Henri de Lubac, *Mémoire sur l'occasion de mes écrits*, Chretiens aujourd'hui 1 (Namur, Belgium: Culture et Verité, 1989). Rudolf Voderholzer suggests that de Lubac's unstarted book on Christ and never-begun book on mysticism were one and the same. Voderholzer, *Meet Henri de Lubac*, trans. Michael J. Miller (San Francisco: Ignatius Press, 2008), 159. The book on Christ is mentioned in *At the Service of the Church*, 147–48.

and incomplete.[9] De Lubac's mysticism is the least defined of his theological engagements because it is the unarticulated context for all of them.[10]

Although he did not write a treatise on mysticism, de Lubac's historical studies on biblical interpretation and sacraments diagnose the problem of recognizing God in the temporal order. *Corpus Mysticum* argues that in the Middle Ages an incipient rationalism replaced what de Lubac calls the "symbolism" of the patristic period. The "ontological symbolism" of the fathers was their recognition of created realities as a reflection of the divine mysteries.[11] Rationality and mystery were aligned. In the Middle Ages, a "new concept of mystery [developed] . . . which managed to quench symbolism while suppressing, even in the understanding of the believer, the momentum that had given birth to it."[12] From the late Middle Ages to the modern age, *mystery* became associated more with the miraculous or special interior experiences of mystics than with the transcendent goal of creation. This "new concept of mystery" prompted the late medieval to modern division of theology into distinct displines: dogmatic theology and mystical theology. Mystery was cut off from

9. As Voderholzer states, his interpretation of Christianity is mystical and the mystical appears as a leitmotif throughout his works. Voderholzer, *Meet Henri de Lubac*, 211.
10. A broader investigation into mysticism in de Lubac is beyond the scope of my investigation. The following observations merely point out the implications of de Lubac's eschatology for a mystical understanding of the present. There are several helpful sources, the most thorough account of which is Bertrand Dumas, *Mystique et théologie d'après Henri de Lubac*, Études Lubaciennes 8 (Paris: Éditions du Cerf, 2013). Dumas argues that de Lubac employs the spiritual sense of Scripture to correlate mysticism and theology. See also Michel Sales, *L'Être humain et la connaissance naturelle qu'il a de Dieu: Essai sur la structure anthropo-théologique fondamentale de la Révélation chrétienne dans la pensée du P. Henri de Lubac* (Paris: Parole et silence, 2003); Francesca Murphy, "De Lubac, Ratzinger and von Balthasar: A Communal Adventure in Ecclesiology," in *Ecumenism Today: The Universal Church in the 21st Century* (Burlington, VT: Ashgate Publishing, 2008), 45–81.
11. Henri de Lubac, *Corpus Mysticum: The Eucharist and the Church in the Middle Ages*, trans. Gemma Simmonds, CJ, Faith in Reason (Notre Dame, IN: University of Notre Dame Press, 2007), 256.
12. Ibid., 230.

rationality or rational content. A mentality that dichotomized mystery and reason, and that could no longer recognize the mystery or perceive the sacred within human existence, was at the root of modern secularization, what de Lubac called the "frightful lack of the sacred."[13] Christianity, de Lubac charged, had unwittingly conspired with secularism in the loss of the transcendent.

Yet the desire for God cannot be suppressed. If human beings do not discover authentic transcendence, their desire is expressed in pathological forms. Atheist humanism and collectivist political organization in the early twentieth century were manifestations of longing for transcendent meaning in historical and human experience. Nazism, he suggests, was a surrogate for the sacred, an effect of the loss of the sacred in the wider culture. Modern forms of historical immanentism—a view of the immanent, material world as complete in itself, intelligible in itself, and lacking all need—are indeed spiritualities of the temporal that sought a revolution of the historical order. European modernity tried to affirm the meaningfulness of human existence by rejecting its transcendent source.

The spiritual challenges today are not so different than those in de Lubac's era, except that the historical immanentism he fought is now so thoroughly entrenched as to no longer be questioned. Contemporary scientific rationalism and atheism are the dominant Western "picture of the world," as David Bentley Hart calls it.[14] This "picture of the world" is no longer manifested primarily in Marxist doctrines of dialectical materialism, philosophies of history,

13. Henri de Lubac, "Internal Causes of the Weakening and Disappearance of the Sense of the Sacred," in *Theology in History*, trans. Anne Englund Nash (San Francisco: Ignatius Press, 1996), 244. Originally published as Henri de Lubac, "Causes de l'atténuation du sens du sacré," *Bulletin des Aumôniers catholiques* 31 (1942), 27-39.
14. David Bentley Hart, *The Experience of God: Being, Consciousness, Bliss* (New Haven: Yale University Press, 2013), 46–84.

or dogmatic totalitarianism, though it remains a powerful cultural undercurrent. The modern condition is that of no longer recognizing the signs of the sacred and, instead, seeing the secular as the default domain of humanity. The loss of the transcendent results in a loss of the meaningfulness of human life, reflected alternatively in excessive consumption, despair, and violence.

Although de Lubac's mystical theology is elusive and incomplete, his understanding of history is the framework for the rediscovery of the mystery of God acting in historical experience. In Christianity, the spiritual interpretation of Scripture communicates that history is part of God's ongoing plan for the world. The spiritual senses of Scripture implied that history is shaped irrevocably by the Christ event and that our lives are oriented to the future completion of the mystery of Christ. Anagogy, the final spiritual sense of Scripture, communicates knowledge of the last things. The anagogical imagination, for de Lubac, represented a whole way of viewing the world that sought a comprehensive knowledge of things in their eschatological destiny. Whereas for the late medieval to modern world, rationality hinges on self-identity, "for the Fathers, the essential mainspring of thought was not identity, or analogy, but *anagogy*."[15] Anagogy is, therefore, the contemplation of the truth about the created world that transcends it and is its destiny. It is the recognition of signs of the transcendent in one's life.

De Lubac's entire work gestures to the transcendent God who can be rediscovered at the center of human historical experience. Historical experience is sacramental in character, propelling us through the mysterious present toward the mystery. For de Lubac, this not merely a mentality or worldview. Historical experience is sacramental structurally and ontologically where the eternal God has

15. De Lubac, *Corpus Mysticum*, 235.

entered into it and drawn it beyond itself. Mysticism is not merely the contemplation of an ahistorical transcendence, but the person's entrance into the mystery of salvation enacted in Christ. It is a personal participation in the mystery of salvation by interiorizing Christ in one's life and through the church.

De Lubac's characteristic writings reflect both the confidence that God can be found in the world and a passionate yearning for the world's consummation, a deep yearning borne by incompleteness. Quoting Charles Péguy in "Le Mystère de la charité de Jeanne d'Arc," he writes,

> May all this earth be like a heaven on earth;
> May all men's hearts beat as one. . . ,
> May the earth be a beginning of heaven,
> A beginning of heaven.[16]

---

16. Henri de Lubac, *A Brief Catechesis on Nature and Grace*, trans. Brother Richard Arnandez, F.S.C. (San Francisco: Ignatius Press, 1984), 103. Quoting Charles Pèguy, "Le Mystère de la charité de Jeanne d'Arc," in *Œvres en Prose complètes, 1898–1914*, vol. 2, 1403.

Bibliography

Antliff, Mark. *Avant-Garde Fascism: The Mobilization of Myth, Art, and Culture in France, 1909–1939.* Durham, NC: Duke University Press, 2007.

Aubert, Roger. "Discussions récentes autour de la théologie de l'histoire." *Collectanea Mechliniensia* 33 (1948): 129–49.

Aumont, Michèle. *Philosophie sociopolitique de Gaston Fessard, S.J.* Paris: Éditions du Cerf, 2005.

Balthasar, Hans Urs von. *Explorations in Theology: The Word Made Flesh.* Translated by A. V. Littledale and Alexander Dru. Vol. 1. San Francisco: Ignatius Press, 1989.

———. *The Glory of the Lord: A Theological Aesthetics.* Vol. 2, *Clerical Styles.* San Francisco: Ignatius Press, 1984.

———. *The Theology of Henri de Lubac: An Overview.* San Francisco: Ignatius Press, 1991.

Baring, Edward. "Humanist Pretensions: Catholics, Communists, and Sartre's Struggle for Existentialism in Postwar France." *Modern Intellectual History* 7, no. 3 (2010): 581–609.

Barmann, Lawrence F. "Defining Historical Consciousness." Paper presented at the Annual Meeting of the American Academy of Religion, Denver, November 2001.

Barth, Karl. *Epistle to the Romans.* Translated by Edwyn C. Hoskyns. 6th ed. Oxford: Oxford University Press, 1933.

Bédarida, Renée. *Les Armes de l'Esprit: Témoignage chrétien (1941–1944).* Paris: Les Éditions Ouvrières, 1977.

Berghaus, Günter. *Futurism and Politics: Between Anarchist Rebellion and Fascist Reaction, 1909–1944.* Oxford: Berghahn Books, 1996.

Bernardi, Peter J. *Maurice Blondel, Social Catholicism, and Action Française: The Clash Over the Church's Role in Society during the Modernist Era.* Washington, DC: Catholic University of America Press, 2009.

Berzosa Martinez, Raúl. *La teología del sobrenatural en los escritos de Henri de Lubac: estudio historico-teológico (1931–1980).* Publicaciones de la Facultad de Teología del Norte de España, Sede de Burgos 57. Burgos, Spain: Ediciones Aldecoa, 1991.

Blondel, Maurice. *The Letter on Apologetics and History and Dogma.* Translated by Alexander Dru and Illtyd Trethowan. Grand Rapids, MI: Eerdmans, 1995.

Boersma, Hans. "The Eucharist Makes the Church." *Crux* 44, no. 4 (Winter 2008): 2–11.

———. *Heavenly Participation: The Weaving of a Sacramental Tapestry.* Grand Rapids, MI: Eerdmans, 2011.

———. *Nouvelle Théologie and Sacramental Ontology: A Return to Mystery.* New York: Oxford University Press, 2009.

———. "Sacramental Ontology: Nature and the Supernatural in the Ecclesiology of Henri de Lubac." *New Blackfriars* 88, no. 1015 (2007): 242–73.

Bonino, Serge-Thomas. *Surnaturel: A Controversy at the Heart of Twentieth-Century Thomistic Thought.* Ave Maria, FL: Sapientia Press of Ave Maria University, 2009.

Braine, David. "The Debate between Henri de Lubac and his Critics." *Nova et Vetera,* English Edition, 6, no. 3 (2008): 543–90.

Calvez, Jean-Yves. *Chrétiens, penseurs du social.* Histoire de la morale. Paris: Éditions du Cerf, 2008.

———. "The French Catholic Contribution to Social and Political Thinking in the 1930s." *Ethical Perspectives: Journal of the European Ethics Network* 7, no. 4 (December 2000): 312–15.

Chenu, Marie-Dominique. *Nature, Man, and Society in the Twelfth Century: Essays on New Theological Perspectives in the Latin West.* Toronto: University of Toronto Press, 1997.

———. *La Théologie au douzième siècle.* Vol. 45. Études de philosophie médiévale 45. Paris: J. Vrin, 1957.

Coffey, David. "The Whole Rahner on the Supernatural Existential." *Theological Studies* 65, no. 1 (March 2004): 95–118.

Congar, Yves. "La Purgatorie." In *Le Mystère de la mort et sa célébration.* Vol. 12. Lex Orandi. Paris: Éditions du Cerf, 1951.

Cullmann, Oscar. *Christ and Time: The Primitive Christian Conception of Time.* Revised Edition. Westminster Press, 1964.

Daley, Brian. "The Nouvelle Théologie and the Patristic Revival: Sources, Symbols and the Science of Theology." *International Journal of Systematic Theology* 7, no. 4 (October 2005): 362–82.

Daly, Gabriel. *Transcendence and Immanence: A Study in Catholic Modernism and Integralism.* Oxford: Clarendon Press, 1980.

Daniélou, Jean. "À travers les revues: Christianisme et progrès." *Études*, no. 255 (1947): 399–402.

———. "Christianisme et histoire." *Études*, no. 254 (1947): 166–84.

———. "Les divers sens de l'Écriture dans la tradition chrétienne primitive." *Ephemerides Theologicae Lovanienses* 24 (1948): 119–26.

———. *Essai sur le mystère de l'histoire.* Paris: Editions du Seuil, 1953.

———. "Les orientations présentes de la pensée religieuse." *Études*, no. 249 (1946): 5–21.

———. *Origène.* Paris: Éditions de la Table Ronde, 1948.

———. *Sacramentum futuri: Études sur les origines de la typologie biblique.* Études de théologie historique. Paris: Beauchesne, 1950.

———. "Traversée de la Mer Rouge et baptême aux premiers siècles." *Recherches de science religieuse* 33 (1946): 492–30.

———. "La typologie d'Isaac dans le christianisme primitif." *Biblica* 28 (1947): 363–93.

De Certeau, Michel. *The Mystic Fable: The Sixteenth and Seventeenth Centuries.* Vol. I. Translated by Michael B. Smith. Religion and Postmodernism. Chicago: University of Chicago Press, 1995.

De Lubac, Henri. *Amida: aspects du Bouddhisme.* Tome 2. Paris: Éditions du Seuil, 1955.

———. "Apologetics and Theology." In *Theological Fragments*, 91–104. Translated by Rebecca Howell Balinski. San Francisco: Ignatius Press, 1989.

———. "Apologétique et théologie." *Nouvelle Revue théologique* 57 (1930): 361–78.

———. "A propos de l'allégorie chrétienne." *Recherches de science religieuse* 47 (1959): 5–43.

———. *Aspects du Bouddhisme.* Tome 1. Paris: Éditions du Seuil, 1951.

———. *At the Service of the Church: Henri de Lubac Reflects on the Circumstances That Occasioned His Writings.* San Francisco: Communio Books, 1993.

———. *A Brief Catechesis on Nature and Grace.* Translated by Brother Richard Arnandez, F.S.C. San Francisco: Ignatius Press, 1984.

———. *Catholicism: Christ and the Common Destiny of Man.* Translated by Lancelot C. Sheppard and Sister Elizabeth Englund, OCD. San Francisco: Ignatius Press, 1988.

———. *Catholicisme: les aspects sociaux du dogme.* Unam Sanctam 3. Paris: Éditions du Cerf, 1938.

———. *The Church: Paradox and Mystery.* Translated by James R. Dunne. Staten Island, NY: Alba House, 1969.

———. *Corpus mysticum: l'eucharistie et l'Église au Moyen âge. Étude historique.* Théologie 3. Paris: Aubier, 1944.

————. *Corpus Mysticum: The Eucharist and the Church in the Middle Ages*. Translated by Gemma Simmonds, CJ. Faith in Reason. Notre Dame, IN: University of Notre Dame Press, 2007.

————. *De Lubac: A Theologian Speaks*. Los Angeles: Twin Circle, 1985.

————. *The Discovery of God*. Translated by Alexander Dru. Grand Rapids, MI: Eerdmans, 1996.

————. *The Drama of Atheist Humanism*. San Francisco: Ignatius Press, 1995.

————. *Exégèse médiévale: Les quatre sens de l'écriture*. Vol. 4. Théologie 59. Aubier: Éditions Montaigne, 1964.

————. "Hellenistic Allegory and Christian Allegory." In *Theological Fragments*, 165–96. Translated by Rebecca Howell Balinski. San Francisco: Ignatius Press, 1989.

————. *Histoire et esprit: l'intelligence de l'Écriture d'après Origène*. Théologie 16. Paris: Aubier, 1950.

————. *History and Spirit: The Understanding of Scripture according to Origen*. Translated by Anne Englund Nash. San Francisco: Ignatius Press, 2007.

————. "Internal Causes of the Weakening and Disappearance of the Sense of the Sacred." In *Theology in History*, 223–40. Translated by Anne Englund Nash. San Francisco: Ignatius Press, 1996.

————. "Joachim de Flore jugé par saint Bonaventure et saint Thomas." In *Pluralisme et œcuménisme en recherches théologiques: Mélanges offerts au R.P. Dockx, O.P.*, 37–49. Bibliotheca Ephemeridum Theologicarum Lovaniensium 43. Leuven: Peeters, 1976.

————. "The Light of Christ." In *Theology in History*, 201–20. Translated by Anne Englund Nash. San Francisco: Ignatius Press, 1996.

————. *Medieval Exegesis: The Four Senses of Scripture*. Translated by Mark Sebanc. Vol. 1. Grand Rapids, MI: Eerdmans, 1998.

————. *Medieval Exegesis: The Four Senses of Scripture*. Translated by E. M. Macierowski. Vol. 2. Grand Rapids, MI: Eerdmans, 2000.

————. *Medieval Exegesis: The Four Senses of Scripture*. Translated by E. M. Macierowski. Vol. 3. Grand Rapids, MI: Eerdmans, 2009.

————. *Mémoire sur l'occasion de mes écrits*. Chretiens aujourd'hui 1. Namur, Belgium: Culture et Verité, 1989.

————. *The Motherhood of the Church: Followed by Particular Churches in the Universal Church and an Interview Conducted by Gwendoline Jarczyk*. San Francisco: Ignatius Press, 1982.

————. "Le Mystère Du Surnaturel." *Recherches de Science Religieuse* 36 (1949): 80–121.

————. *Le mystère du surnaturel*. Théologie. Paris: Aubier, 1965.

————. *The Mystery of the Supernatural*. Translated by Rosemary Sheed. New York: Crossroad, 1998.

————. "On an Old Distich: The Doctrine of the 'Fourfold Sense' in Scripture." In *Theological Fragments*, 109–28. Translated by Rebecca Howell Balinski. San Francisco: Ignatius Press, 1989.

————. *Paradoxes of Faith*. Translated by Paule Simon and Sadie Kreilkamp. San Francisco: Ignatius Press, 1987.

————. *Petite catéchèse sur nature et grâce*. Communio. Paris: Fayard, 1980.

————. *La Posterité spirituelle de Joachim de Flore: de Joachim à Schelling*. Vol. 1. Paris: Éditions Lethielleux, 1979.

————. "Remarques sur l'histoire du mot 'Surnaturel.'" *Nouvelle Revue théologique* 61 (1934): 225–249; 350–370.

————. *La rencontre du Bouddhisme et de l'Occident*. Vol. 24. Théologie 24. Paris: Aubier, 1952.

————. "La Révélation divine: Commentaire du préambule et du chapitre I de La Constitution 'Dei Verbum' du Concile Vatican II." In *Révélation divine—Affrontements mystiques—Athéisme et sens de l'homme*, 4:580. Œuvres complètes. Paris: Éditions du Cerf, 2006.

————. *La Révélation divine: Église Catholique Romaine, Concile Vatican II (1962–1965)*. Lyon: La Bonté, 1966.

————. *Scripture in the Tradition.* Translated by Luke O'Neill. New York: Crossroad, 2001.

————. *The Splendor of the Church.* Translated by Michael Mason. San Francisco: Ignatius Press, 1986.

————. *Surnaturel: Études historiques.* Théologie 8. Paris: Aubier-Montaigne, 1946.

————. "'Typologie' et 'Allégorisme.'" *Recherches de Science Religieuse* 34 (1947): 180–226.

————. "Typology and Allegorization." In *Theological Fragments*, 129–64. Translated by Rebecca Howell Balinski. San Francisco: Ignatius Press, 1989.

Desmazières, Agnès. "La nouvelle théologie, prémisse d'une théologie herméneutique? La controverse sur l'analogie de la vérité (1946–1949)." *Revue Thomiste* 104, no. 1/2 (2004): 241–72.

Doran, Robert M. "Social Grace." In *Essays in Systematic Theology: An E-Book*, 1–14, 2011. http://www.loneranresource.com/pdf/books/1/35 – Social Grace.pdf

Doyle, Dennis M. *Communion Ecclesiology: Vision and Versions.* Maryknoll, NY: Orbis Books, 2000.

————. "Henri de Lubac and the Roots of Communion Ecclesiology." *Theological Studies* 60, no. 2 (1999): 209–27.

Dumas, Bertrand. *Mystique et théologie d'après Henri de Lubac.* Études Lubaciennes 8. Paris: Éditions du Cerf, 2013.

Duval, André. "Aux origines de l'Institut historique d'études thomistes' du Saulchoir (1920 et ss): notes et documents." *Revue des sciences philosophiques et théologiques* 75, no. 3 (1991): 423–48.

Falque, Emmanuel. "La postérité spirituelle de Joachim de Flore ou le principe d'immunité chez Henri de Lubac." *Revue des sciences religieuses* 77, no. 2 (April 2003): 183–98.

Fédou, Michel. "Henri de Lubac, lecteur d'Origène: l'hospitalité de la théologie et sa source mystique." *Revue des sciences religieuses* 77, no. 2 (April 2003): 133–46.

Feingold, Lawrence. *The Natural Desire to See God according to St. Thomas Aquinas and His Interpreters.* Dissertationes Series Theologica 3. Rome: Apollinare studi, 2001.

———. *The Natural Desire to See God according to St. Thomas and His Interpreters.* Washington, DC: Sapientia Press, 2010.

Féret, Henri-Marie. "Apocalypse, histoire, et eschatologie chrétiennes." *Dieu Vivant* 2 (1945): 117–34.

———. *L'Apocalypse de saint Jean: Vision chrétienne de l'histoire.* Paris: Corrêa, 1943.

———. *The Apocalypse of St. John.* Translated by Elizabethe Corathiel. Westminster, MD: The Newman Press, 1958.

Fessard, Gaston. *De l'actualité historique.* Paris: Desclée de Brouwer, 1960.

———. *Autorité et bien commun.* Paris: Aubier, 1944.

———. *Le Dialogue catholique-communiste est-il possible?* Paris: Grasset, 1937.

———. *Épreuve de force: Réflexions sur la crise internationale.* Paris: Bloud et Gay, 1939.

———. *France, prends garde de perdre ta liberté.* Paris: Éditions du Témoignage chrétien, 1946.

———. *"Pax nostra": Examen de conscience international.* Paris: Grasset, 1936.

———. "Théologie et histoire: à propos du temps de la conversion d'Israël." *Dieu Vivant* 8 (1947): 37–65.

Flannery, OP, Austin, ed. "Dei Verbum." In *Vatican Council II: The Conciliar and Postconciliar Documents.* Revised edition. Vol. 1. Northport, NY: Costello, 1996.

———. "Gaudium et Spes." In *Vatican Council II: The Conciliar and Postconciliar Documents.* Revised edition. Vol. 1. Northport, NY: Costello, 1996.

Flynn, Gabriel, and Paul D. Murray, eds. *Ressourcement: A Movement for Renewal in Twentieth-Century Catholic Theology*. New York: Oxford University Press, 2012.

Fouilloux, Étienne. "'Nouvelle Théologie' et Théologie Nouvelle (1930–1960)." In *L'histoire religieuse en France et en Espagne: Colloque international, Casa de Velázquez, 2–5 avril 2001: Actes*, edited by Benoît Pellistrandi, 87:411–25. Collection de la Casa de Velázquez. Madrid: Casa de Velázquez, 2004.

———. "Une vision eschatologique du christianisme: Dieu vivant (1945–1955)." *Revue d'histoire de l'Église de France* 57, no. 158 (1971): 47–72.

Garrigou-Lagrange, OP, Reginald. "La nouvelle théologie où va-t-elle?" *Angelicum* 23 (1946): 126–45.

Gerlach, Matthew T. "Lex Orandi, Lex Legendi: A Correlation of the Roman Canon and the Fourfold Sense of Scripture." PhD diss., Marquette University, 2011.

Giao, Nguyen Hong. *Le Verbe dans l'histoire: la philosophie de l'historicité du Pere Gaston Fessard*. Bibliothèque des Archives de philosophie 17. Paris: Beauchesne, 1974.

Gilson, Étienne. *The Spirit of Medieval Philosophy*. Notre Dame, IN: University of Notre Dame Press, 1991.

Gotcher, Robert Franklin. "Henri de Lubac and Communio: The Significance of His Theology of the Supernatural for an Interpretation of Gaudium et Spes." PhD diss., Marquette University, 2002.

Grumett, David. "Eucharist, Matter, and the Supernatural: Why de Lubac Needs Teilhard." *International Journal of Systematic Theology* 10, no. 2 (2008): 165–78.

———. "Yves de Montcheuil: Action, Justice and the Kingdom in Spiritual Resistance to Nazism." *Theological Studies* 68, no. 3 (2007): 618–41.

Gutiérrez, Gustavo. *A Theology of Liberation: History, Politics, Salvation*. Maryknoll, NY: Orbis Books, 1973.

Hankey, Wayne J. "Neoplatonism and Contemporary French Philosophy." *Dionysius* 23 (December 2005): 161–90.

Harnack, Adolf von. *History of Dogma.* Vol. 2. London: Williams and Norgate, 1896.

Hart, David Bentley. *The Experience of God: Being, Consciousness, Bliss.* New Haven: Yale University Press, 2013.

Harvey, David. *The Condition of Postmodernity: An Enquiry into the Origins of Cultural Change.* Cambridge, MA: Blackwell, 1989.

Healy, Mary. "Inspiration and Incarnation: The Christological Analogy and the Hermeneutics of Faith." *Letter and Spirit* 2 (2006): 27–42.

Healy, Nicholas J. "Henri de Lubac on Nature and Grace: A Note on Some Recent Contributions to the Debate." *Communio* 35, no. 4 (2008): 535–64.

Hemming, Laurence Paul. "Henri de Lubac: Reading Corpus Mysticum." *New Blackfriars* 90, no. 1029 (September 2009): 519–34.

Hollon, Bryan C. *Everything Is Sacred: Spiritual Exegesis in the Political Theology of Henri de Lubac.* Eugene, OR: Cascade Books, 2009.

———. "Ontology, Exegesis, and Culture in the Thought of Henri de Lubac." PhD diss., Baylor University, 2006.

Holsinger, Bruce W. *The Premodern Condition: Medievalism and the Making of Theory.* Chicago: University of Chicago Press, 2005.

Huby, Joseph. "Apocalypse et Histoire." *Construire* 15 (1944): 80–100.

———. "Autour de l'Apocalypse." *Dieu Vivant* 5 (1946): 119–30.

Hughes, Kevin L. "The 'Fourfold Sense:' De Lubac, Blondel and Contemporary Theology." *The Heythrop Journal* 42, no. 4 (2001): 451–62.

Hütter, Reinhard. "*Desiderium Naturale Visionis Dei—Est Autem Duplex Hominis Beatitudo Sive Felicitas*: Some Observations about Lawrence Feingold's and John Milbank's Recent Interventions in the Debate over the Natural Desire to See God." *Nova et Vetera,* English Edition, 5, no. 1 (2007): 81–132.

Jones, Tamsin. "Dionysius in Hans Urs von Balthasar and Jean-Luc Marion." In *Re-Thinking Dionysius the Areopagite*, edited by Sarah Coakley and Charles M. Stang, 213–24. Malden, MA: Wiley-Blackwell, 2009.

Kern, Stephen. *The Culture of Time and Space, 1880–1918*. Cambridge, MA: Harvard University Press, 1983.

Kerr, Fergus. *Twentieth-Century Catholic Theologians: From Neoscholasticism to Nuptial Mysticism*. Malden, MA: Blackwell Publishing, 2007.

Kerr, Nathan R. *Christ, History and Apocalyptic: The Politics of Christian Mission*. Eugene, OR: Cascade Books, 2009.

Koma, Elie. "Le mystère de l'Eucharistie et ses dimensions ecclesiales dans l'oeuvre d'Henri de Lubac." ThD, Pontificia Universita Gregoriana, 1990.

Komonchak, Joseph A. "Modernity and the Construction of Roman Catholicism." *Cristianesimo nella Storia* 18, no. 2 (1997): 353–85.

Larsen, Sean. "The Politics of Desire: Two Readings of Henri de Lubac on Nature and Grace." *Modern Theology* 29, no. 3 (2013): 279–310.

Laurance, John D. *Priest as Type of Christ: The Leader of the Eucharist in Salvation History according to Cyprian of Carthage*. American University Studies, VII: Theology and Religion 5. New York: Peter Lang, 1984.

Lee, Anthony. "From Sacrament of Salvation to Sign That Interrupts: The Evolution in Edward Schillebeeckx's Theology of the Relationship between the Church and the World." PhD diss., Notre Dame, 2011.

Livingston, James C. *Modern Christian Thought: The Enlightenment and the Nineteenth Century*. 2nd ed. Minneapolis: Fortress Press, 2006.

Lonergan, Bernard J. F. "The Transition from a Classicist World-View to Historical-Mindedness." In *A Second Collection*, 1–10. Toronto: University of Toronto Press, 1996.

Malloy, Christopher J. "De Lubac on Natural Desire: Difficulties and Antitheses." *Nova et Vetera*, English Edition, 9, no. 3 (2011): 567–624.

Mansini, Guy. "The Abiding Theological Significance of Henri de Lubac's Surnaturel." *The Thomist* 73, no. 4 (2009): 593–619.

Marinetti, Filippo Tommaso. "Fondazione e manifesto del Futurismo." *Gazetta dell'Emilia*. February 5, 1909.

McCool, Gerald. *From Unity to Pluralism: The Internal Evolution of Thomism.* New York: Fordham University Press, 1992.

———. *Nineteenth-Century Scholasticism: The Search for a Unitary Method.* 2nd ed. New York: Fordham University Press, 1989.

McGinn, Bernard. *Apocalypticism in the Western Tradition.* Brookfield, VT: Ashgate, 1994.

McIntosh, Mark A. *Mystical Theology: The Integrity of Spirituality and Theology.* Challenges in Contemporary Theology. Malden, MA: Wiley-Blackwell, 1998.

McPartlan, Paul. "Catholic Perspectives on Sacramentality." *Studia Liturgica* 38, no. 2 (January 2008): 219–41.

———. "The Eucharist, the Church, and Evangelization: The Influence of Henri de Lubac." *Communio* 23, no. 4 (1996): 776–85.

Mettepenningen, Jürgen. *Nouvelle Théologie—New Theology: Inheritor of Modernism, Precursor to Vatican II.* New York: T & T Clark, 2010.

———. "Truth, Orthodoxy, and The Nouvelle Théologie: Truth as Issue in a 'Second Modernist Crisis' (1946–1950)." In *Orthodoxy, Liberalism, and Adaptation: Essays on Ways of Worldmaking in Times of Change from Biblical, Historical and Systematic Perspectives,* edited by Bob Becking, 149–84. Leiden: Brill, 2011.

Milbank, John. "Henri de Lubac." In *The Modern Theologians: An Introduction to Modern Theology since 1918,* edited by David F. Ford. Malden, MA: Blackwell, 2005.

———. *The Suspended Middle: Henri de Lubac and the Debate Concerning the Supernatural.* Grand Rapids, MI: Eerdmans, 2005.

———. *Theology and Social Theory: Beyond Secular Reason.* 2nd ed. Malden, MA: Blackwell Publishing, 2006.

————. *The Word Made Strange: Theology, Language, Culture.* Oxford: Wiley-Blackwell, 1997.

Moloney, Raymond. "De Lubac and Lonergan on the Supernatural." *Theological Studies* 69, no. 3 (Spring 2008): 509–27.

Montcheuil, Yves de. "Communisme." *Courrier français du Temoignage chretien,* no. 5 (1943): 2–3.

————. "Perspectives." *Courrier Français du Témoignage chrétien,* no. 9 (1944): 1.

Muir, Mary Alice. "Gaston Fessard, S.J.: His Work Towards a Theology of History." MA thesis, Marquette University, 1970.

Mulcahy, OP, Matthew Bernard. *Aquinas's Notion of Pure Nature and the Christian Integralism of Henri de Lubac: Not Everything Is Grace.* American University Studies. New York: Peter Lang, 2011.

Murphy, Francesca. "De Lubac, Ratzinger and von Balthasar: A Communal Adventure in Ecclesiology." In *Ecumenism Today: The Universal Church in the 21st Century,* 45–81. Burlington, VT: Ashgate Publishing, 2008.

Nichols, OP, Aidan. "Thomism and the Nouvelle Théologie." *The Thomist* 64 (2000): 1–19.

O'Regan, Cyril. *Theology and the Spaces of Apocalyptic.* Milwaukee, WI: Marquette University Press, 2009.

O'Sullivan, Noel. "Henri de Lubac's Surnaturel: An Emerging Christology." *Irish Theological Quarterly* 72, no. 1 (2007): 3–31.

Pecknold, C. C., and Jacob Wood. "Augustine and Henri de Lubac." In *T & T Clark Companion to Augustine and Modern Theology,* 197–222. New York: Bloomsbury T & T Clark, 2013.

Peddicord, OP, Richard. *The Sacred Monster of Thomism: An Introduction to the Life and Legacy of Reginald Garrigou-Lagrange, O.P.* South Bend, IN: St. Augustine's Press, 2004.

Pelchat, Marc. *L'Église mystère de communion: l'ecclésiologie dans l'œuvre d'Henri de Lubac*. Collection Brèches théologiques 2. Montréal: Éditions Paulines, 1988.

Pelikan, Jaroslav. *The Emergence of the Catholic Tradition (100—600)*. Vol. 1. of *The Christian Tradition: A History of the Development of Doctrine*. Chicago: University of Chicago Press, 1971.

Pépin, Jean. *Mythe et allégorie: Les origines grecques et les contestations judéo-chrétiennes*. Philosophie de l'esprit. Paris: Éditions Montaigne, 1958.

Pickstock, Catherine. *After Writing: On the Liturgical Consummation of Philosophy*. Oxford: Wiley-Blackwell, 1998.

Pseudo-Dionysius the Areopagite. *Pseudo-Dionysius: The Complete Works*. Edited by Colm Luibhéid. Translated by Paul Rorem. The Classics of Western Spirituality. Mawah, NJ: Paulist Press, 1987.

Ratzinger, Joseph. *Eschatology, Death and Eternal Life*. 2nd ed. Washington, DC: Catholic University of America Press, 1988.

Ruggieri, Giuseppe. "The First Doctrinal Clash." In *History of Vatican II: The Formation of the Council's Identity: First Period and Intersession, October 1962–September 1963*, edited by Giuseppe Alberigo and Joseph A. Komonchak. Vol. 2. Maryknoll, NY: Orbis Books, 1997.

Sales, Michel. *L'Être humain et la connaissance naturelle qu'il a de Dieu: Essai sur la structure anthropo-théologique fondamentale de la Révélation chrétienne dans la pensée du P. Henri de Lubac*. Paris: Parole et silence, 2003.

———. *Gaston Fessard, 1897–1978: Genèse d'une pensée*. Presences 14. Brussels: Culture et Vérité, 1997.

Schillebeeckx, Edward. *The Mission of the Church*. Translated by N. D. Smith. New York: Herder and Herder, 1973.

———. *The Real Achievement of Vatican II*. New York: Herder and Herder, 1967.

Schindler, David L. *Heart of the World, Center of the Church: Communio Ecclesiology, Liberalism, and Liberation*. Grand Rapids, MI: Eerdmans, 1996.

Schloesser, Stephen. "Vivo Ergo Cogito: Modernism as Temporalization and Its Discontents: A Propaedeutic to This Collection." In *The Reception of Pragmatism in France and the Rise of Roman Catholic Modernism, 1890–1914*, 21–58. Washington, DC: Catholic University of America Press, 2009.

Schnackers, Hubert. *Kirche als Sakrament und Mutter: Zur Ekklesiologie von Henri de Lubac*. Vol. 22. Regensburger Studien zur Theologie. Frankfurt am Main: Peter Lang, 1979.

Schoof, T. M. *A Survey of Catholic Theology, 1800–1970*. Glen Rock, NJ: Paulist Newman Press, 1970.

Séguy, Jean. "Sur l'apocalyptique catholique." *Archives de sciences sociales des religions*, no. 41 (1976): 165–72.

Sobel, Dana. *Longitude: The True Story of a Lone Genius Who Solved the Greatest Scientific Problem of His Time*. New York: Walker and Company, 1995.

Voderholzer, Rudolf. *Meet Henri de Lubac*. Translated by Michael J. Miller. San Francisco: Ignatius Press, 2008.

Wang, Lisa. "Sacramentum unitatis ecclesiasticae: The Eucharistic Ecclesiology of Henri de Lubac." *Anglican Theological Review* 85, no. 1 (2003): 143–58.

Webster, John. *Confessing God: Essays in Christian Dogmatics II*. New York: T & T Clark, 2005.

Weir, David. *Decadence and the Making of Modernism*. Amherst, MA: University of Massachusetts Press, 1996.

Williams, A. N. "The Future of the Past: The Contemporary Significance of the Nouvelle Théologie." *International Journal of Systematic Theology* 7, no. 4 (2005): 347–61.

Williams, David M. *Receiving the Bible in Faith: Historical and Theological Exegesis*. Washington, DC: Catholic University of America Press, 2004.

Wood, Susan K. "The Church as the Social Embodiment of Grace in the Ecclesiology of Henri de Lubac." PhD diss., Marquette University, 1986.

———. "The Nature-Grace Problematic within Henri de Lubac's Christological Paradox." *Communio* 19, no. 3 (1992): 389–403.

———. *Spiritual Exegesis and the Church in the Theology of Henri de Lubac.* Grand Rapids, MI: Eerdmans, 1998.

Index

Action française, 51–52, 55

Aelred of Rievaulx, 154

Aeterni Patris, 30, 40n37, 41–42

Albert the Great, 181, 188

Alexandrian theology, 132, 132n3, 140

allegorical sense of scripture, 11, 93–95, 97, 100–115, 119–22, 130–44, 149, 152, 154, 159, 161n23, 162–63, 169–73, 175–78, 213, 231–34; and typology, 130–35

allegorization. *See* allegorical sense of scripture

anagogical sense of scripture, 11, 93–95, 97, 117, 120–22, 140–41, 144, 148, 152–70, 176, 178, 181–84, 186–90, 231–34, 309; definition, 120, 153–55, 157; as heavenly and future, 163–69; as objective and subjective, 158–63

anagogy. *See* anagogical sense of scripture

antichrist, 38, 43

antimodernism (Roman Catholic), 18, 36, 43–45. *See also* Modernism

apocalyptic, 12–15, 18–19, 27–28, 36–46, 57–73, 90, 153, 189–201, 210, 305; and Catholicism, 13, 18–19, 36–46; and modern culture, 18, 27–28, 90; and theology of history, 12–15, 57–73, 153, 189–201, 305

Aquinas. *See* Thomas Aquinas

Aristotle, 47, 109, 177n60, 180n71, 183, 188, 259, 291

atheism, 80, 83, 308

Augustine, Aurelius, 77, 95, 111, 118n65, 137, 154, 178, 186–87, 219, 264, 283

Balthasar, Hans Urs von, 6, 8, 11–12, 17, 19, 185, 239
Báñez, Domingo, 266
Barmann, Lawrence F., 31
Barth, Karl, 21–22
Baudelaire, Charles, 26
Bede (Venerable), 154, 159n17
Bergson, Henri, 26–27, 27n12, 35n30, 76
Bernanos, Georges, 13, 54–55, 56n15
Billot, Louis, 262
Blondel, Maurice, 53, 118n69, 136n12, 166n38
Boersma, Hans, 10, 10n21, 10n23, 107n39, 109–10, 110nn46–47, 207, 209
Bonaventure, 181, 190, 192
Boniface VIII, 188
Bouillard, Henri, 35, 206
Boyer, Charles, 271
Braine, David, 276–77, 277n36
Bultmann, Rudolf, 201–2

Cajetan, Thomas, 266, 268, 275, 288
Carolingian Renaissance, 179

Chaillet, Pierre, 54–55, 69
Chenu, Marie-Dominique, 5, 45, 48–49, 57, 57n18, 87, 176, 181, 193n108, 206, 259n2
chronos, 10–11
Claudel, Paul, 12, 54n9
Comte, Auguste, 81, 270
Congar, Yves, 5, 45, 48, 53, 57, 181, 189, 193n108, 205–6, 220n23
Crocco, Antonio, 192n104
Cullmann, Oscar, 211

Daley, Brian, 12
Daly, Gabriel, 262
Daniélou, Jean, 5, 12–13, 19, 34, 48–50, 56, 68, 75–80, 87, 109, 111n51, 126, 131, 132n3, 133–34, 205; and de Lubac, 11n51, 133–34; theology of history, 75–80
de Blic, Jacques, 271
de Broglie, Guy, 267n11, 271
Decadent Movement, 29, 45
de Certeau, Michel, 238–39, 239n61
De fontibus Revelationis, 221
Dei Filius, 40–41, 221, 261
Dei Verbum, 201, 211, 221–27, 304
de Lubac, Henri: anthropology of, 7, 11–12, 260–65, 286–92, 299;

antiplatonism of, 108, 100–112, 127; on Christ, 226–234; on the church, 234–246; eschatology of (*see* eschatology); and liberation theology, 246–54; on Marxism, 80–86, 92, 104n29, 126, 129, 131, 150; on mystery, 210–20; on the mystical body (*corpus mysticum*), 4, 238–39; mysticism, 7, 14, 264, 305–310; on natural desire (*see* natural desire [for God]); on nature and the supernatural (*see* nature and the supernatural); on pure nature (*see* pure nature); sacramental structure of his theology, 210, 213–20; on revelation, 220–26; on the temporal interim, 150, 160, 210–13; *totus Christus*, 231, 254

de Montcheuil, Yves, 55

Denis the Carthusian, 266

Didymus the Blind, 154

Dionysius the Areopagite, 153–54, 178, 182–89, 190, 201, 280

Divino afflante Spiritu, 98

Dodd, C. H., 211

Donnelly, Philip, 270–72

Drey, Johann Sebastian von, 129

Dreyfus Affair, 51

eschatology, 11–14, 17–19, 20–22, 37–46, 62–65, 73–74, 86–88, 131, 151–52, 160, 167, 187–90, 193, 197, 200–202, 211, 214, 217, 220, 234–46, 253, 279–300; and anagogy, 187–90; and the church, 134–46; and the supernatural, 279–300

eternalism, 30–36, 44–45, 186

Eucharist, 125, 238–39, 291

exegesis, 12, 49, 70, 96–104, 98n12, 104n28, 108, 111–13, 115–27; historical-critical, 98–100; spiritual, 12, 49, 70, 96–104, 104n28, 111–13, 115–27. *See also* allegorical sense of scripture; Origen

extrinsicism, 118n69, 136n12, 389

Falque, Emmanuel, 191

fascism, 28, 45, 56, 61, 74, 87

Feingold, Lawrence, 273–74, 277, 293

Féret, Henri-Marie, 13, 19, 49–50, 53, 57–70, 73–74, 87; theology of history, 57–70

Fessard, Gaston, 13, 19, 49–50, 53–56, 68–74, 87, 303; theology of history, 68–74

Feuerbach, Ludwig, 270

fideism, 261–62

First Vatican Council. *See* Vatican I

First World War. *See* World War I

Flaubert, Gustave, 26

Frenay, Henri, 54

Fumet, Stanislaus, 54–56

Futurist Movement, 28, 45

Garnier of Rochefort, 187–88

Garrigou-Lagrange, Reginald, 35, 35n30, 271

Gaudium et Spes, 249, 285, 304–5

Greek philosophy. *See* Hellenism

Giles of Rome, 188, 266

Gregory of Nyssa, 75, 77, 132, 154, 162, 172, 283

Grumett, David, 109, 290

Guillaume de Saint-Amour, 188

Gutiérrez, Gustavo, 86, 247n81, 253, 299

Harnack, Adolf von, 100–101, 101nn17–18, 107

Harvey, David, 23, 25

Hankey, Wayne J., 109

Heidegger, Martin, 76, 109

Hellenistic allegorization and Christian allegory, 96, 104n27, 106–15, 125, 127, 132–33, 134n8, 152

Hellenistic understanding of time, 77, 92, 96, 101–3, 133, 185, 199

Hellenization thesis, 100–109

Hemming, Laurence Paul, 238–40, 240n62

hermeneutics. *See* exegesis

Hilduin, 280

historical consciousness, 15, 18, 30–31, 36, 44–46, 48, 88, 302

historical sense of scripture. *See* literal sense of scripture

historicism, 36, 118n69

Holocaust. *See* Shoah

Hollon, Bryan C., 9, 9n19

Huby, Joseph, 13, 19, 49, 49n3, 50, 61–68, 87; theology of history, 61–68

Hugh of Balma, 188, 188n93

Hugh of Saint Victor, 154, 177–78, 186

Humani generis, 97, 272, 292–94, 293n82

International Meridian Conference, 24

Irenaeus of Lyons, 132, 134, 194

Jerome, 98, 121, 154

Joachim of Fiore, 3, 14, 49, 153, 164–66, 181, 189–203, 231, 249, 251, 255; eternal gospel, 165–66, 195–96; three ages, 196–97
John Cassian, 95, 154, 172, 186
John of Paris, 180
John Scotus Eriugena, 183, 280
John of Torquemada, 188
Johnson, Elizabeth, 299
Journet, Charles, 70, 70n50, 73–74
Joyce, James, 26

kairos, 10–11, 207
Kant, Immanuel, 23, 27n13, 33, 107, 261
Kasper, Walter, 34n26
Kern, Stephen, 22, 25, 27n12
Kleutgen, Joseph, 38–40
Komonchak, Joseph, 30, 37, 41
Kung, Hans, 258

Lacroix, Jean, 55–56, 83n82, 303
Lagrange, Marie-Joseph, 32
Labourdette, Marie-Michelle, 34–35, 206, 271
Lamentabili sane exitu, 19, 32–33
Leibniz, Gottfried Wilhelm, 23
Leo XIII (Pope), 30, 40–42, 45, 53
Larsen, Sean, 275–76
Leonine Prayers, 42

Lessing, G. E., 106–7
liberation theology, 246–54, 249n86
Liberatore, Matteo, 38, 38n34, 40n37, 45
literal sense of scripture, 11, 70, 93, 100–103, 114, 137, 139, 142, 177–78, 180, 233; as a historical sense, 39; New Testament as a, 233
Lonergan, Bernard, 31n21, 44, 290
Lumen gentium, 243–44

Malevez, Leo, 271
Malloy, Christopher J., 272–73, 293, 293n83
Manning, Henry Edward Cardinal, 38
Mansini, Guy, 109, 259, 259n2
Marcel, Gabriel, 27n12, 54n9
Marinetti, Filippo Tommaso, 28
Maritain, Jacques, 27n12, 53n8, 55, 70, 87, 303
Marx, Karl, 76, 85, 87, 129, 150, 202, 249n86
Marxism, 45, 48, 53, 59, 61, 79–86, 87, 92, 104n29, 126, 129, 131, 150
Mary (mother of Jesus), 12, 44
Maurras, Charles, 51

McGinn, Bernard, 192n104, 192n108, 193

Meister Eckhart, 188

metaphysics. *See* ontology

Mettepenningen, Jürgen, 49nn3–4, 57n18, 61, 205

Metz, Johann Baptist, 253

Milbank, John, 2, 6, 8–9, 109, 206–7, 237–38, 237nn58–59, 239n61, 274–75, 275n29, 281–82, 293n82

modernism (culture), 24–26, 45; Roman Catholic Modernism, 19, 35, 272

Modernist Crisis, 19, 31, 34

Möhler, Johann Adam, 129

Mondésert, Claude, 205

moral sense of scripture. *See* tropology

Mouroux, Jean, 49, 285, 303

Mulcahy, Matthew B., 9

mystical body of Christ (*corpus mysticum*). *See* de Lubac, Henri

Nazism, 50, 54–55, 54n10, 68, 308; Christian resistance to, 54–57, 54n11

natura pura. See pure nature

natural desire (for God), 11, 110, 110n48, 260–61, 264–67, 266n11, 271–73, 298

nature and the supernatural, 2, 8–10, 206–7, 237, 246–55, 247n81, 265–70, 275–300

Neoplatonism, 109–11, 110n46, 186, 199, 207, 282n49

neoscholasticism, 5, 12, 18, 30–36, 38, 44–48, 87, 107n39, 179n68, 205, 259, 266, 279, 289

neothomism. *See* Thomism

Newman, John Henry, 32

Newton, Sir Isaac, 23, 25

Nichols, Aidan, 35

Nietzsche, Friedrich, 270

nouvelle théologie, 1–2, 5, 10–12, 13–15, 18–19, 34–36, 47–88, 109–11, 129, 205–7, 271, 302–3; and neoscholasticism, 34–36, 47–48, 205–6; and platonism, 110–111

ontology (metaphysics), 2, 8–12, 10n21, 10n, 20–22, 32, 35–36, 101–7, 109, 118, 125, 134, 206–7, 209, 236–38, 259–60, 275–76, 281–83, 285, 299; and history, 20, 104–15, 134, 259–60; platonic/Neoplatonic, 9n10, 10, 10n23, 109–15, 182, 282; sacramental, 10, 10n21, 110–11, 207, 209

ontos, 10–11, 207, 299

O'Regan, Cyril, 13

Origen of Alexandria, 15, 49, 83,
83n86, 89–90, 92, 94, 95–104,
106, 108, 111–13, 115, 120,
125–27, 129–59, 162–70, 172,
178, 181, 183, 186–87, 189,
190, 198 195–96, 203–4, 209,
212, 244, 283; allegorization,
101, 115, 129–150; anagogy,
155–58, 163–68, 181, 198;
apocatastasis, 157; on Christ,
145–49; Christian newness,
135–39; on the Eternal Gospel,
163–69, 195–96; exemplarism,
140–44; and Neoplatonism, 89,
97, 101n17, 102, 108, 112, 183;
significance of, 95, 151–52,
158; spiritual meaning, 94, 98,
111n50 (*see also* allegorization);
threefold division of history,
120, 163–68

Papal States, 38, 41, 43

Pascendi dominici gregis, 19, 32–33,
43

Pastor aeternus, 40–41

Paul (apostle), 43, 71–72, 74, 87,
115, 119, 133, 140–41, 170,
183, 194, 214–15

Péguy, Charles, 27n12, 51, 54n9,
310

Pépin, Jean, 97, 104n27, 131

Perrone, Giovanni, 38

Peter Comestor, 187

Philo of Alexandria, 101n17,
103n24, 104, 111–12, 111n50,
133, 159

Pius X (Pope), 33, 43, 51–53

Pius XI (Pope), 52

Pius XII (Pope), 97–98, 272, 292,
293n82

platonism, 105, 108–10, 140–44,
144n32, 177. *See also*
Neoplatonism

Plotinus, 106

Porphyry, 104n27

Poulat, Emile, 37, 37n31

Preparatory Theological
Commission, 220, 220n23

Proudhon, Pierre-Joseph, 81,
81n79, 134, 270

Pseudo-Dionysius the Areopagite.
See Dionysius the Areopagite

pure nature, 9, 109–10, 251, 265,
268–69, 274–75, 275n29,
288–90, 290n77, 293

radical orthodoxy, 9, 238

Rahner, Karl, 214n8, 221, 223,
223n28, 258, 277n36

rationalism, 39, 192, 261, 271, 299,
307–8

Ratzinger, Joseph, 21, 305

Reeves, Marjorie, 192n104

Richard of Saint Victor, 162,
178–79

Ritschl, Albrecht, 107

Robert Grosseteste, 188, 234n50

Robert of Melun, 154

Rousselot, Pierre, 12

Rupert of Deutz, 187

Russo, Francesco, 192

Sallust, 104n27, 106, 134n8

Schillebeeckx, Edward, 221,
249–50, 258, 286, 299

Schoof, T. M., 33

Schweitzer, Albert, 17, 21, 210

Scola, Angelo, 6

scholasticism. 4, 32, 34, 41–42, 48,
109, 176, 181, 189–92,
193n108, 221, 259, 265–69,
278–279, 283, 288; *nouvelle
théologie* and, 34–36, 47–48,
205–6. *See also*
neoscholasticism

Second Vatican Council. *See*
Vatican II

Second World War. *See* World
War II

Semaines Sociales, 53, 56, 80, 83,
83n86, 86, 131

Shoah, 13

Sillon, 53

Sobel, Dana, 23–24

Social Catholicism, 45, 50, 53–54,
61

Sources Chrétiennes (series of
translations), 34, 56, 75, 84n86,
109, 132n3, 133n6, 205–6

Spengler, Oswald, 29, 76, 77n66

spiritual exegesis. *See* exegesis

spiritual interpretation *See* exegesis

spiritual senses of scripture. *See*
exegesis

Stöckl, Albert, 39

Suárez, Francisco, 266, 268, 271,
288

supernatural. *See* nature and the
supernatural

supersessionism, 84n86, 138–39

Théologie (book series), 34, 56

theology of history (debate),
47–57

Thomas Aquinas, 30, 38, 47, 70,
109, 157, 181, 192, 206,
234n50, 265–66, 266n11, 274,
280, 283, 289, 291

Thomas of Verceil, 188

Thomism, 2, 19, 34–35, 56, 70,
79, 109, 121, 176, 188, 193,
271, 274, 278n37, 279, 288,
293, 303

Tondelli, Leone, 192

tropology, 117n64, 120, 122, 159–62, 169–75, 178, 232–34

Tübingen School, 129

typology, 96; and allegory, 131–35

Vatican I, 40–41, 40n37, 221, 261–63

Vatican II, 1, 5, 49n4, 87, 220–22, 220n23, 243, 249, 258–59, 272, 285, 303–5

Vichy, 50, 54n11, 68

Webster, John, 236–37

Weir, David, 29

Weiss, Johannes, 17n1, 21, 210

Wells, H. G., 29

Williams, David, 3, 98n12

William of Ockham, 188

Wood, Susan K., 8n16, 11–12, 104n28, 108n41, 138n16, 144n32, 240nn62–63, 244

World War I, 22, 45, 52, 54n9

World War II, 13, 15, 19, 28n15, 46, 50, 53–54, 74, 78, 80, 86–87, 303; theological responses to, 53–57, 86–87